Foreign Mining Investment Law

Richard W. Roeder

Foreign Mining Investment Law

The Cases of Australia, South Africa and Colombia

Springer

Richard W. Roeder
Rosenheim, Germany

ISBN 978-3-319-31216-3 ISBN 978-3-319-31217-0 (eBook)
DOI 10.1007/978-3-319-31217-0

Library of Congress Control Number: 2016940845

Printed on acid-free paper

This Springer imprint is published by Springer Nature
The registered company is Springer International Publishing AG Switzerland

Acknowledgments

This book is a result of research supervised by Professor Dr. Stephan Hobe, LL.M. (McGill), chair of Public International Law, European Law, and European and International Economic Law and managing director of the International Investment Law Centre at the University of Cologne, Germany (http://www.iilcc.uni-koeln.de), between January 2012 and September 2015.

This volume includes research undertaken in Brisbane and Canberra, Australia, specifically at the University of Queensland, Brisbane; Donezk and Lugansk, Ukraine; Johannesburg and Cape Town, South Africa, specifically at the Mining INDABA and the University of Cape Town; Bogota and Medellin, Colombia, specifically at the Universidad Nacional de Colombia; and at the International Investment Law Centre of the University of Cologne, Germany.

I owe my special gratitude to my father, Rainer Röder, for being such a constant source of motivation to me to finish this project.

I owe my gratitude to Stephan Hobe for his quick and candid responses to my questions and him and Marc Bungenberg for allowing me to present at the International Conference on Permanent Sovereignty over Natural Resources in January 2013, which assessed *the evolution of the principle of permanent sovereignty over natural resources into a principle of customary international law, as well as related developments* of the UN General Assembly resolution 1803 (XVII) on the principle of Permanent Sovereignty over Natural Resources. This helped me to frame my thinking, introduced me to an academic environment of researchers interested in a similar academic realm, and provided an early milestone for this thesis.

To Joern Griebel of the International Investment Law Centre Cologne, for his insights and help with the academic resources of the International Investment Law Centre, and Burkhard Schöbener of the University of Cologne, Germany, for his suggestions for the future study of International Mining Investment Law.

To Tillmann Rudolf Braun of the Federal Ministry of Economics and Energy of Germany, for supervising my first internship in the field of foreign direct investments and his dedication to the cause that inspired me.

To Frank Leschhorn of RWE Australia, who explained the technical aspects of mining projects to me in words a lawyer was able to understand. To Chantelle Doerksen, for the introduction.

To Martin Klapper at HopgoodGanim's Resources and Energy practice group in Brisbane, Australia, who has accompanied the development of this thesis with challenging suggestions and advice and was willing to dedicate his time in the very end of the project to make sure none of my findings got lost in translation. To Jonathan Fulcher at HopgoodGanim's Resources and Energy practice group in Brisbane, Australia, who introduced me to the importance of issues around the social license to operate and native title. To both, to be able to work with HopgoodGanim's Resources and Energy practice group in 2012 to gain firsthand experience.

To Saleem Ali, director of the Centre for Social Responsibility in Mining of the Sustainable Minerals Institute of the University of Queensland who supervised my final thesis of my master's of international studies with a focus on the interplay between public and private governance of mining projects and who offered me to stay on as a visiting scholar to undertake further research after my master's was over.

To Robert Milbourne, professor of the class *mining law* at the University of Queensland, for his insights and for supervising my paper "UN General Assembly resolution 1803 on 'permanent sovereignty over natural resources' – an Australian perspective of today" that become the basis for my presentation at the Conference on Permanent Sovereignty over Natural Resources.

To Tina Hunter, head of the Centre for International Minerals and Energy Law at the University of Queensland, for her insights and for pointing out crucial literature.

To Richard Devetak, head of the School of Political Science and International Studies of the University of Queensland, whose lecture on the purpose of science motivated me to attempt to define International Mining Investment Law as a distinct field of study.

To Joseph Hongoh for teaching the class *resolving deep-seated conflict resolution* and for supervising my paper "Conflicts in mining operations – a challenge of fair distribution of benefits, impacts and risks" that helped to frame my thinking on the various stakeholders involved in international mining projects.

To David Earl, manager of the International Investment and Trade Policy Unit of the Foreign Investment and Trade Policy Division of the Treasury of the Commonwealth of Australia and his team, for the dedication to answer my numerous questions regarding the foreign investment review process in Australia and for welcoming me at the Treasury in Canberra in 2013. To Jon Richardson, Australian high commissioner to Nigeria, for the introduction.

To Bruce Harvey, global practice leader of the Communities and Social Performance branch of Rio Tinto, for his insights on issues regarding the social license to operate and corporate social responsibility policies in Australia.

To Tim Foote for his insight on foreign mining activities of Australian mining companies.

To Jon Womersley, former director of the Regulatory Support and Practice of the Queensland Department of Environment and Resource Management, and his wife, John Simpson and his wife, and Graeme Lewis and the Rotary Club of Cleveland, Australia, for their advice and hospitality.

To Mark Leeman and Adrian Deitz of Skadden, Arps, Slate, Meagher & Flom LLP for their insights on current legal developments in the realm of foreign mining investments in Australia. To Lutz Zimmer and Bernd Mayer and my colleagues at Skadden, Arps, Slate, Meagher & Flom LLP who allowed me to take time for the finalization of this project.

To Hanri Mostert of the University of Cape Town for explaining to me the changes of the mineral ownership and mineral rights ownership from the Mining Law 1991 to the MPRDA 2002. Professor Mostert, I did my best to get it right. To Richard Cramer and Janine Howard for their help with accessing South African academic resources.

To Eberhard Gschwindt of the European Investment Bank for his insights and the material on Africa's mineral law regimes.

To Otsile Matlou of Edward Nathan Sonnenbergs Law Firm for his insights on legal developments in the realm of international mining investments in South Africa.

To Lisa Chamberlain and Megan Geldenhuys of the University of the Witwatersrand, Johannesburg, for their insights on governance issues relating to natural resources.

To Jessica van Onselen of AngloGold Ashanti for her insights on issues regarding the social license to operate and corporate social responsibility policies in South Africa.

To Sureiya Adam for her insights in the ICSID negotiations of the South African government in the early 1990s.

To Michael Schroeder of Old Mutual South Africa for his insights on the political and business landscape for international mining investments in South Africa. To him and his wife, the Rotary Club of am Kap, and the Rotary Club of Cape Town for their hospitality.

To Guillermo Parada of the Radio Universidad Nacional de Colombia for inviting me to his radio show to discuss International Mining Investment Law and the introductions that followed. To Thomas Dittrich, alumni of the German National Academic Foundation, for the introduction.

To María del Pilar of Gestion Ambiental Estrategica for her insights on artisanal mining. To Diana Arbeláez-Ruiz of the Centre for Social Responsibility in Mining for the introduction.

To Ana Maria Rodriguez Contreras for her insights on the executive branch of the mineral regulators in Colombia.

To Tamara Romero Restropo of the law firm Alianza W.J.S.A., for her insight on current legal issues for foreign direct investments in Colombian mining projects.

To Nathan Monash, vice president, Sustainability of AngloGold Ashanti Americas, Inc., for his insights on AngloGold Ashanti's corporate social responsibility policies.

To the Rotary Club of Cartagena and the Rotary Club of Bogota Occidente, specifically to Beatriz Lizarazu for the hospitality.

To Manuela Dollinger, of the newspaper Münchner Merkur, for her insights on natural resources available in Germany.

To Oliver Kloss for his insights on double-tax treaties.

To Raimonda Miglinaite, Astrid Schaffland, Aura Gariela Negret, and Marina Calderón for their feedback and help with translations.

To Thomas Gutschlag and Titus Gebel of the Deutsche Rohstoff AG for a firsthand mining experience at the Camp Wolfram mine opening in Queensland, Australia.

To Vladimir Polienko of the Renova Group for his insights from an investor's perspective.

To Rotary International for the fellowship that funded the master's of international studies focused on conflicts around international mining projects that allowed me to undertake research for parts of this thesis.

To all those who I could not mention.

To my family, for everything.

Rosenheim, Germany
February 2016

Richard W. Roeder

Contents

Table of Statutes

Australia

South Africa

Colombia

International Law

Table of Cases

Australia

South Africa

Colombia

International Arbitration

List of Abbreviations

ACCC	Australian Competition and Consumer Commission
ADMPAMPA	Argyle Diamond Mine Participation Agreement: Management Plan Agreement
ADR	Alternative dispute resolution
AEC	Australian Employment Covenant
AGAC	AngloGold Ashanti Colombia
AMIC	Australian Mining Industry Council
ANC	African National Congress
ANCERTA	Australia New Zealand Closer Economic Relations Trade Agreement
ASM	Artisanal and small-scale mining
AUSFTA	Australia–United States Free Trade Agreement
B-BBEE	Broad-Based Black Economic Empowerment
B-BBEE Act 2003	Broad-Based Black Economic Empowerment Act 53 of 2003
BIT	Bilateral investment treaty
CCA	Conduct and Compensation Agreements
CEO	Chief executive officer
COMPES	Consejo Nacional de Politica Economica y Social
CREE	Colombian Additional Annual Income Tax
CSR	Corporate social responsibility
EDR	Economic demonstrated resources
FATA	Foreign Acquisition and Takeovers Act 1975
FATAA	Foreign Acquisitions and Takeovers Amendment Act 2010
FATNR	Foreign Acquisition and Takeovers (Notices) Regulations 1975
FATR	Foreign Acquisition and Takeovers Regulations 1989
FIRB	Foreign Investment Review Board
HDSA	Historically disadvantaged South Africans

ICMM	The International Council on Mining and Metals
ICSID	International Centre for Settlement of Investment Disputes
ILUA	Indigenous land use agreement
IMIL	International Mining Investment Law
IMISL	International Mining Investment Soft Law
JSE	Johannesburg Stock Exchange
JV	Joint venture
LUPO	Land Use Planning Ordinance 15 of 1985
Mining Charter 2002	The Broad-Based Socio-Economic Empowerment Charter for the South African Mining Industry 2002
Mining Charter 2010	Amendment of the Broad-Based Socio-Economic Empowerment Charter for the South African Mining and Minerals Industry of 2010
MNE	Multi-national enterprises
MPRDA 2002	Mineral and Petroleum Resources Development Act 2002
MPRDA 2008	Mineral and Petroleum Resources Development Amendment Act, No. 49 of 2008
MQRA	Modernizing Queensland's Resources Acts
MRA 1989	Mineral Resources Act 1989
MRRT	Mineral Resource Rent Tax
NGO	Nongovernmental organizations
NNTT	National Native Title Tribunal
NSW	New South Wales, Australia
PAICI	Plan de Ayuda Integral a las Comunidades Indígenas
PGSA	Petroleum and Gas (Production and Safety) Act 2004
QLD	Queensland, Australia
RSPT	Resource Super Profit Tax
RTN	Right to negotiate
SACCAWU	South African Commercial, Catering and Allied Workers Union
SLO	Social license to operate
SLP	Social and labor plan
STC	Secondary tax on companies
Streamlining Act	Mines Legislation Streamlining Amendment Act 2012
UNCED	United Nations Conference on Environment and Development
UNCITRAL	United Nations Commission on International Trade Law Arbitration Rules
UNCTAD	United Nations Commission for Trade and Development

Chapter 1
Introduction

1.1 Subject Matter and Hypothesis

The boom of foreign investments in mining projects over the last 2 decades is only a herald of the global competition for access to mineral resources in the decades to come.

In its report "*The Resource Revolution*: *Meeting the world's energy*, *materials*, *food and water needs*", the McKinsey Global Institute estimates that the demand for steel alone will increase by about 80 % from 1270 million tonnes in the year 2010 to 2290 million tonnes in 2030.[1] This development is driven by an increasing demand for mineral resources from a materializing middle class in China, India and other emerging markets.[2]

Several other minerals, especially critical minerals like rare earths, tin, tungsten, phosphate and potash have already shown high price volatility between 2004 and 2009. Additionally their supply is geographically focused, complicating access for many countries and companies alike.[3] This is especially challenging for countries like Germany that require large quantities of minerals for their industries, specifically rare earths for its pronounced "*Green Revolution*" and have little Economic Demonstrated Resources ("**EDRs**") of crucial minerals.

This shortage and concentration of supply of minerals creates a field of tension:

One the one hand, countries and companies that do not possess a sufficient amount of minerals aim to secure access to these minerals for their industry, constituents and projects at the best price possible—with the help of foreign investment in mining projects.

One the other hand, resource rich countries have an interest to best use their mineral wealth for their own industry and constituents.

---

[1] McKinsey Global Institute (2011), p. 42.

[2] McKinsey Global Institute (2011), p. 36.

[3] McKinsey Global Institute (2011), p. 43.

R.W. Roeder, *Foreign Mining Investment Law*, DOI 10.1007/978-3-319-31217-0_1

The hypothesis is (i) that the realization of and the investment in international mining projects creates complex legal challenges, (ii) that these challenges are similar wherever the international mining investments take place; and (iii) that these specific legal challenges cannot sufficiently be analyzed by the legal framework provided for by general foreign investment law.

1.2 Purpose of the Study

The aim of this work is to explore the past and the status quo of the current legal framework for foreign direct investments in mining projects as well as possible future developments. The work then intends to understand what these findings mean for the further study of the legal framework for foreign investments in mining projects.

1.3 Scope

Mining can take place in geographic locations that fall under the sovereignty of a nation as well as in other geographic locations such as the Deep Sea Bed or Outer Space.

Under international law, besides the territory on land, nations have the exclusive right to undertake mining activities in deep sea in an exclusive economic zone that stretches 200 nautical miles from the coastal baseline, beyond their territorial waters that stretch up to 12 nautical miles from the coastal baseline.[4]

Article 55 of the United Nations Conventions on the Law of the Sea states: "*In the exclusive economic zone, the coastal State has sovereign rights for the purpose of exploring and exploiting, conserving and managing the natural resources, whether living or non-living, of the waters superjacent to the seabed and of the seabed and its subsoil*, (. . .);"

Investments in mining projects outside of the sovereign territory of nations, whilst not yet common, are also developing and deserve academic interest in the years to come.

Deep-sea bed mining that takes place outside of any exclusive economic zone is governed by United Nations Conventions on the Law of the Sea and is regulated by the International Seabed Authority.[5]

---

[4] Hobe (2014), p. 81.

[5] For a discussion of the current framework see: Oude Elferink (2005) and Harrison (2011).

Mining in Outer Space is yet to be regulated.[6] Notwithstanding its technical feasibility in the years to come,[7] commercial interest has already been voiced.[8]

This work focuses on foreign investment in mining projects within the sovereign territory of nations and their exclusive economic zones.

From the legal challenges the realization of an international mining project creates this work discusses the admission of foreign mining investments, the corporate structure requirements of foreign mining investments, mineral ownership and mineral rights ownership, mining licenses, land access for foreign mining investments, performance requirements for foreign mining investments, distribution of profits from foreign mining investments, repatriation of profits from foreign mining investments, resolution of conflicts in relation to foreign mining investments, the question of the Social License to Operate and the Corporate Social Responsibility policy answer of mining companies. The terminology, the specific relevance of each aspect and the reason to select it above other aspects will be discussed in the respective chapter.

1.4 Limitations

In a legal sphere with such complexity as the legal framework for foreign investments there are more questions than answers, and any research is prone to be limited in scope.

The author acknowledges that there are further fields of the law that the legal framework for foreign investments touches upon: Environmental Law is one of these. In all jurisdictions encountered, international and national Environmental Law are present and an environmental license is obligatory in one form or another before commencing mining activities. The complexity and technical nature of international and national environmental law would easily double the volume of this work and International,[9] Australian,[10] South African[11] and Colombian[12] environmental law, also with specific reference to mining projects[13] has been discussed in depth elsewhere.

Health and safety laws were left to experts with the necessary technical and engineering expertise.[14]

---

[6] For the discussion of a possible future framework see: Lee (2012), p. 16.

[7] Sonter (2014).

[8] National Geographics (2014).

[9] Beyerlin and Marauhn (2011), Pevato (2003), Kiss and Shelton (2004) and Sands et al. (2012).

[10] Fisher (2010) and Bates (2009).

[11] Brauteseth (1995) and McAuslan (2002).

[12] Rey (2010), Galvis (2012), with further references.

[13] Marcus (1997) and Hester and Harrison (1994).

[14] Gunningham and Sinclair (2012) and Yang (2012).

For those interested in the engineering side of a mining project, the project cycle of a mining project and its technical aspects the Northern Miner provides substantive guidance.[15]

Furthermore the legal framework for the financing of mining projects[16] and the question of access to infrastructure such as railways and ports[17] is not being discussed, as each topic has its own compilations.

The research is focused on the time frame between 1992 and 2013, but also includes past and more recent developments where they are helpful for an understanding of the status quo. The laws reflect their state as of June 30, 2013 if not noted otherwise. References such as today, now and current refer to June 30, 2013.

This particular time span was chosen with reference to fluctuations in the development of the commodity prices between 1992 and 2013 as a possible stimulus for investment, without attempting to draw conclusions regarding the impact of the development of the commodity prices on the changes in the law.

The time span furthermore was useful as the *Mabo case* in Australia (see infra) the end of Apartheid in South Africa (see infra) and the economic liberalization in Colombia (see infra) all took place in the early 1990s and strongly influenced how the legal framework for foreign investments in mining projects applicable to the respective countries developed.

Each specific question raised takes into account the status quo as of June 30, 2013. If applicable, it will then show how this status quo was reached by analysing the key legal developments of the past and conclude by analysing current political trends to point towards possible legal developments in the future.

1.5 The Choice of Australia, South Africa and Colombia as Jurisdictions to be Analysed in Depth

Considering the wealth of nations that possess some or substantial reserves of minerals and the limit of this volume a choice had to be made for nations that are so central for the world's mining landscape that developments in their respective jurisdiction have the potential to represent the global legal regime for mining investments.

This first and foremost is based on the Economic Demonstrated Resources ("***EDR***") of crucial minerals.

At the same time it was crucial to guarantee geographic and economic differentiation to avoid that developments only reflect location specific legal developments or a certain level of industrial development.

[15] Whyte et al. (2012).

[16] Runge (1998), GMF (2014) and Annels (2004).

[17] Livermore (2011).

Furthermore the data and legal material needed to be accessible to the author in respect of language and cooperation of the respective academic, public and private sources for information.

The choice fell for Australia, South Africa and Colombia. The countries, their regulatory regime and the reasons why they became the focus of a work on international mining investments are introduced in the following paragraphs and further detailed in the respective case studies:

1.5.1 Australia

1.5.1.1 Overview Over the Regulatory Regime for Mining in Australia

In various former British colonies on the Australian continent, democratic systems were established over 150 years ago. The Commonwealth of Australia was established in 1901.[18]

Today Australia can be described as a national federation of states and territories with representative democracies at national, state and local level.

The Commonwealth of Australia (to be distinguished from the Commonwealth (of formerly British Nations) includes six states (Queensland, Tasmania, Victoria, Western Australia and New South Wales) and several internal (the Australian Capital Territory which includes Canberra, and the Northern Territory) and external (Norfolk Island, Christmas Island and Cocos (Keeling) Islands) territories. The population of Australia is approximately 22 million people.[19]

The Australian Constitution provides specific powers to the national government, with the residual power of government retained by the states. Local governments are then creations of the state legislatures.

The states and territories retain jurisdictional power over natural resources such as minerals, onshore petroleum and offshore petroleum up to the three nautical mile limit from the baseline, while the national government shares jurisdictional power with the states and territories in other classes of natural resources and autonomously regulates offshore petroleum outside the three nautical mile limit from the baseline.[20]

Whilst the regulation of mining activities in the several states and territories differs between the various jurisdictions, the focus of this work will be on the State of Queensland. The reason for choosing Queensland lies in its importance for the mining sector in Australia overall, especially with regard to the production of coal, and the accessibility of data.

---

[18] For an overview over the history of the Commonwealth of Australia see: Australian History (2014).

[19] PWC (2013), p. 4.

[20] Australian Government (2013).

In Queensland, Australia, the State Minister responsible for the legislation governing the management of natural resources is the Minister for Natural Resources and Mines. The Minister is assisted by the Department of Natural Resources and Mines.[21] Further key departments include the Department of Energy and Water Supply,[22] the Department of State Development, Infrastructure and Planning[23] and the Queensland Treasury.

When this report refers to Indigenous Australians, it refers to Aboriginal and Torres Strait Islander Australians.[24]

1.5.1.2 Importance of Australia in the Global Mining Landscape

Australia has been a global centre for mining for decades: The history of modern mining activities in Australia started when gold was discovered in New South Wales in April 1851.[25] Today, Australia is referenced as the No. 3 on the World's Top Mining Countries.[26]

Whilst Australia is still a key producer and net exporter of gold, today iron ore and coal production and export are even more important.

Australia possesses one of the largest EDR of Iron ore in the world. Of the global EDR of Iron ore that totals 168 billion tonnes, Australia accounts for 28 billion tonnes, or 16.7 %. Russia with 13 % holds the next biggest share of global EDR of Iron ore.[27]

Australia is also one of the world's largest producers of Iron ore. In 2009 Australia's Iron ore production (including concentrate) was 423 million tonnes, with only China producing more Iron ore. [28] In 2009 Australia exported 390 million tonnes of Iron ore, with over two thirds of it being exported to China.[29]

EDR of Coal in Australia as of 2012 was calculated to be 76,400 million tonnes. Of the world's EDR of Coal totalling 860 billion tonnes, Australia's share is 9 %. Its reserves rank fourth behind the United States, Russia and China.[30]

Australia is also one of the world's largest producers for Coal. Australia's production in 2012 was 241 million tonnes, with a global share of coal production of 6.3 % and with only China and the United States of America producing more Coal.[31]

---

[21] Queensland Government (2014).

[22] Queensland Government (2014).

[23] Queensland Government (2014).

[24] Australian Government (2014), p. 2.

[25] La Croix (1992b).

[26] O'Donnell (2014).

[27] Geoscience Australia (2014a).

[28] Geoscience Australia (2014b).

[29] Australian Bureau of Agricultural and Resource Economics and Sciences (2014), p. 23.

[30] BP, p. 30.

[31] BP, p. 32.

Compared to China's vast economic resources of rare earth oxides, the Australian share of the world's economic resources of rare earth oxides is small and estimated at less than 2 %.[32] Considering the quasi monopoly position of China, any substantial production site outside of China is however crucial for the global mining landscape. Australia does have several potential and some realized rare earth projects.

The Mount Weld project already produces rare earths,[33] the Cummins Range project[34] is under construction in Western Australia and further feasibility studies underway in the Northern Territory and New South Wales.[35]

The development of these projects to commercial production would make Australia one of the few countries in the world actually producing rare earth oxides.[36] Fully state-owned mining companies do not exist in Australia.

1.5.2 *South Africa*

1.5.2.1 Overview Over the Regulatory Regime for Mining in South Africa

South Africa has a hybrid legal system, having incorporated parts of a civil law system through Dutch influence, parts of a common law system through British influence and parts of South African customary law.[37]

According to section five, six and seven of the Constitution of South Africa the levels of governmental hierarchy in South Africa are the national (federal) level, the provinces and the local level.

The Minister responsible for governing the management of natural resources is the federal Minister Mineral Resources. The Mission statement of the Department of Mineral Resources reads as follows: "[*To*] *Promote and Regulate the Minerals and Mining Sector for transformation, growth, development and ensure that all South Africans derive sustainable benefits from the country's mineral wealth.*"[38]

Its mineral policy and promotion branch is responsible for designing and implementing mineral related policies that encourage investments, at the same time it ensures that environmental standards are observed. Its mineral regulation branch deals with regulating the mining industry's process of post-Apartheid

[32] Geoscience Australia (2014b).

[33] Rarus (2014).

[34] Navigator Resources Navigator Resources Limited (2014).

[35] Geoscience Australia (2014b).

[36] Geoscience Australia (2014b).

[37] Du Bois (2004), p. 15.

[38] Department of Mineral Resources South Africa (2011), p. 4.

transformation. Health and safety legislation is implemented by the mine health and safety inspectorate.[39]

Further public entities and agencies relevant in the South African mining sector are: the South African Diamond and Precious Metals Regulator, the State Diamond Trader, the Council for Geoscience and the Council for Mineral Technology and Research.

When this work refers to Historically Disadvantaged South Africans ("***HDSAs***"), it refers to "*any person, category of persons or community, disadvantaged by unfair discrimination before the Constitution of the Republic of South Africa, 1993 (Act No. 200 of 1993) came into operation.*"[40]

1.5.2.2 Importance of South Africa in the Global Mining Landscape

In 1867 the discovery of diamonds on the banks of the Orange River close to South Africa's Northern Cape Region's capital Kimberley ignited the mining history in South Africa. The discovery of the world's largest gold deposits in Witwatersrand shortly thereafter in 1886 led to the first gold rush in South Africa. The wealth of the region in part also triggered the Anglo-Boer Wars, which in the end led to the annexation of South Africa by the British Empire by 1910.[41] Today, South Africa is referenced as the No. 1 on the World's Top Mining Countries.[42]

Up to today diamonds and gold play a key role in the South African mining industry, but iron ore, coal and platinum also gained importance.

South Africa is probably most renown in the mining industry for its quasi-monopoly on Platinum. South Africa is estimated to possess EDR of Platinum of 63,000 tonnes and therefore about 95 % of the global EDR.[43] With a production of 131 tonnes it produces more than five time of the second largest producer Russia—and has an abundant reserve to maintain the production on a similar level for decades to come or even increase it.[44]

South Africa is estimated to possess Economically Developable Resources (EDR) of Iron ore of about 1000 million tonnes of the global EDR of Iron ore. This is about 0.9 % of the global EDR. The importance of South Africa for the global Iron Ore market derives from its high production levels. It currently produces about 72 million tonnes of Iron Ore a year of which is more than the United States.[45]

South Africa's estimated EDR of coal is about 30,200 million tonnes. With an approximate 3.5 % of the world's coal reserves of 860,938 million tonnes it is

[39] Government of South Africa (2012), p. 370.

[40] Government of South Africa (2004), p. 2.

[41] Projects IQ (2014).

[42] O'Donnell (2014).

[43] USGS (2014a), p. 121.

[44] USGS (2014a), p. 121.

[45] USGS (2014a), p. 85.

therefore ranked 9th on the global scale.[46] With a production of about 147 million tonnes it produces about 3.8 % of the global market.[47]

South Africa's estimated EDR of gold is about 6 tonnes. This is about 13 % of the global EDR of gold, ranking South Africa as No. 2. It's production is at about 160 tonnes, ranking South Africa fifth on a global production scale.[48]

Being the world leader in rare earth production in the 1950s, South Africa now again has a great potential for rare earth projects.[49] Construction and small-scale production have already started at Steenkampskraal[50] and Zandkopsrift[51] and separation plants are being constructed.[52]

Another key player in the South African mining industry is the chamber of mines. It is an industry employers' organization with the purpose to extract, promote and protect the collective interests of its members.[53]

There are some state-owned mining companies, such as Alexkor and the newly founded African Exploration Mining & Finance Corporation ("***AEMFC***"), that explore coal and uranium.[54] Both do not have a major stake in the South African mining industry landscape so far.

1.5.3 Colombia

1.5.3.1 Overview Over the Regulatory Regime for Mining in Colombia

According to article 1 of the Constitution of Colombia of 1991. Colombia is organized as a social State of law, organized as a unitary, decentralized, democratic, participatory and pluralistic Republic with autonomous territorial entities.[55]

[46] BP (2014), p. 30.

[47] BP (2014), p. 32.

[48] USGS (2014a), p. 67.

[49] Jepson (2014), p. 17.

[50] Great Western Minerals Group (2014).

[51] Frontier Rare Earths (2014).

[52] Jepson (2014), p. 10.

[53] Chamber of Mines (2014).

[54] Creamer's Media Mining Weekly (2014).

[55] Article 1 of the Constitution of Colombia of 1991: Colombia es "(...) *un Estado social de derecho, organizado en forma de República unitaria, descentralizada, con autonomía de sus entidades territoriales, democrática, participativa y pluralista, fundada en el respeto de la dignidad humana, en el trabajo y la solidaridad de las personas que la integran y en la prevalencia del interés general.*" [(...) a social State of law, organized as a unitary, decentralized, democratic, participatory, and pluralistic Republic, with autonomous territorial entities, founded on respect for human dignity, work and the solidarity of the persons composing it, and the prevalence of the general interest.]

According to article 286 of the Constitution of Colombia of 1991, below the federal level the political power is organized in the levels of: "(...) *departamentos, los distritos, los municipios y los territorios indígenas*." [(...) departments, districts, municipalities, and Indigenous territories.][56]

In Colombia, mineral resources are generally managed at the federal level. There is one exception however: The government of the departments of Antioquia has the capacity to grant and control mining concession agreements for all minerals in their territory, and the governments of the departments of Cesar, Norte de Santander, Caldas and Boyacá have the capacity to grant and control mining concession agreements for all minerals, except emeralds and coal.[57] Yet the applicable law remains the same.

The Minister responsible for governing the management of natural resources is the Minister of the (federal) Ministerio de Minas y Energía [Ministry of Mines and Energy]. The Mission statement of the ministry is to create and adopt policies aimed at sustainable utilization of mineral and energy resources and thereby to contribute to economic and social development of the country.[58]

By decree 4134 of 2011 the government has founded the Agencia Nacional de Minería [National Mining Agency]. The Agencia Nacional de Minería become operational May 3rd, 2012 and was established to manage the day-to-day administration of the mineral sector for the government.[59] The mission statement of the agency states is to manage the mineral resources owned by the State efficiently and effectively to promote productivity and competitiveness of the mining sector and in order to maximize the contribution of the mineral resources to the sustainable development of the country.[60]

Prior to its establishment these tasks, such as awarding mining titles and solving related disputes, had been administrated by "*Ingeominas*"[61] [Colombian Institute of Geology and Mining]—which had received substantial criticism for its management of Colombia's natural resources.[62]

---

[56] Article 286 of the Constitution of Colombia of 1991 "(...) *departamentos, los distritos, los municipios y los territorios indígenas*." [(...) departments, districts, municipalities, and Indigenous territories.]

[57] Law Business Research Ltd (2014), p. 2.

[58] Agencia Nacional de Minería (2014), *Misión y Visión*: "*Formular y adoptar políticas dirigidas al aprovechamiento sostenible de los recursos mineros y energéticos para contribuir al desarrollo económico y social del país*." [To create and adopt policies aimed at sustainable utilization of mineral and energy resources to contribute to economic and social development of the country.]

[59] Agencia Nacional de Minería (2014).

[60] Agencia Nacional de Minería (2014), *Misión y Visión*: "*Administrar en forma eficiente y eficaz los recursos minerales de propiedad del Estado para promover la productividad y competitividad del sector, a fin de maximizar su contribución al desarrollo sostenible del país*." [To manage the mineral resources owned by the State efficiently and effectively to promote productivity and competitiveness of the sector, in order to maximize their contribution to the sustainable development of the country.]

[61] Amortegui and Jiménez (2013).

[62] Amortegui and Jiménez (2013).

Other public entities and agencies relevant in the Colombian mining sector are the Servicio Geológico Colombiano [Geological Service Colombia] which aims to perform scientific research to generate geoscientific knowledge of the national territory[63] and the "*Unidad de Planeación Minero Energética*" [Mining and Energy Planning Unit] that helps the government to determine economic information for tax/policy choices.[64]

1.5.3.2 Importance of Colombia in the Global Mining Landscape

While between the 1980s and the 2000s foreign direct investors were careful to invest in Colombia because of the security situation,[65] the higher level of safety in the last years has redrawn interest to Colombia[66] and several new projects to explore the mineral wealth of Colombia are on their way.[67] Colombia has become renowned as key mining country in Latin America for its combination of mineral wealth and accessibility for foreign investors.[68]

The mining industry plays a steadily increasing important role in the overall Colombian economy. By 2012 in Colombia the value derived from the exploitation of mines and quarries was about USD 20 billion, which equals 7.7 % of Colombia's GDP.[69] Coal, Nickel and Gold play a key role in the Colombian mining market.

Colombia is estimated to possess EDR of coal of about 6746 million tonnes. Of the world's EDR of Coal totalling 860 billion tonnes, Colombia's share is 0.6 %.[70] The specific importance derives from the fact that is possesses the largest reserves in Latin America, making it indispensable for the local industry for accessing Coal without substantial transport costs. With a steadily increasing production of about 59 million tonnes in 2012 it produces about 1.5 % of the global market.[71]

Colombia is estimated to possess EDR of Nickel of about 1,100,000 tonnes. With a production of 72,000 tonnes in 2012 it is ranked 11th with request to global production.[72]

---

63 Servicio Geológico Colombiano (2014), *Objetivos y Funciones*: "*Realizar investigación científica básica para generar conocimiento geocientífico integral del territorio nacional.*" [Perform basic scientific research to generate comprehensive geoscientific knowledge of the national territory].

64 La Unidad de Planeación Minero Energética UPME (2014).

65 For on overview over the historical developments see: Pascuzzi (1994), p. 451; Federal Research Division (2014).

66 Germany Trade and Invest (2014).

67 Resource Investing News (2014).

68 Walther-Meade (2014).

69 Wacaster (2014), p. 2.

70 BP (2014).

71 BP (2014).

72 USGS (2014b), p. 2.

For Colombia it is difficult to determine a reliable estimate of EDR of gold as to the various illegal and small-scale mining projects. The estimate in regards to the production based on export/sale statistics shows a production of 66 tonnes in 2012.[73]

There are no major state-owned companies active in the Colombian mining business. Ecopetrol is a major player, but only in the energy business.[74] The former state-owned mining company Minercol was privatized[75] and eventually liquidated against strong union-led public protest.[76]

Other key players in the Colombian mining scene are artisanal, local, Indian and Afro-Colombian miners whose role is discussed in detail infra.

1.5.4 Acknowledged Exemplary Nature of Case Studies

While results derived from the comparison Australia, South Africa and Colombia will always be of exemplary nature only, the specific combination of Australia, South Africa and Colombia provided additional advantages:

Australia, South Africa and Colombia substantially differ in their geographic location, size, level of industrial development in general and the development of their mining industry, their legal systems and legal history, the number and ethnic background of their citizens, their culture, language and their (non-)colonial history. Any result found to equally exist in these three jurisdictions is therefore more likely to be a result of a global, rather than a region specific development.

---

[73] Wacaster (2014), p. 4.

[74] Ecopetrol (2014).

[75] Issued by article 358 Mining Law 2001: "*La Empresa Nacional Minera, Minercol Ltda., debera en un plazo no mayor a seis (6) meses, contados a partir de la expedicion del presente Codigo, reestructurar su organizacion administrativa y su planta de personal, de conformidad con los lineamientos establecidos por el Gobiemo Nacional.*"

[The National Mining Company Ltd.- MINERCOL LTDA should in a term not over six (6) months, counted as from the issuing of the present Code, restructure its administrative organization and its staff, according with the guidelines established by the National Government.];

The English translations of Spanish Acts are based on Minminas, *English translation Mining Law 2001*. In the case of the Mining Law 2001 and Colombia Commercial Code on the translation provided by Foreign Tax Law, Inc, *Colombia Commercial Code English* in the case of the Colombian Commercial Code 1971. Further translation and modifications were undertaken were done by the author, if so deemed necessary.

[76] Labournet (2014).

1.6 Methodology

This work uses a legal science approach regarding the analyses of the status quo and a political science approach regarding the analysis of future political trends. Past developments required a hybrid approach, combining both a legal science and a political science approach for their understanding.

Legal science has been defined as the science:

> (. . .) die sich mit der Lösung von Rechtsfragen im Rahmen und auf der Grundlage einer bestimmten, historisch gewachsenen Rechtsordnung befasst, also die herkömmlicherweise so genannte Jurisprudenz.[77]

[(. . .) which deals with the resolution of legal issues in the framework and on the basis of a specific, historically developed legal system, conventionally known as jurisprudence.]

For the purpose of this work, the legal science approach includes taking into account the legislated status quo and legislative developments such as past acts as well as executive orders and judgments by the judiciary.

Political science has been defined as:

> (. . .) including studies of political structures, processes and policies in (. . .) societies, the contemporary ideas, ideologies and theories that determine the framework for political decision making, and the organizational and diplomatic approaches to cooperation and conflict resolution in the international system.[78]

For the purpose of this work, the political science approach includes taking into account political power structures, processes and policies that are likely to impact on the legal framework for foreign investments in mining projects in the future.

The research is based on primary and secondary sources.

Primary sources were gathered whilst living in Brisbane, Queensland, Australia from January 2012 to July 2013, specifically while working at HopgoodGanim's Resources and Energy practice group, as a student of the University of Queensland and as a Visiting Scholar at the Centre for Social Responsibility in Mining of the Sustainable Minerals Institute. Primary sources were furthermore gathered from research field trips to the Ukraine in January 2013, South Africa in February 2013 and Colombia in June 2013.

No formal interviews were conducted, but numerous discussions with and feedback on my writing from professors, lawyers, foreign investors, mining engineers, mining company staff, NGO activists, politicians, public servants and members of local/indigenous populations helped me to frame my thinking and to focus my research on the most pressing issues in the context of International Mining Investments.

Secondary resources were mostly gathered at the International Investment Law Centre at the University of Cologne, Germany, the University of Queensland,

---

[77] Larenz and Canaris (1995), p. 7.

[78] University of Queensland (2014).

Brisbane, Australia, the University of Cape Town, South Africa and the Universidad Nacional in Bogota, Colombia.

1.7 Line of Inquiry and Outline of the Study

This chapter discusses the approach and outlines the theoretical framework of the study. It outlines what the legal challenges of the realization of international mining projects are. From the numerous legal challenges likely to be found it was then necessary to select those that are key challenges and require scholarly attention in this work and beyond.

Chapters 2–11 discuss the key questions to be asked for international mining investments. Each of these chapters introduces the question and its relevance in the context of international mining investments and determines the horizon of the observations. It then presents the results of the research in the three chosen jurisdictions by presenting first the legal status quo and then past legal and likely future political developments that might alter the legal environment in the near future. When analyzing the legal challenges of the realization of international mining projects in different host countries the work then shall analyze the differences and similarities in the answers to the legal challenges posed, focusing on the identification of similarities and common trends.

Chapter 12 summarizes and compares the finding of Chaps. 2–11 and undertakes them a thorough analysis. The question arises what the results mean for the future of the study of the legal framework for foreign investments in international mining projects. The work finds the introduction of a sub-category of foreign investment law to be called "*International Mining Investment Law*" ("***IMIL***") to be a necessary next step and concludes Chap. 12 and the work by sketching the pillars of such International Mining Investment Law as a framework to capture and resolve the specific legal challenges international mining investments face as of today and in the future.

References

Agencia Nacional de Minería (2014) Misión y Visión. Available online at: https://www.anm.gov.co/?q=agencia/mision. Last checked on 15 February 2014

Amortegui NM, Jiménez PP (2013) Mining National Agency. Available online at: http://www.palacioslleras.com/en/the-mining-national-agency-one-step-closer-to-an-effective-mining-institutionalization/, updated on 6/27/2013. Last checked on 15 February 2014

Annels AE (2004) Mineral deposit evaluation. Springer, Dordrecht

Australian Government (2013) Indigenous business Australia. Available online at: http://www.iba.gov.au/. Last checked on 15 February 2014

Australian Bureau of Agricultural and Resource Economics and Sciences (2014) Australian mineral statistics 2011. Available online at: http://adl.brs.gov.au/data/warehouse/pe_abares99010607/AMS11.2_Marchqtr_2011_lowres_REPORT.pdf. Last checked 22 March 2015

Australian History (2014) Australian history. Available online at: http://www.australianhistory.org/. Last checked on 1/5/2014

Australian Government, Paper indigenous economic development strategy 2011–2018 (2014) Available online at: http://www.fahcsia.gov.au/sites/default/files/documents/09_2012/ieds_2011_2018.pdf. Last checked on 15 February 2014

Bates GM (2009) Environmental law in Australia, 7th edn. LexisNexis Butterworths, Chatswood

Beyerlin U, Marauhn T (2011) International environmental law. Hart/Beck, Oxford/Portland/Munich

BP, BP statistical review of world energy 2013 (2014) Available online at: http://www.bp.com/content/dam/bp/pdf/statistical-review/statistical_review_of_world_energy_2013.pdf. Last checked 22 March 2015

Brauteseth N (1995) Environmental law in South Africa. Int Bus Law 23:409

Chamber of Mines (2014) About. Available online at: http://www.bullion.org.za/content/?pagename=About&pid=4. Last checked 10 April 2015

Creamer's Media Mining Weekly (2014) South Africa's new State mining company pursuing coal, uranium. Available online at: http://www.miningweekly.com/article/south-africas-new-state-mining-company-pursuing-coal-uranium-ceo-2008-10-28. Last checked on 10 April 2015

Department of Mineral Resources South Africa (2011) Annual Report 2010/2011. Available online at: http://www.info.gov.za/view/DownloadFileAction?id=177944. Last checked on 15 February 2014

Du Bois F (2004) Introduction: history, system and sources. In: Van Der Merwe CG, Du Plessis JE (eds) Introduction to the law of South Africa. Kluwer Law International, The Hague, pp 1–54

Ecopetrol (2014) About us. Available online at: http://www.ecopetrol.com.co/english/. Last checked on 11 April 2015

Federal Research Division (2014) Colombia: a country study. Available online at: http://lcweb2.loc.gov/frd/cs/pdf/CS_Colombia.pdf. Last checked on 10 April 2015

Fisher DE (2010) Australian environmental law. Norms, principles and rules, 2nd edn. Thomson Reuters (Professional) Australia Limited, Rozelle

Frontier Rare Earths (2014) Rare metal mining exploration and development stock. Available at: http://www.frontierrareearths.com/. Last checked on 22 March 2015

Galvis SR (2012) La regulacíon ambiental y social de la minería en Colombia. In FES publicás (38), p 1. Available online at: http://library.fes.de/pdf-files/bueros/kolumbien/09382.pdf. Last checked on 15 February 2014

Geoscience Australia, Iron ore (2014a) Available online at: http://www.ga.gov.au/minerals/mineral-resources/iron-ore.html. Last checked 22 March 2015

Geoscience Australia, Rare earths (2014b) Available online at: http://www.ga.gov.au/minerals/mineral-resources/rare-earth-elements.html. Last checked 22 March 2015

Germany Trade and Invest GmbH (2014) Colombia - mining struggle. Available online at: http://www.gtai.de/GTAI/Navigation/DE/Trade/maerkte,did=781730.html. Last checked on 11 April 2015

GMF (2014) Global mining finance. Available online at: http://www.globalminingfinance.com/documents/gmf-2011.pdf. Last checked on 15 February 2014

Government of South Africa (2004) South African Mining Charta - broad-based socio-economic empowerment charter for the South African mining industry. Available online at: http://www.cidafund.co.za/charters/miningCharter.pdf. Last checked on 15 February 2014

Government of South Africa (2012) SA yearbook mineral resources. Available online at: http://www.gcis.gov.za/sites/www.gcis.gov.za/files/docs/resourcecentre/yearbook/2011/21_Mineral%20resources.pdf, updated on 1/11/2013. Last checked on 15 February 2014

Great Western Minerals Group (2014) Steenkampskraal Mine (Rareco), Western Cape, South Africa. Available online at: http://www.gwmg.ca/html/projects/mining/index.cfm. Last checked: 22 March 2015

Gunningham N, Sinclair D (2012) Managing mining hazards - regulation, safety and trust. Federation Press, Annandale

Harrison J (2011) Making the law of the sea. A study in the development of international law. Cambridge University Press (Cambridge studies in international and comparative law), Cambridge/New York

Hester RE, Harrison RM (1994) Mining and its environmental impact, vol 1. Royal Society of Chemistry (Issues in environmental science and technology), Cambridge

Hobe S (2014) Einführung in das Völkerrecht, 10th edn. Francke, Tübingen

Jepson N (2014) A 21st century scramble: South Africa, China and the rare earth metals industry. Occasional paper no. 113, South African Institute of International Affairs 2012, p 17

Kiss A, Shelton D (2004) International environmental law, 3rd [rev.] edn. Transnational, Ardsley

La Croix SJ (1992) Property rights and institutional change during Australia's gold rush. Explor Econ Hist 29(2):204–227. doi:10.1016/0014-4983(92)90011-K

La Unidad de Planeación Minero Energética UPME (2014) Quienes somos. Available online at: http://www1.upme.gov.co/index.php/la-upme/quienes-somos.html. Last checked on 15 February 2014

Labournet, Colombia: stop the closing of Minercol Ltd (2014) Available online at: http://www.labournet.net/world/0111/colomb1.html. Last checked on 11 April 2015

Larenz K, Canaris C-W (1995) Methodenlehre der Rechtswissenschaft. 3 Aufl., Dritte, neu bearbeitete Aufl. Springer, Berlin/New York

Law Business Research Ltd (2014) http://www.lbresearch.com: Colombia - mining - reference - Latin lawyer. Available online at: http://www.cardenasycardenas.com/archivos/52.M2013%20-%20Colombia%20%282%29.pdf. Last checked on 15 February 2014

Lee RJ (2012) Law and regulation of commercial mining of minerals in outer space, vol 7. Springer (Space regulations library), Dordrecht/New York

Livermore J (2011) Transport law in Australia. Kluwer Law International, Alphen aan den Rijn

Marcus JJ (1997) Mining environmental handbook. Effects of mining on the environment and American environmental controls on mining. Imperial College Press/World Scientific Pub. Co. [distributor], London/Singapore/River Edge

McAuslan P (2002) Environmental law in South Africa. J Environ Law 14(2):266

McKinsey Global Institute (2011) The resource revolution: meeting the world's energy, materials, food and water needs. Available online at: http://www.mckinsey.com/insights/energy_resources_materials/resource_revolution. Last checked on 15 February 2014

National Geographics, Lunar mining activities (2014) Available online at: http://news.nationalgeographic.com/news/2013/11/131113-lunar-property-rights-bigelow-nasa/. Last checked on 15 February 2014

Navigator Resources Navigator Resources Limited (2014) Cummins range. Available online at: http://www.navigatorresources.com.au/Projects/Cummins-Range-%28REE%29. Last checked 22 March 2015

O'Donnell C (2014) The world's top 5 mining countries. Available online at: http://www.wealthwire.com/news/global/2372. Last checked: 22 March 2015

Oude Elferink AG (2005) Stability and change in the law of the sea. The role of the LOS convention, vol 24. Martinus Nijhoff (Nova et vetera iuris gentium. Series A, modern international law), Leiden/Boston

Pascuzzi DJ (1994) International trade and foreign investment in Colombia: a sound economic policy amidst crisis. Fla J Int Law 9:443–478

Pevato PM (2003) International environmental law. Ashgate/Dartmouth (The library of essays in international law), Aldershot/Burlington

Projects IQ (2014) Mining in South Africa. Available online at: http://www.projectsiq.co.za/mining-in-south-africa.htm. Last checked 22 March 2015

PWC (2013) Doing business in Australia - business guide. Available online at: http://www.pwc.com.au/legal/assets/GuideBusiness2011.pdf, updated on 3/18/2013. Last checked on 15 February 2014

Queensland Government, Department of energy and water supply (2014a) Available online at: http://www.dews.qld.gov.au/. Last checked on 15 February 2014

Queensland Government, Department of state development, infrastructure and planning (2014b) Available online at: http://www.dsdip.qld.gov.au/. Last checked on 15 February 2014

Queensland Government, Executive directory (2014c) Available online at: http://www.qgd.qld.gov.au/min-minister.html. Last checked on 15 February 2014

Rarus (2014) Mount weld project. Available online at: http://www.rarus.com.au/irm/ShowStaticCategory.aspx?CategoryID=216&masterpage=3. Last checked on 22 March 2015

Resource Investing News (2014) Gold mining in Colombia. Available online at: http://resourceinvestingnews.com/60342-gold-mining-in-colombia.html?utm_source=Resource+Investing+News&utm_campaign=44151025fd-RSS_EMAIL_CAMPAIGN&utm_medium=email&utm_term=0_f83d87db0f-44151025fd-248794225. Last checked on 11 April 2015

Rey JPG (2010) Minería y Medio Ambiente en Colombia. In Lexbase Colombia. Available online at: http://www.portafolio.co/opinion/blogs/juridica/mineria-y-medio-ambiente-en-colombia-la-nueva-regulacion-del-2010. Last checked on 15 February 2014

Runge IC (1998) Mining economics and strategy. Society for Mining, Metallurgy, and Exploration, Littleton

Sands PJ, Peel J, Fabra Aguilar A, Mackenzie R (2012) Principles of international environmental law, 3rd edn. Cambridge University Press, Cambridge/New York

Servicio Geológico Colombiano (2014) Objetivos y Funciones. Available online at: http://www.sgc.gov.co/Nosotros/Objetivos-y-Funciones.aspx. Last checked on 15 February 2014

Sonter M (2014) The technical and economic feasibility of mining the near-earth asteroids. Available online at: http://mining.about.com/gi/o.htm?zi=1/XJ&zTi=1&sdn=mining&cdn=b2b&tm=26&f=00&tt=2&bt=3&bts=14&zu=http%3A//www.spacefuture.com/archive/the_technical_and_economic_feasibility_of_mining_the_near_earth_asteriods.shtml. Last checked on 15 February 2014

University of Queensland (2014) What is political science? Available online at: http://www.polsis.uq.edu.au/major-in-political-science. Last checked on 15 February 2014

USGS, Mineral commodities summary (2014a) Available online at: http://minerals.usgs.gov/minerals/pubs/mcs/2015/mcs2015.pdf. Last checked 22 March 2015

USGS, Nickel (2014b) Available online at: http://minerals.usgs.gov/minerals/pubs/commodity/nickel/mcs-2012-nicke.pdf. Last checked 11 April 2015

Wacaster S (2014) The mineral industry of Colombia. Available online at: http://minerals.usgs.gov/minerals/pubs/country/2012/myb3-2012-co.pdf. Last checked on 11 April 2015

Walther-Meade C (2014) Colombia. Available online at: http://latinlawyer.com/reference/topics/46/jurisdictions/8/colombia/. Last checked: 22 March 2015

Whyte J, Brockelbank T, Cooke J (2012) Mining explained: a Layman's guide. The Northern Miner, Don Mills

Yang B (2012) Regulatory governance and risk management. Occupational health and safety in the coal mining industry, vol 47. Routledge (Routledge advances in management and business studies), New York

Chapter 2
May I Invest? The Question of the Admission of Foreign Investments

2.1 Introduction and Disambiguation

Foreign direct investment has been defined as involving "*the transfer of tangible or intangible assets from one country to another for the purpose of their use in that country to generate wealth under the total or partial control of the owner of the assets*".[1]

International law distinguishes between foreign direct investment and portfolio investments. Portfolio investments, such as buying foreign shares, bonds or other instruments, are generally accepted to not fall under the scope of international law and are therefore not protected by customary international law.[2] It is possible to include portfolio investments under the regime for foreign investment through treaties,[3] such as bilateral investment treaties and investor state treaties.

This work will focus on foreign direct investment[4] as defined supra and neglect portfolio investments as they do not fall within the scope of the close, more often than not long-term relationship between a foreign direct investor and a host state created by an international mining investment that is at the heart of this work.[5]

Foreign investment in mining projects discussed in this work can be further distinguished as "*Greenfield investments*" and "*Brownfield investments*".

Greenfield investments have been defined as a "*form of foreign investment where a parent company starts a new venture in a foreign country by constructing new operational facilities from the ground up*".[6]

---

[1] Sornarajah (2010), p. 8.

[2] Sornarajah (2010), p. 9.

[3] Sornarajah (2010), p. 9.

[4] For the purpose of readability, the work will infra refer to foreign direct investment as "*foreign investment*" and to foreign direct investors as "*foreign investors*".

[5] Sornarajah (2010), p. 9.

[6] Investopedia (2014).

R.W. Roeder, *Foreign Mining Investment Law*, DOI 10.1007/978-3-319-31217-0_2

In the case of an investment in a mining project, this refers to investment into prospecting and exploration of a possible target area, but can also include investment in the development phase of a first time mining project, such as investments in early mining activities.

Brownfield investments take place "*when a company or government entity purchases or leases existing production facilities to launch a new production activity*".[7]

In case of an investment in a mining project Brownfield investment may refer to investments into further prospecting and exploration of an existing mining project as well as investments in the development or exploitation of an existing mining project to either increase production or to resume production after the mining project had a shutdown, e.g. because of lost profitability due to low commodity prices.

2.2 Relevance

The question of the admission of foreign investment lies at the centre of the sovereignty of a host state and is a precondition for realizing any international mining project.

2.3 Observation Horizon

The discussion of the admission of foreign investment in this section relates to the question "*if and to what extent*" the investment is allowed into a country.

The question of "*how*" the investment is allowed into a country, which is also referred to as "*establishment*"[8] of foreign investment, is discussed in various other questions infra.

States are not obliged by international law to admit foreign investment into their economies. The choice to admit foreign direct investments or not is protected by the international principle of national sovereignty that expands to economic decisions.[9] States can decide to be bound to allow foreign investments from another state or enterprise by contract, e.g. by including the question of admission in bilateral investment treaties.[10] An example can be found in article 2 (1) of the German Model BIT from 2008. It obliges the contracting state to promote as far as possible

[7] Investopedia (2013).

[8] Juillard (2000).

[9] Dolzer and Schreuer (2008), p. 79.

[10] Dolzer and Schreuer (2008), p. 81.

foreign investments and admit such investments in its territory in accordance with its legislation.[11]

The terminology "*as far as possible*" often relates to an approach that limits foreign investments in type or scope.

One way of regulating the inflow of foreign investment is to identify sectors that are not open to foreign investment ("*negative list*"), or to only allow foreign investment in specific sectors ("*positive list*").[12]

Another way is to establish a regulatory system that will review application for foreign investment approvals on a case-by-case basis.[13]

The host state can therefore allow all, some or specific types of foreign investments only. The host state may also decide to review some or each investment on a case-by-case-basis.

For the options of allowing some foreign investment or deciding to review some or each investment on a case-by-case-basis, the host state may choose either to establish objective criteria or to provide its administration with discretion. Furthermore, the host state can determine whether judicial review of investment approval decisions will be available to foreign investors or not.

2.4 Countries

2.4.1 Australia

2.4.1.1 Current Situation

In the Australian legal system, the power over the admission of foreign investment is exercised by the Commonwealth of Australia.

2.4.1.1.1 Policy of Admission of Foreign Investment

The official Foreign Investment Policy of Australia states that Australia "*welcomes foreign investment as it has helped to build Australia's economy and is thought to furthermore enhance the wellbeing of Australians by fostering economic growth and prosperity*".[14] At the same time it states that "*Australia does however review*

[11] Federal Ministry of Economics and Technology, *German Model BIT*: "*Each Contracting State shall in its territory promote as far as possible investments by investors of the other Contracting State and admit such investments in accordance with its legislation.*"

[12] Dolzer and Schreuer (2008), p. 81.

[13] An example is the Australian FIRB system, see infra.

[14] Foreign Investment Review Board (2014a), p. 1.

investment proposals on a case-by-case basis to ensure that Australia's national interest is protected".[15]

2.4.1.1.2 Acts and Regulations

Foreign investment into Australia is regulated by the Foreign Acquisition and Takeovers Act 1975 (FATA), the Foreign Acquisition and Takeovers Regulations 1989 ("**FATR**") and the Foreign Acquisition and Takeovers (Notices) Regulations 1975 ("**FATNR**") as well as Australia's Foreign Investment Policy.[16] Furthermore, the Australian Treasury regularly announces the government's approach towards foreign investment and provides guidance notes to aid foreign investors.[17]

Under sections 18—21A of the FATA the Treasurer of Australia has a wide discretion to allow or block various types of foreign investments or takeovers in Australia.

According to section 18(2) of the FATA the treasurer has discretion to restrict or prohibit the proposed transaction.[18] Section 21A of the FATA gives the Treasurer specific power to examine proposals to acquire interests in urban land, including land acquisitions that may be necessary or desirable to support mining explorations.

While the Treasurer has the power to review and decide upon investment proposals, in practice the Treasurer seeks and generally relies on the assistance of the Assistant Treasurer who in turn is advised by the Foreign Investment Review Board ("***FIRB***").[19] The FIRB comprises three part-time Members and a full-time Executive Member.[20]

2.4.1.1.3 Process of Approval for Foreign Investments

2.4.1.1.3.1 Who Needs to Apply for Approval?

Foreign government investors receive special attention in the screening process of the Foreign Investment Review Board. After substantive debate and fears voiced of Australians, especially in regard to investments by Chinese State-owned

---

15 Foreign Investment Review Board (2014a), p. 1.

16 Foreign Investment Review Board (2014a), p. 1.

17 Foreign Investment Review Board (2014b).

18 Section 18(2) FATA states: "*Where the Treasurer is satisfied that*: (*a*) *a person proposes*, *or persons propose*, *to acquire shares in a corporation or a corporation proposes to issue shares*; (*b*) *the proposed acquisition or acquisitions or the proposed issue would have the result that*: (...) [*foreign control over the corporation is established*] (...); *and that result would be contrary to the national interest*; *the Treasurer may make an order prohibiting the proposed acquisition or all or any of the proposed acquisitions*, *or the proposed issue*, *as the case may be*."

19 Foreign Investment Review Board (2014a), p. 2.

20 Foreign Investment Review Board (2014c).

enterprises,[21] the investment policy was adapted to cover all types of government investors. Government investors are required to notify the FIRB—regardless of the value of the investment.[22]

These related entities include political bodies of that foreign country; companies or other entities in which foreign governments, their agencies or related entities have a total of more than 15 % interest; or companies or entities that are controlled by foreign governments, their agencies or related entities by other means.[23]

For privately owned legal entities, certain thresholds for investment review exist: the investor is required to notify the FIRB only when acquiring a substantial interest in an Australian business or corporation with a value of more than $AUD 248 million.[24]

Under the AUSFTA, United States sourced investment and, since March 1st, 2013 under the ANCERTA, New Zealand sourced investment has been liberalized. For a transaction with any entity from the US or New Zealand, this general threshold increases to $AUD 1078 million, while for investments in prescribed sensitive sectors the threshold remains at $AUD 248 million.[25]

Those sensitive sectors are: media, telecommunications, transport, the supply of training or human resources, the manufacture or supply of military goods or equipment or technology to the Australian Defence Force or other Defence forces, the manufacture or supply of goods, equipment or technology able to be used for a military purpose, the development, manufacture or supply of, or the provision of services relating to encryption and security technologies and communications systems, the extraction of (or the holding of rights to extract) uranium or plutonium or the operation of nuclear facilities.[26]

In order to invest in residential real estate, vacant land or to buy shares in Australian urban land corporations or trusts, all foreign persons are required to notify the FIRB.[27]

This is also the case for investment in developed commercial real estate with a value of AUD$ 54 million or above, whereas US and NZ investors will only have to notify the FIRB if the investment in developed commercial real estate reaches the threshold of AUD$ 1078 million.[28]

---

[21] Industry Search (2014).

[22] Foreign Investment Review Board (2014a), p. 2.

[23] Foreign Investment Review Board, *Australia's Investment Policy 2013*, p. 15 details: "*A body politic of a foreign country; entities in which governments, their agencies or related entities from a single foreign country have an aggregate interest (direct or indirect) of 15 per cent or more; entities in which governments, their agencies or related entities from more than one foreign country have an aggregate interest (direct or indirect) of 40 per cent or more; or entities that are otherwise controlled by foreign governments, their agencies or related entities, and any associates, or could be controlled by them including as part of a controlling group*".

[24] Foreign Investment Review Board (2014a), p. 2.

[25] Foreign Investment Review Board (2014a), p. 2.

[26] Foreign Investment Review Board (2014a), p. 17.

[27] Foreign Investment Review Board (2014a), p. 4.

[28] Foreign Investment Review Board (2014a), p. 4.

2.4.1.1.3.2 Timeline

The FIRB provides assistance in presenting in how to best present a project for notification.[29]

After the notification of a proposed investment is given, the Treasurer has 30 days to consider the application and make a decision. The Treasurer can extend that period by up to a further 90 days by publishing an interim order.[30]

2.4.1.1.3.3 The National Interest Test

The decision to allow or block foreign investment is based on whether or not the investment is considered to be contrary to Australia's national interest. The term "*national interest*" is not defined in the FATA or FATR, giving the Treasurer a wide discretion. The Australian Government does give guidance for orientation though:

> The Treasurer will take into account questions of national security, healthy market competition, the impact on the Australian tax revenue, the economy, the environment, the community and the character of the investor.[31]

For a national security assessment, the Australian Government relies on an assessment provided by the relevant security agencies, such as the Australian Secret Intelligence Service.

The assessment of the impact of foreign investment on healthy competition in Australia and on a global scale aims to guard against an investor gaining control over market pricing and production of a good or service.

As stated, FIRB will consult with the relevant agencies before making a decision whether to admit foreign investment or not. Regarding the question of competition law FIRB therefore may consult with the Australian Competition and Consumer Commission ("***ACCC***").[32]

The extent of tax revenues and the impact on the economy as a whole will be taken into consideration, as will potential environmental and social impacts on Australian communities. The Australian Government also considers the Australian participation in the mining project, but there is no specific "*local ownership*" criterion (see infra).

The "*character*" of the investor refers to the transparency of the commercial actions of the investor, its corporate governance practices and its track record.[33]

The mentioned (see supra) differentiation between private and government owned (or influenced) business entities also plays a role in determining the question of alignment with the national interest.

---

[29] FIRB (2014d).

[30] Foreign Investment Review Board (2014a), p. 5.

[31] Foreign Investment Review Board (2014a), p. 7.

[32] Australian Competition and Consumer Commission (2013).

[33] Foreign Investment Review Board (2014a), p. 8.

This is in line with the enhanced public awareness and concerns regarding foreign investments by state-owned enterprises and sovereign wealth funds.[34] While foreign investments from the United States total over half a trillion dollar Australian in assets, making the United States by far the biggest contributor of total foreign investment in Australia,[35] the public perception is focused on investment from China.[36] Recent rises of Chinese investment—passing $AUD 50 billion between 2007 and 2012 alone—have brought the perception of investment from China into sharper relief.[37]

The Australian government reacted to those developments by releasing a set of new principles that are now considered when determining whether investments by state owned or affiliated entities are consistent with the national interest.[38]

When determining whether or not foreign investment by state owned enterprises or sovereign wealth funds is in the national interest, the Australian Treasurer also considers whether the foreign investment is of commercial nature, or whether the investor might use the investment to pursue further political or strategic objectives.[39]

The Australian Treasurer will also try to assess whether the contractual or funding arrangements are established in a way that allow for control—at the time of the application or later—by a foreign government.[40]

The Australian Government is more restrictive towards investments that are closely aligned or influenced by foreign governments.[41] The Australian Government does take into account mitigating factors such as external (non-governmental) partners, continuous listing on an internationally recognized stock exchange and other arrangements preventing non-commercial activities.[42]

While the Treasurer does have the power to formally prohibit a proposal, most applicants withdraw their proposals if they receive (informal) notice from the FIRB that the proposal faces challenges or is likely to be considered not to be in line with the national interest.[43]

For example: In the time between 2010 and 2011 out of a total of 11,420 applications, 534 were withdrawn whereas only 13 were formally rejected.[44] And even within the 534 withdrawn proposals some might have been withdrawn for business reasons and overlapping applications.

---

[34] Industry Search (2014).

[35] Industry Search (2014).

[36] Industry Search (2014).

[37] Industry Search (2014).

[38] Foreign Investment Review Board (2014a), p. 8.

[39] Foreign Investment Review Board (2014a), p. 8.

[40] Foreign Investment Review Board (2014a), p. 8.

[41] Foreign Investment Review Board (2014a), p. 8.

[42] Foreign Investment Review Board (2014a), p. 8.

[43] Foreign Investment Review Board (2013), p. 10.

[44] Foreign Investment Review Board (2013), p. 10.

The possibility of judicial review of decisions of the Treasurer is limited due to the wide discretion of the Treasurer in respect of the national interest. An example of judicial review is the judgment in *Canwest Global Communications Corp v Treasurer of the Commonwealth of Australia* where a decision of the Treasurer was overruled on the basis that the Treasurer failed to consider the test of foreign control in FATA section 18(4)(a)(ii).[45]

2.4.1.2 Past Legal Developments and Future Political Trends

No major reforms are currently in sight for the FATA. The latest major amendment, the Foreign Acquisitions and Takeovers Amendment Act 2010 ("***FATAA***"), dealt with new investment structures and clarified the voting requirements.[46] This was done to broaden the applicability of the FATA by making sure that corporate restructuring of voting rights would not avoid application of the FATA and thus the Treasurer' power to prohibit an investment.[47]

The question of what is and what is not the right policy of foreign investment in the natural resources sector was and remains a matter of diverse public debate. The opinions of Australia's political leaders are especially split regarding foreign investments from China and possibly state-owned enterprises originating there.[48]

While Tony Abbott is quoted stating: "*It would rarely be in Australia's interest to allow a foreign government or its agencies to control an Australian business.*",[49] Bob Carr, former Minister of Foreign Affairs of Australia replied by calling Abbott's position "*dangerously dumb*".[50]

Somewhere in the middle stands a statement by the Chairman of the Foreign Investment Review Board, Brian Wilson: "*Australian businesses, however they are owned, should be run on a purely commercial basis and not as an extension of the policy, political or economic agenda of a foreign government*".[51]

[45] Federal Court of Australia (2014).

[46] Department of Finance and Deregulation (2013), p. 1.

[47] Department of Finance and Deregulation (2013), p. 2.

[48] Walsh (2012).

[49] The University of Sydney (2012).

[50] The University of Sydney (2012).

[51] The University of Sydney (2012).

2.4.2 *South Africa*

2.4.2.1 Current Situation

In the South African legal system the power over the decision of admitting foreign investments is vested with the government of South Africa at the federal level.

2.4.2.1.1 Policy of Admission of Foreign Investments

The latest policy update regarding foreign investments was announced in connection with a new policy regarding future international investment treaties. It states that the policy: "(...) *will ensure South Africa remains open to foreign investment, provides adequate security and protection to all investors, while preserving the sovereign right of the South African Government to pursue developmental public policy objectives.*"[52]

2.4.2.1.2 Acts and Regulations

A specific admission and screening process examining the reconcilability of a foreign investment with the South African national interest as such does not exist. The South African Reserve Bank explains that non-residents may freely invest in South Africa if the respective transactions are concluded at arm's length and in the form of introducing foreign currency.[53]

The Competition Act of 1998 though does give the South African Government a tool to screen and approve foreign investments. It is important to note that besides the more common goals to promote and maintain competition in South African, section 2 of the Competition Act of 1998 furthermore demands from the South African authorities to promote a greater spread of ownership, in particular to increase the ownership stakes of HDSAs.[54] One could see this drafting of the law as a way to introduce a partial national interest test.

---

[52] Government of South Africa (2014).

[53] South African Reserve Bank (2014), *Financial surveillance and exchange controls* details: "*Non-residents may freely invest in South Africa, provided that suitable documentary evidence is viewed by the bank concerned, in order to ensure that such transactions are concluded at arm's length, at fair market related prices and are financed in an approved manner.*" and that "*Such financing must be in the form of the introduction of foreign currency or Rand from a Non-Resident account* (*i.e. a Rand account opened by a non-resident at a South African bank*)."

[54] Section 2 of the Competition Act of 1998: "(...) *the purpose of this act is to promote and maintain competition in the Republic in order to promote the efficiency, adaptability and development of the economy*; (...); *to promote employment and expense the social and economic welfare of South Africa*; (...) [*and*] *to promote a greater spread of ownership, in particular to increase the ownership stakes of historically disadvantaged persons.*"

2.4.2.2 Past Legal Developments and Future Political Trends

South Africa has a long history of putting effort into attracting foreign investment. For the time under the Apartheid regime, it has been said: "*The problem for South Africa was not that it rejected foreign investments. Instead, foreign investors rejected South Africa.*"[55]

This was not only true for the Apartheid regime, although related international economic sanctions and isolation made it more difficult for South Africa to attract foreign investment. It was also because of the effects of laws such as the Group Areas Act of 1950 that restricted the free movement of blacks in South Africa, and therefore also the free movement of capital and labour within the country.[56]

Attracting foreign investment was a crucial aspect of the re-internationalization of South Africa after the Apartheid regime.[57] Early on after the end of the Apartheid regime and even before he had become the president of South Africa, Nelson Mandela voiced the will to attract foreign investment in his vision for the future foreign policy of South Africa. In an article in "*Foreign Affairs*" he stated:

> It is obvious to me that the primary components of our international economic relations, which must feed our development strategy, are the strengthening of our trade performance and our capacity to attract foreign investment. (. . .) We do not expect foreign investment to solve our economic problems, but we understand that [it] can play a valuable role in our economic development. (. . .) The ANC believes the most important way to attract foreign investment is to create a stable and democratic political environment. Also important is the development of legitimate, transparent, and consistent economic policies."[58]

The legislature followed the path drawn by Nelson Mandela and introduced new regulations promoting foreign investment in private and public projects that included tax cuts, lower import tariffs and a more liberal approach towards currency exchange that step by step led to the very liberal approach of today outlined supra.[59] South Africa also concluded several bilateral investment treaties with European countries in the years after Apartheid (see infra).

Considering this development—and the fact that South Africa has never considered foreign investment as an "*imperialistic form of domination*" as other countries have[60]—it is unlikely that we shall see a stringent restriction of the South African economy towards foreign investment anytime soon.

The broad and political purpose of the Competition Law Act 1998 outlined supra allows for governmental discretion to an extent that creates legal uncertainty for foreign investors. It has been alleged that via the power vested in the Competition Commission according to sections 11–18 of the Competition Act of 1998:

[55] Hunter and Bogran (1999), p. 340.

[56] Hunter and Bogran (1999), p. 341.

[57] Eisenberg (1994), p. 6.

[58] Mandela (1993), p. 95.

[59] Hunter and Bogran (1999), p. 344.

[60] Hunter and Bogran (1999), p. 339.

"*Political interference has, at times, imposed requirements that discriminated against foreign investors*".[61] A case that is referenced in supporting this claim is: "*Minister of Economic Development and Others v Competition Tribunal and Others, South African Commercial, Catering and Allied Workers Union v Wal-Mart Stores Inc. and Another*".[62] In this case, the court dismissed an appeal by the Government of South Africa from the decision of the Competition Tribunal to approve the Wal-Mart purchase of a stake in the South African company Massmart Holding Ltd. While not specifically concerning the mining industry, the case demonstrates the power to limit or condition foreign investments that exists in the Competition law. In the specific case the appeal was dismissed, but Wal-Mart was ordered to reemploy 503 workers fired before the merger.[63]

2.4.3 Colombia

This section regarding Colombia highlights the key points of the statutes, case law, administrative orders and statements in-text and provide the Spanish original text directly followed by a translation in English in "[. . .]" or in the footnote.[64]

2.4.3.1 Current Situation

In the Colombian legal system the power over the decision to admit foreign investment is vested with the government of Colombia at the national level.

2.4.3.1.1 Policy of Admission of Foreign Investments

The Government of Colombia established its own portal, "*Invierta-en-Colombia*" [Invest in Colombia], to attract foreign investment and uses the platform to advertise itself as an attractive market for foreign investments.[65] It states the open

---

[61] US Department of State (2013).

[62] South African Competition Law Appeal Court (2012).

[63] South African Competition Law Appeal Court (2012).

[64] Unless otherwise indicated translations are based on English versions of the statutes, case law, administrative orders and statements provided by the Government of Colombia or its agencies. If those were not available translation are those of the author.

[65] Invierta en Colombia (2014), *Portal Oficial de Inversión de Colombia—Invierta en Colombia*: "*La inversión extranjera es permitida en todos los sectores de la economía, salvo en actividades de defensa y seguridad nacional y el procesamiento, disposición y desecho de basuras tóxicas, peligrosas o radiactivas, no producidas en el país*". [Foreign investment is allowed in all sectors of the economy except in defence activities, national security and the processing and disposal of toxic, hazardous or radioactive waste not produced in the country.]

Colombian policy towards foreign investment that allows foreign investments in all sectors of the economy except in defence activities, national security and the processing and disposal of certain type of waste.

2.4.3.1.2 Acts and Regulations

There is no specific foreign investment review process in place.[66] In theory, Act 1340 of 2009, the Colombian Competition Law Act, could be used by the government as an indirect vehicle to regulate foreign investment in the mining sector by arguing against an investment from a competition law basis.

Article 18 Mining Law 2001 even provides a specific guarantee to foreign investors that guarantees that foreign investors applying for a mining license in Colombia will have the same rights and obligations as Colombian natives, save some exceptions like specific registration requirements.[67]

2.4.3.2 Past Legal Developments and Future Political Trends

Before the 1990s Colombia was governed by a restrictive policy towards foreign investment which included a screening process that required the prior approval of the Departamento Administrativo de Planeación [the Planning Department].[68]

The screening process was based upon the criteria set out in article 107 decree 444 of 1967, which included questions of the effect of the investment to the level of employment in the country, local production, the participation of Colombian investors and further factors picked by the Planning Department ensuring that the investment corresponds to the economic and social development programs.[69]

---

[66] Cárdenas et al. (2012), p. 187.

[67] Article 18 Mining Law 2001 "*Las personas naturales y jurídicas extranjeras, como proponentes contratistas de concesiones mineras, tendrán los mismos derechos y obligaciones que los nacionales colombianos. Las autoridades minera y ambiental no podrán, en el ámbito de sus competencias, exigirles requisitos, condiciones y formalidades adicionales o diferentes, salvo las expresamente señaladas en este Código.*" [Foreign individuals and foreign legal entities acting as applicants to be contractors of mining concessions will have the same rights and obligations as Colombian natives. The mining and environmental authorities cannot, in their field of competence, demand from them any additional or different requirements, conditions and formalities, save those expressly appointed in this Code.].

[68] Article 107 decree 444 of 1967: "*Las inversiones de capital extranjero que se proyecte hacer en el país requerirán la aprobación del Departamento Administrativo de Planeación.*" [Foreign investment into the country requires the approval of the Planning Department.].

[69] Article 107 decree 444 of 1967: "*El Consejo Nacional de Política Económica (...) tomará en cuenta: Contribución de la inversión al nivel de empleo del país; (...); Grado de utilización inicial y posterior de materias primas nacionales y de partes o elementos fabricados o que se vayan a fabricar en el país; (...); Vinculación de capitales e inversionistas nacionales; Grado de competencia en el mercado del respectivo renglón de producción, Contribución al proceso de*

Decision 24 of 1973 of the Commission of the Andean Pact and Decision 220 of 1987 of the Commission of the Andean Pact altered this rigid regime, but left a restrictive regime in place.[70]

In the 1990s Colombia's foreign investment policy changed. In August 1990 Cesar Gaviria became president of Colombia. The president initiated an economic reform program called "*Apertura*" that included changes in the foreign investment, foreign exchange, trade, labour and tax regimes.[71]

Decision 291 of 1991 of the Commission of the Andean Pact gave back the power to the members of Andean Pact to adopt their own rules regarding foreign investment.[72]

Law 9 of 1991 mandated the Consejo Nacional de Politica Economica y Social ("***COMPES***"), a consulting agency of the Colombian government, to establish a new investment regime in Colombia. Step by step[73] the remainder of the rigid direct investment screening process regimes outlined supra were abolished.

Cases of the use of competition law rules to regulate the admission of foreign investment could not be found.

References

Australian Competition and Consumer Commission (2013) ACCC. Available online at: http://www.accc.gov.au/, updated on 9/9/2013. Last checked on 15 February 2014

Cárdenas BP, Bejarano D, Guerra D (2012) Colombia. In: Sutcliffe S (ed) Mining law: jurisdictional comparisons. Thomson Reuters, London pp 175–190

integración latinoamericana; Características técnicas del proyecto, de su manejo y administración, e Las demás circunstancias que el Consejo juzgue pertinentes para asegurar que la inversión corresponda a los programas de desarrollo económico y social y a la conveniencia de vincular capital foráneo a determinadas actividades que no puedan desarrollarse adecuadamente con recursos internos." [The National Economic Council (...) has to take into account: The contribution of investment to the level of employment in the country; (...); the degree of initial and subsequent use of domestic raw materials and parts or components manufactured or to be manufactured in the country; (...); the inclusion of national capital and investors; the degree of competition in the relevant market and the production line, the contribution to the Latin American integration processes; technical characteristics of the project, its management and administration, and other circumstances that the board considers appropriate to ensure that the investment corresponds to the economic and social development programs and to the benefit of linking foreign capital to certain activities that cannot develop properly with internal resources.]

[70] Gomez (2001), p. 12.

[71] Gomez (2001), p. 13.

[72] Pascuzzi (1994), p. 451.

[73] Resolution 51 of 1991, modified by resolution 52 of 91, 53 of 92, 55 of 92, 56 of 92 and 57 of 92, 60 of 93 of COMPES and the governmental decrees 2348 of 93, 98 of 94, 1812 of 94, 2012 of 94, 2764 of 94, 517 of 95, Decree 1295 of 96, 1874 of 98 and 241 of 99.

Department of Finance and Deregulation (2013) Post-implementation review of the Foreign Acquisitions and Takeovers Amendment Act 2012 and it's associated regulations. Available online at: http://ris.finance.gov.au/files/2013/02/03-FATA-2010-amendments-PIR.pdf, updated on 2/27/2013. Last checked on 15 February 2014

Dolzer R, Schreuer C (2008) Principles of international investment law. Oxford University Press, Oxford

Eisenberg GS (1994) The policy and law of foreign direct investment in the New South Africa. A preliminary assessment for a country in transition. J World Trade: Law Econ Public Policy 28 (1):5–25

Federal Court of Australia (2014) The court's jurisdiction. Available online at: http://www.fedcourt.gov.au/about/jurisdiction. Last checked on 15 February 2014

Foreign Investment Review Board (2013) Annual Report 2011–12. Available online at: http://www.firb.gov.au/content/Publications/AnnualReports/2011-2012/_downloads/FIRB-Annual-Report-2011-12_v4.pdf, updated on 1/16/2013. Last checked on 15 February 2014

Foreign Investment Review Board, Australia's investment policy 2013 (2014a) Available online at: http://www.firb.gov.au/content/policy.asp. Last checked on 15 February 2014

Foreign Investment Review Board, Foreign investment guidance notes (2014b) Available online at: http://www.firb.gov.au/content/guidance.asp?NavID=85. Last checked on 15 February 2014

Foreign Investment Review Board, Foreign Investment Review Board hierarchy (2014c) Available online at: http://www.firb.gov.au/content/who.asp?NavID=48. Last checked on 15 February 2014

FIRB, Foreign investment review board: how to apply (2014d) Available online at: http://www.firb.gov.au/content/how_to_apply/how_to_apply.asp. Last checked on 15 February 2014

Gomez J (2001) Foreign direct investment in Colombia. LLM Theses and Essays, paper 14. In Digital Commons @ Georgia Law, LLM Theses and Essays 2001. Available online at: http://digitalcommons.law.uga.edu/cgi/viewcontent.cgi?article=1017&context=stu_llm. Last checked on 15 February 2014

Government of South Africa (2014) The South African government's approach to future international investment treaties. Available online at: http://www.jadafa.co.za/LinkClick.aspx?fileticket=9A6eXZstRl0%3D&tabid=432. Last checked on 15 February 2014

Hunter CR, Bogran A (1999) Foreign direct investment in South Africa. Denver J Int Law Policy 27(3):337–358

Industry Search (2014) Could Chinese investment really hurt Australia? In industry search. Available online at: http://www.industrysearch.com.au/Could-Chinese-investment-really-hurt-Australia/f/10158. Last checked on 15 February 2014

Investopedia (2013) Brown field investment. Available online at: http://www.investopedia.com/terms/b/brownfield.asp, updated on 9/19/2013. Last checked on 15 February 2014

Investopedia, Green field investment (2014) Available online at: http://www.investopedia.com/terms/g/greenfield.asp. Last checked on 15 February 2014

Invierta en Colombia (2014) Portal Oficial de Inversión de Colombia - Invierta en Colombia. Available online at: http://www.inviertaencolombia.com.co/index.php. Last checked on 15 February 2014

Juillard P (2000) Freedom of establishment, freedom of capital movements, and freedom of investment. ICSID Rev 15(2):322–339. doi:10.1093/icsidreview/15.2.322

Mandela N (1993) South Africa's future foreign policy. Foreign Aff 72(5):86–97

Pascuzzi DJ (1994) International trade and foreign investment in Colombia: a sound economic policy amidst crisis. Fla J Int Law 9:443–478

Sornarajah M (2010) The international law on foreign investment, 3rd edn. Cambridge University Press, Cambridge

South African Competition Law Appeal Court (2012) Minister of economic development and others v competition tribunal and others, case number 110/CAC/Jul11

South African Reserve Bank (2014) Financial surveillance and exchange controls. Available online at: http://www.resbank.co.za/RegulationAndSupervision/FinancialSurveillanceAndExchangeControl/Pages/Financial%20Surveillance%20and%20Exchange%20Control-Home.aspx. Last checked on 15 February 2014

The University of Sydney (2012) What's really wrong with Chinese investment? The University of Sydney. Available online at: http://sydney.edu.au/business/news/2012/whats_really_wrong_with_chinese_investment, updated on 8/20/2012. Last checked on 15 February 2014

US Department of State (2013) 2013 investment climate statement - South Africa. Available online at: http://www.state.gov/e/eb/rls/othr/ics/2013/204733.htm. Last checked on 15 February 2014

Walsh M (2012) Abbott's foreign investment policy shuns reality. Financial Review, 8/2/2012. Available online at: http://afr.com/p/opinion/abbott_foreign_investment_policy_GQwJ72DyM1YYdy2EczeE6I. Last checked on 15 February 2014

Chapter 3
How to Set Up? The Question of Corporate Structure Requirements

3.1 Introduction and Disambiguation

Corporate structure requirements refer to the options on how a foreign investor can legally structure foreign investment in mining projects in a particular country.

3.2 Relevance

Corporate structure requirements limit the choice of a foreign investor on how to implement the foreign investment in a mining project. The choice on how to legally structure its foreign investment in the mining project has financial and tax impacts at home and abroad.

3.3 Observation Horizon

The corporate law of a host state will have a *Numerus clausus* of corporate structures available to national investors to conduct their business.

The host state may decide to allow foreign investors to conduct their business in all or only some of the corporate structures available to national investors. Also, host states may create specific corporate structures for foreign investors and chose to limit their business activities to those specific corporate structures.

Conducting preliminary or all business activities within the jurisdiction of the host state may be allowed without or only by establishing a new local entity.

Furthermore, various levels of registration requirements may be established.

Corporate structure requirements can be a tool for enforcing state participation in the mining project, inter alia by requiring state or local ownership via

R.W. Roeder, *Foreign Mining Investment Law*, DOI 10.1007/978-3-319-31217-0_3

shareholding or requiring a joint venture with a state-owned or nationally-owned business entity.

The work will not analyse Corporate Finance aspects, such as listing requirements and furthermore not deal with specific national corporate takeover rules, such as rules regarding the squeeze-out of minority shareholdings.

Corporate governance issues will only be touched upon where they become relevant for the relationship of the foreign investor with external stakeholders.

3.4 Countries

3.4.1 Australia

3.4.1.1 Current Situation

The corporate structure requirements in Australia are administered by the Corporations Act of 2001. The Act came into effect on July 15th, 2001.

A foreign company generally needs to be registered before conducting business in Australia.[1]

The Australian law therefore does not allow foreign companies to conduct business in Australia under their foreign legal entity directly and immediately.

The most common approaches to conduct business in Australia as a foreign investor are: to establish an own Australian legal entity, e.g. in the form of a subsidiary, to form a joint-venture with a local partner (established Australian legal entity) in the form of a incorporated joint-venture or to register itself as a foreign legal entity and then conclude contractual arrangements such as a farm-in agreement or an unincorporated Joint-Venture.

3.4.1.1.1 Subsidiary

To incorporate a wholly owned or a partly owned subsidiary is one way to conduct business as a foreign investor in Australia. A foreign investor may choose to acquire a so-called shelf company (a company that has been duly incorporated, but not yet engaged in business activities) or form and register a new company. According to section 112 of the Corporations Act 2001 an investor has the choice between a proprietary company and a public company.

[1] Section 601CD of the Corporations Act of 2001 state that a "*(...) foreign company must not carry on business in [the Australian Commonwealth's] jurisdiction unless it is registered under Part 5B division 2 of the Corporations Act of 2001 or it has applied to be so registered and the application has not been dealt with*". Although section 601CD subsection 2 Corporations Act of 2001 refers to: "*(...) offering debentures in [Australia]*" it is read to relate to the conduct of any kind of business.

3.4.1.1.2 Incorporated Joint-Venture

A joint-venture requires a joint-venture agreement between the two entities. This agreement includes the purpose, the scope and the timeline for the project. Both parties will have to agree what assets, such as money, intellectual property and staff they are willing to contribute to the project. In the mining industry it is common to form a joint-venture for the foreign investor to get a partner that is savvy of the local laws and administrative procedures. The joint-venture agreement will then outline the interest of the parties and design how the operation and the control of the venture will be structured. It is a common occurrence to have one of the two parties to take a lead on the operation.[2]

An incorporated joint-venture consists of a special purpose vehicle owned by the parties who own its shares. The special purpose vehicle has a legal entity separate from its parent companies. A shareholder agreement that regulates the rights derived from the shareholding positions should be entered into. As the incorporated joint-venture requires an Australian subsidiary as vehicle, this option could also be summarized as a subsidiary with additional contractual obligations with a third party.

The advantage of an incorporated joint-venture is the absence of direct liabilities for the parties regarding debt and other liabilities of the special purpose vehicle. It should be noted that the principles on piercing the corporate veil do exist in Australia as well.

3.4.1.1.3 Unincorporated Joint-Venture/Farm-In Agreements

An unincorporated joint-venture is a mere contractual relationship between the joint-venture parties. The joint-venture agreement determines how the two parties are planning to cooperate in the mining endeavor. Assets and entitlements remain with the parties; no legal entity separate from the original parties is created.

One form to cooperate in the form of a joint-venture is a farm-in agreement. A farm-in agreement generally involves two parties: one party, the farmee, who is providing capital necessary to make use of a mining license. And another party, the farmor, who holds the license and more often than not conducts the actual mining. In return for providing capital for the mining project to farmor receives an interest in the mining project. Unlike a loan this interest will not be an interest on the money invested, but for example a previously agreed percentage of the profits derived from the minerals or even a part of the minerals themselves.[3] The foreign entity will have to be registered under Part 5 B division 2 of the Corporations Act of 2001.

---

[2] AMPLA (2014).

[3] Clayton Utz (2014).

If the foreign investor does not want to establish a distinct Australian legal entity, e.g. to consolidate the financial results overseas,[4] it may register a branch office of its foreign legal entity.

The branch office needs to be registered according to section 601CE of the Corporations Act 2001. An application needs to be launched with the Australian Securities and Investments Commission, which examines its due incorporation in its place of origin. Furthermore, according to section 601CF Corporations Act 2001 a local agent needs to be appointed. The local agent, inter alia, needs to be "*authorized to accept on the foreign company's behalf service of process and notices*" according to section 601CG Corporations Act 2001.

3.4.1.1.4 State/Local Ownership Requirements

There are no legal requirements, neither legal nor factual, to include the Commonwealth of Australia or a State as an owner in order to realize a mining project. While not legally required, the participation of the indigenous population in the mining industry is an important consideration to take into account (for details see infra).

3.4.1.2 Past Legal Developments and Future Political Trends

In its beginning mining was done by individuals that were awarded only a very small area to mine. The commencement of the first underground mining made higher capital expenditure and more close cooperation between miners necessary. In 1855 the Legislative Council reacted to this development by allowing limited liability mining companies by Act 18 Victoria No. 42.[5] The law on companies developed ever since. The last major change was the enactment of the Corporations Act 2001 analyzed supra.

3.4.2 South Africa

3.4.2.1 Current Situation

The corporate law and corporate structure requirements in South Africa are administered by the Companies Act 2008. The Act came into effect on May 1st,

[4] PWC (2013), p. 11.

[5] La Croix (1992), p. 216.

2011. The Companies Act 2008 requires foreign companies to register within 20 days after it begins to conduct business in South Africa.[6]

Foreign investors may also decide to establish a South African legal entity, e.g. in the form of a subsidiary, to form a joint venture/partnership with a local partner (an established South African legal entity), to register a branch office or to conclude a farm-in agreement.

3.4.2.1.1 Subsidiary

According to section 8 of the Companies Act 2008 there are three relevant types of companies for a foreign investor to choose from[7]:

Any type of company will have to set up at least one office in South Africa and has to register this office with the Government according to section 23(3) Companies Act 2008.

3.4.2.1.2 Joint Venture

Joint Ventures are an option used in the South African business landscape. For a foreign investor a joint venture agreement with a local and already established player is well trodden path to follow.[8]

3.4.2.1.3 Branch Office

If the foreign investor does not want to establish a distinct South African legal entity in the form of a subsidiary (e.g. to consolidate the financial results overseas[9]) it may register a branch office of its foreign legal entity and continuously maintain it.[10]

---

[6] Section 23(1) of the Companies Act 2008 states that "*(...) external [foreign] company must register with the Commission within 20 business days after it first begins to conduct business, (...) within the Republic (...) as an external profit company, if, within the jurisdiction in which it was incorporated, it meets legislative or definitional requirements that are comparable to the legislative or definitional requirements of a profit company incorporated under* [the Companies Act 2008]."

[7] Government of South Africa (2014), p. 90.

[8] Mokoduo Attorneys (2014).

[9] PwC (2013), p. 11.

[10] Section 23(3) of the Companies Act 2008 states that "*(...) each (...) external company must continuously maintain at least one office in the Republic and register the address of its office (...) by providing the required information when filing its registration (...).*"

3.4.2.1.4 Farm-in Agreements

A typical form of participation in a mining project for a foreign investor is a so-called farm-in agreement. A farm-in agreement does not create a new legal entity, but is a mere contractual arrangement.[11]

3.4.2.1.5 State or Local Ownership Requirements

The Companies Act 2008 specifically mentions state-owned companies, inter alia in section 8(2) (a) of the Companies Act 2008. While there are state owned competitors such as Alexkor and the African Exploration Mining & Finance Corporation, there are no requirements, either legal or factual, to include the state of South Africa as an owner in order to realize a mining project.

There is a requirement for the participation of at least 26 % of Historically Disadvantaged South Africans in the ownership of South African mining assets by 2014. This restricts the freedom of business choice of foreign investors. The details of the relevant Black Economic Empowerment laws and policy will be explained infra in Sect. 7.4.2.1.1.

3.4.2.2 Past Legal Developments and Future Political Trends

Based upon the document: *South African Company Law for the 21st Century: Guidelines for Corporate Law Reform* (May 2004), a policy document developed by the Department of Trade and Industry, the Companies Act 2008 was enacted after a broad discussion.[12] So far, there has been little critique of this. It is therefore unlikely that this legal regime will see any changes any time soon.

When investing in South Africa, it is important to note that South Africa is dealing with an ongoing nationalization debate. Demands to nationalize the industry were voiced when the Apartheid regime started, and again when it collapsed in the early 1990s.[13]

The post-Apartheid attitude in the society can be characterized as a consensus demanding black economic empowerment, but refraining from the option of nationalization.[14]

Not everybody agrees though. Plans to require 51 % HDSA ownership of international mining projects, something that will have a similar effect than nationalization, were more or less freely discussed some years ago.[15] One of the most

[11] For a detailed description, please see supra.

[12] Department of Trade and Industry South Africa (2004).

[13] Nevin (2010).

[14] Smith (2010).

[15] Worthington (2002).

famous voices over the last few years was Julius Malema, the former leader of the African National Congress Youth League that again and again demanded nationalization of the mining industry.[16] Many others took up the discussion from where Julius Malema, expelled from the ANC for other reasons, had left it.[17]

The development of state owned entities comes from an attempt of the government to head off demands for the nationalization of the mining industry—and the "*No*" to nationalization was recently reconfirmed by the ANC.[18]

Whether or not the debate will continue, strengthen or ease will very much depend on the economic achievements for Historically Disadvantaged South Africans.

The restriction of the transfer of the controlling interests of an unlisted company that holds a mining right by requiring the consent of the Minister of Mineral Resources also impacts on corporate structure considerations.[19] For foreign investors this requirement could currently be circumvented by listing the investment vehicle though.

The MPRDA Amendment Bill 2011 aims to expand this requirement to listed companies. Considering the corporate structures of many mining projects this provision could lead to a situation in which a multinational company would need the consent of the South African Minister for Mineral Resources to trade shares. A detailed account of the impact of the current situation, the situation after the enactment of the MPRDA Amendment Bill 2008 and on the impact of the MPRDA Amendment Bill 2011 has been provided elsewhere.[20,21]

3.4.3 Colombia

3.4.3.1 Current Situation

Corporate law in Colombia is governed by decree 410 of 1971, the Código de Comercio 1971 [Corporate Law Act 1971].

The Mining Law 2001 provides additional specific guidance for structuring the corporate aspects of a mining project in Colombia.

Foreign investors have several options for engaging in mining activities in Colombia. They may act through a representative domiciled in Colombia, or, if

[16] Lapper (2010).

[17] African Business (2011).

[18] Clarke (2012).

[19] Section 11 of the MPRDA 2002 states: "*A prospecting right or mining right or an interest in any such right, or a controlling interest in a company or close corporation, may not be ceded, transferred, let, sublet, assigned, alienated or otherwise disposed of without the written consent of the Minister, except in the case of change of controlling interest in listed companies.*"

[20] Moore and Veldsman (2013), p. 85.

[21] Leon (2013).

they start to execute a concession contract, a branch, affiliate or subsidiary is to be established in Colombia that needs to assure that its liabilities are covered by e.g. a bank guarantee.[22] The obligation to present this public assurance has been eliminated for Simplified Shared Corporations.[23]

Accordingly, for an application for a mining concession the designation of a representative suffices. The representative can be an individual or corporate entity that is authorized to act on the foreign investor's behalf. For conducting actual business, a branch/affiliate office or a subsidiary has to be established. Joint ventures and farm-in agreements are further possible options.

3.4.3.1.1 Subsidiary

The Código de Comercio 1971 allows a foreign investor to choose from the Sociedad Colectiva [Partnership], the Sociedad en Commandita [Limited Partnership], the Sociedad en Comandita Simple [Simple Limited Partnership], the Sociedad en Comandita por Acciones [Company Limited by Shares], the Sociedad de Responsabilidad Limitada [Limited Liability Company], the Sociedad Anónima [Stock Corporation] and the Sociedad por Acciones Simplificada [Simplified Share Corporation].

The most common corporate structures are the Sociedad de Responsabilidad Limitada [Limited Liability Company], the Sociedad Anónima [Stock Corporation] and the Sociedad por Acciones Simplificada [Simplified Share Corporation] that each differ, specifically in relation to the personal responsibilities of the shareholders.

3.4.3.1.1.1 Sociedad de Responsabilidad Limitada

The shareholders of such a Limited Liability Company are together liable (only) for their contributions.[24]

[22] Article 19 of the Mining Law 2001 states "*Las personas jurídicas extranjeras podrán, a través de representante ante domiciliado en Colombia, presentar y tramitar propuestas. Para la celebración del contrato de concesión deberán establecer una sucursal, filial subsidiaria, domiciliada en el territorio nacional. (…). Deberán asegurar debidamente ante la autoridad concedente, las obligaciones que contraigan en el país, bien sea con la garantía de la persona beneficiaria de la obra o servicio o con el aval de una entidad bancaria o de una compañía de seguros que opere en Colombia.*" [Foreign corporate persons will be able, through a representative domiciled in Colombia, to present and transact proposals. For the execution of the concession contract, a branch, affiliate or subsidiary is to be established, domiciled in the national territory. (…). They should duly assure to the granting authority, the liabilities contracted in Colombia, either by a guarantee of the work's or service's beneficiary or an endorsement of a banking institution or an insurance company that operates in Colombia.].

[23] Triana and Escobar (2014).

[24] Article 353 of the Código de Comercio 1971 states for the Sociedad de Responsabilidad Limitada [Limited Liability Company]: "*En las compañías de responsabilidad limitada los socios responderán hasta el monto de sus aportes.*" [In the limited liability company the shareholders shall be responsible up to the amount of their contributions.].

3.4.3.1.1.2 Sociedad Anónima

The shareholders of such Stock Corporation are responsible up to the amount of their respective contributions.[25]

3.4.3.1.1.3 Sociedad por Acciones Simplificada

The Simplified Share Corporation is a separate legal entity from the parent company and has the advantage that liabilities for both for contractual and tax/labour obligations of the company are separated from the liability of the investing individual/parent company.[26] It can not finance itself on the stock market though.[27]

3.4.3.1.2 Joint Venture

Joint ventures are generally recognized in the Colombian Corporate Code[28] and specifically recognized form of structuring mining operations in Colombia according to the Colombian Mining Law.[29]

---

[25] Article 373 of the Código de Comercio 1971 for the Sociedad Anónima [Stock Corporation] states: "*La sociedad anónima se formará por la reunión de un fondo social suministrado por accionistas responsables hasta el monto de sus respectivos aportes; será administrada por gestores temporales y revocables y tendrá una denominación seguida de las palabras "Sociedad Anónima" o de las letras "S A.""* [The stock corporation is formed by the creation of a corporation fund furnished by shareholders who shall be responsible up to the amount of their respective contributions; it shall be administered by temporary and removable promoters and shall have a name followed by the words "stock corporation" or the letters "S.A.".].

[26] Article 10 of law 1258 of 2008 (Corporate Law Act), enacted December 05th, 2008 a Sociedad por acciones simplificada [Simplified Share Corporation]: "*(...) podrá constituirse por una o varias personas naturales o jurídicas, quienes sólo serán responsables hasta el monto de sus respectivos aportes.*" [May be constituted by one or more natural or legal persons who are liable only up to the amount of their contributions.]

[27] Triana and Escobar (2014).

[28] Article 507 Código de Comercio 1971 states: "*La participación es un contrato por el cual dos o más personas que tienen la calidad de comerciantes toman interés en una o varias operaciones mercantiles determinadas, que deberá ejecutar uno de ellos en su solo nombre y bajo su crédito personal, con cargo de rendir cuenta y dividir con sus partícipes las ganancias o pérdidas en la proporción convenida.*" [A joint venture is a contract by which two or more persons who are qualified as merchants take an interest in one or more determined mercantile operations, which one of them must execute in his own name and under his personal credit, with the duty to render account and divide the gains or losses with his partners in the agreed proportion.].

[29] Article 17 Mining Law 2001 states: "*Cuando Uniones Temporales reciba concesiones deberán constituirse en figura societaria, con la misma participación que se derive de la propuesta presentada. También podrán presentar propuestas y celebrar contratos de concesión los consorcios, caso en el cual sus integrantes responderán solidariamente de las obligaciones consiguientes.*" [When joint ventures receive concessions, those should incorporate a company, with the same shares that might result from the submitted proposal. The joint ventures may also present proposals and be granted concession contracts, in which case its members will be jointly liable (obligatio in solidum).].

3.4.3.1.3 Foreign Company Branch

Under Colombian corporate law a foreign branch office is considered a legal extension of the company established in accordance with the laws of another country[30] that requires a license to operate in Colombia by the Superintendence of Corporations.[31]

3.4.3.1.4 Farm-In Agreements

A typical form of participation in a mining project for a foreign investor are so-called farm-in agreements. A farm-in agreement does not create a new legal entity, but is a mere contractual arrangement.[32]

3.4.3.1.5 State/Local Ownership Requirements

There are no requirements, either legal or factual, to include the State of Colombia or local groups as an owner in order to undertake a mining project.

3.4.3.2 Past Legal Developments and Future Political Trends

Before 2008 the two most common corporate structures where the Stock Corporation and the Limited Liability Company.[33]

---

[30] Article 469 of the Código de Comercio 1971 states foreign companies: "*Son extranjeras las sociedades constituidas conforme a la ley de otro país y con domicilio principal en el exterior.*" [Foreign companies are established in accordance with the laws of another country and having their main domicile abroad.].

According to article 471 Code Commercial: "*Para que una sociedad extranjera pueda emprender negocios permanentes en Colombia, establecerá una sucursal con domicilio en el territorio nacional, para lo cual cumplirá los siguientes requisitos:*" [In order that a foreign company may carry out permanent business in Colombia, it shall set up a branch domiciled in the national territory, and to this effect shall fulfil the following requisites:] "*Protocolizar en una notaría del lugar elegido para su domicilio en el país, copias auténticas del documento de su fundación, de sus estatutos, la resolución o acto que acordó su establecimiento en Colombia y de los que acrediten la existencia de la sociedad y la personería de sus representantes, y obtener de la Superintendencia de Sociedades (...), permiso para funcionar en el país.*" [Register with an official Notary in the place chosen for its domicile in the country, authenticated copies of the public instrument of its incorporation, its by-laws, the resolution or decree which authorized its establishment in Colombia and of the documents evidencing the existence of the company and the legal character of its representatives; and to obtain from the Superintendence of Corporations (...), a license to operate in the country.].

[31] Diaz Reus (2014).

[32] For a detailed description please see supra.

[33] Triana and Escobar (2014).

Recently, the Simplified Share Corporation has proven very popular amongst investors as it reduces the administrative burdens for investors. Within 6 months after its enactment by section 10 of law 1258 of 2008 more than 5000 entities were incorporated[34] and between January 2009 and August 2010, a total of 42,207 Simplified Share Corporations were registered.

Law 1258 of 2008 did not replace the Código de Comercio 1971, but the new regulations amend the old Código de Comercio 1971.[35]

References

African Business (2011) Is nationalization inevitable? African business, 5/1/2011. Available online at: http://search.proquest.com.ezproxy.library.uq.edu.au/docview/873589807. Last checked on 15 February 2014

AMPLA (2014) Model documents model mining joint venture agreement (minerals). Available online at: https://www.ampla.org/modeldocuments/documents/model-documents65. Last checked on 15 February 2014

Clarke W (2012) ANC say no to mine nationalization. Think Africa Press, 2/10/2012. Available online at: http://thinkafricapress.com/south-africa/anc-say-no-mine-nationalization. Last checked on 15 February 2014

Clayton Utz (2014) New farm-in exemption for the mining sector has a sting in the tail - energy and natural resources - Australia. Available online at: http://www.mondaq.com/australia/x/252260/Mining/New+farmin+exemption+for+the+mining+sector+has+a+sting+in+the+tail. Last checked on 15 February 2014

Department of Trade and Industry South Africa (2004) South African Company Law for the 21 century. Available online at: http://www.pmg.org.za/bills/040715companydraftpolicy.pdf, updated on 12/26/2004. Last checked on 15 February 2014

Diaz Reus (2014) Setting up a foreign corporation in Colombia. Available online at: http://www.diazreus.com/news-articles-setup-foreign-business-in-colombia.html. Last checked on 15 February 2014

Government of South Africa (2014) South Africa's Investor Handbook. Available online at: http://www.thedti.gov.za/DownloadFileAction?id=742. Last checked on 15 February 2014

La Croix SJ (1992) Property rights and institutional change during Australia's gold rush. Explor Econ Hist 29(2):204–227. doi:10.1016/0014-4983(92)90011-K

Lapper R (2010) South Africa plans state mining company. Financial Times 2010, 31 March 2010

Leon P (2013) Confusion over new mining laws. Available online at: http://www.moneyweb.co.za/moneyweb-safm-market-update/r-1300. Last checked on 15 February 2014

Mokoduo Attorneys (2014) Partnerships and joint ventures. Available online at: http://www.mokoduo.co.za/partnerships-and-joint-ventures/. Last checked on 15 February 2014

Moore GJA, Veldsman J (2013) Big brother and the holding company: ministerial consent to dispose of indirect controlling interests in mining companies. S Afr J Law 130(1):85–124

Nevin T (2010) South Africa's mine-nationalization jitters. Afr Bus (361): 34, 36, 38. Available online at: http://search.proquest.com.ezproxy.library.uq.edu.au/docview/598611989. Last checked on 15 February 2014

[34] Diaz Reus (2014).

[35] Triana and Escobar (2014).

PWC (2013) Doing business in Australia - business guide. Available online at: http://www.pwc.com.au/legal/assets/GuideBusiness2011.pdf, updated on 3/18/2013. Last checked on 15 February 2014

PwC PricewaterhouseCoopers Australia (2013) Mine 2013: a confidence crisis - review of global trends in the mining industry. Edited by PricewaterhouseCoopers. Available online at: http://www.pwc.com.au/industry/energy-utilities-mining/publications/mine-a-confidence-crisis.htm, updated on 8/5/2013. Last checked on 15 February 2014

Smith AD (2010) Why FW de Klerk let Nelson Mandela out of prison. In The Guardian/The Observer, 1/31/2010. Available online at: http://www.guardian.co.uk/world/2010/jan/31/nelson-mandela-de-klerk-apartheid. Last checked on 15 February 2014

Triana JP, Escobar J (2014) Simplified joint stock companies – new corporate structure. Available online at: http://www.tumnet.com/_literature_135344/Simplified_Joint_Stock_Companies-Article_for_the_IBA. Last checked on 15 February 2014

Worthington T (2002) South Africa flirts with nationalization. Eng Min J 9:4

Chapter 4
Mine or Not? The Question of Ownership of Minerals and Mineral Rights

4.1 Introduction and Disambiguation

Firstly, in the context of mineral ownership a distinction needs to be made between the ownership of the minerals per se, the ownership of mineral rights and mining licenses.[1] Questions regarding the ownership of land are dealt with infra in Sect. 5.4.

Mineral ownership refers to the actual ownership of the minerals in the ground. Mineral ownership is either vested with the nation or a federal state or lies with a private party.

Mineral rights describe rights that a party has in respect of those minerals, e.g. the right to explore or extract certain minerals.[2] Mineral rights also can be owned by the state or by a private party.

Mining licenses are dealt with in more detail infra in Chap. 5 and entail governmental permission to conduct actual prospecting and mining activities.

In some jurisdictions, the grant of a mining license encompasses the grant of mineral rights.[3] This is only possible if the state also owns the mineral right or is willing to expropriate the mineral right in favour of the mining license applicant.

4.2 Relevance

From the host state's point of view, mineral and/or mineral rights ownership by the state provides a higher extent of sovereignty over its natural resources[4] and—in the case of state ownership of mineral rights—the possibility to demand royalties for its

[1] Badenhorst et al. (2014), p. 292.

[2] Mostert (2012), p. 1.

[3] Southalan (2012), p. 43.

[4] Southalan (2012), p. 42.

R.W. Roeder, *Foreign Mining Investment Law*, DOI 10.1007/978-3-319-31217-0_4

use (see infra). Resource nationalism—a key challenge for foreign investors—often manifests itself in the form of changes in the mineral and mineral rights ownership structures.

For a foreign investor, ownership of mineral rights is more relevant than the actual ownership of the minerals in situ. A foreign investor may be able to develop the mining project when he holds the mineral rights and the necessary mining licenses, but does not need to be the actual owner of the minerals. At the moment the minerals are severed from the land they are treated as personal property and ownership of the mineral passes to the owner of the mineral right.[5]

Private ownership of minerals and/or mineral rights may still be regulated by the state via mining licenses (see infra), but give the foreign investor the opportunity to purchase the mineral and/or the mineral right directly.

For a foreign investor the structure and especially changes in the ownership structure of minerals and changes in the ownership of mineral rights are therefore of key interest.

4.3 Observation Horizon

Ownership of minerals can lie either with the state or with private parties. It may also be the case that the state owns some minerals and private parties other minerals at the same geographic location, or that the state owns all minerals in a certain area and the private party all minerals in another area.

One form of private mineral ownership has been summarized by the common law principle "*Cuius est solum eius est usque ad coelum et ad inferos*" [Whoever owns [the] soil, [it] is theirs all the way [up] to Heaven and [down] to Hell].

This form of private mineral ownership attaches the ownership of the minerals to the ownership of the land underneath which the mineral is found.[6]

This form of private mineral ownership allows the owner of the land to give other private parties minerals rights, such as to explore or extract such minerals. The right to explore or extract minerals is then established as a form of servitude to the land—called a mineral right—and can be transferred separately from the mineral ownership of the owner of the land.[7] As shown infra this notion was the starting point of many mineral governance regimes, but has been amended intensively by statutory law.

Under this doctrine, regarding the ownership of the actual mineral (the deposit) itself, the owner of the land remains owner of the mineral until the mineral rights holder severs the mineral.

[5] Supreme Court of South Africa (Appellate Division), *Trojan Exploration Company (Pty) Ltd and Another v Rusteburg Platinum Mines Ltd and Another*.

[6] Mostert (2012), p. 7.

[7] Mostert (2012), p. 1.

Before that severance, the holder of the mineral right can have a contingent right to the ownership of the mineral.[8]

In the moment the minerals become movables, the ownership of the mineral passes from the landowner to the owner of the mineral right.[9]

Broad distinctions regarding the management systems of mineral and mineral rights ownership can be made between the "*accession*" system, the "*regalia*" system and a system of absolute state control.

The "*accession*" system refers to a management system whereby the right to explore and extract minerals is based on private ownership of minerals and private party contracts determine exploration and production rights.[10]

Another system is the "*regalia*" system, where the state owns all minerals and mineral rights, and assigns or leases the mineral rights to private parties.[11]

A third possibility is a system where the state owns the minerals and mineral rights, and that state ownership of minerals and mineral rights is inalienable.[12] Therefore mineral resources need to be developed by the state, either via state-owned enterprises or via contract mining.[13] Therefore privatization by the sale of previously state-owned minerals to private parties can create opportunities for foreign investors.[14]

Nationalization of the mining industry or an expropriation of specific mining projects creates risks for foreign investors.[15]

4.4 Countries

4.4.1 Australia

4.4.1.1 Current Situation

Section 8 of the MRA 1989 declares (with very limited exceptions) the Crown's property in coal and other minerals. According to section 52 of the Acts Interpretation Act 1954: "*In every Act reference to the Sovereign reigning at the time of the passing of such Act, or to 'Her Majesty', 'His Majesty', 'the Queen', 'the King', or 'the Crown', shall be construed as references to the Sovereign for the time being,*

[8] North Gauteng High Court South Africa (2014), p. 29.

[9] Supreme Court of South Africa (Appellate Division), *Trojan Exploration Company (Pty) Ltd and Another v Rusteburg Platinum Mines Ltd and Another.*

[10] Southalan (2012), p. 41.

[11] Australian Industry Commission (2007), p. 10.

[12] Australian Industry Commission (2007), p. 10.

[13] Kirk (2007).

[14] Princeton (2014).

[15] Oxford Dictionary (2014).

and, where necessary, shall include the heirs and successors of such Queen or King; (...)." Today the Crown refers to the relevant sovereign, in the case of Queensland the state of Queensland.

In Queensland, Australia, the ownership of gold and coal on or below the surface of land is the property of the state. In respect to coal there is an exception as in that land that was alienated in fee simple by the Crown before 1 March 1910 and the grant of that land did not contain a reservation to the Crown of the property in that coal.[16]

All minerals other than coal and gold on or below the surface of land in Queensland other than land alienated in fee simple by the Crown pursuant to the Alienation of Crown Lands Act 1860, section 22; or the Crown Lands Alienation Act 1868, section 32; or the Mineral Lands Act 1872, section 21; are the property of the Crown.

4.4.1.2 Past Legal Developments and Future Political Trends

With the Case of Mines it was so decided that so called "*royal minerals*", such as silver and gold were property of the crown. In the *Case of Mines* the Court of Exchequer Chamber[17] in 1568 found that:

> [In] respect of the Excellency of the thing, for of all things which the soil within this realm produces or yields, gold and silver is the most excellent; and of all persons in the realm the King is in the eye of the law most excellent. And the common law, which is founded upon reason, appropriates everything to the persons whom it best suits, as common and trivial things to the common people, things of more worth to persons in a higher and superior class, and things most excellent to those persons who excel all other; and because gold and silver are the most excellent things which the soil contains, the law has appointed them (as in reason it ought) to the person who is most excellent, and this is the King.[18]

While the Australian legal regime evolved from the British common law the case now provides historical context rather than legal guidance, as the case has been superseded by the declaration of the Crown's property in minerals (see supra). As section 9 of the MRA 1989 details the: "*Exclusive right of the Crown to grant mining leases etc. irrespective of ownership of mineral*", the licensing process for coal mining is not different to the licensing that applies to mining coal that is owned by the Crown. The difference is in the royalties regime: royalties—after being

[16] Section of the 8 MRA 1989 specifies: "*(...) Gold on or below the surface of land is the property of the Crown. Coal on or below the surface of land that was acquired by the Crown (...) and subsequently alienated in fee simple by the Crown is the property of the Crown; [Coal] on or below the surface of land (other than land referred [supra]) is the property of the Crown except where that land was alienated in fee simple by the Crown before 1 March 1910 and the grant of that land did not contain a reservation to the Crown of the property in that coal.*"

[17] Williams (2003).

[18] Court of Exchequer Chamber, *The Case of Mines*.

collected by the state of Queensland—are paid to the private owner of the coal (less taxes) according to section 320(2)(b) of the MRA 1989.

In 1980, New South Wales decided to expropriate the remaining private coal rights in favour of state ownership of the minerals. In 1985, it established the New South Wales Coal Compensation Board. The New South Wales Coal Compensation Board was structured as "*a NSW Government organization under the provisions of the Coal Acquisition (Compensation) Arrangements Act 1985 to administer legislation providing for compensation to former owners of private coal compulsorily acquired by the Crown.*"[19] The basis for the expropriation was the *Coal Acquisition Act 1981* (NSW).[20]

In Australia there is no major debate ongoing on the expropriation of the remaining private mineral rights. But the fact that the state of Queensland lately decided to claim that "*All geothermal energy on or below the surface of any land in the State is, and is taken always to have been, the property of the State*" according to section 28 of the Geothermal Energy Act 2010 as well as "*All Greenhouse Gas storage reservoirs [an ownership in the mere potential] in land [are] taken always to have been the property of the State*" according to section 27 of the Greenhouse Gas Storage Act 2009 shows that the interest of the state to own any type of natural resources in Queensland, Australia, remains high.

4.4.2 *South Africa*

4.4.2.1 Current Situation

According to section 3 (1) of the MPRDA 2002: "*Mineral and petroleum resources are the common heritage of all the people of South Africa and the State is the custodian thereof for the benefit of all South Africans.*"

While the concept of "*state custodianship*" is currently undergoing further academic analysis elsewhere,[21] section 3(2) of the MPRDA 2002 further specifies it by determining that: "*as the custodian of the nation's mineral and petroleum resources, the State, acting through the Minister, may—grant, issue, refuse, control, administer and manage any reconnaissance permission, prospecting right, permission to remove, mining right, mining permit, retention permit, technical co-operation permit, reconnaissance permit, exploration right and production right.*"

[19] The Government of New South Wales (2013).

[20] Section 5 of the Coal Acquisition Act 1981 (NSW): "*(1) All coal that, but for this Act, would be vested in: an instrumentality or agency of the Crown, or any person other than the Crown, is vested in the Crown freed and discharged from all trusts, leases, licenses, obligations, estates, interests and contracts.*".

[21] Mostert (2012).

By stating that the state can provide both the mineral right and the license to use it, this provision excludes (the use of) private ownership rights in regards to minerals. The explanation of the impact of such exclusion shall follow infra.

4.4.2.2 Past Legal Developments and Future Political Trends

Mostert presents an extensive account of the development of ownership of minerals and mineral rights under South African soil.[22] This work will therefore focus on the key developments that are a necessary for today's understanding of ownership of minerals and mineral rights in South Africa.

The latest development was a legal proceeding regarding the question whether or not the MPRDA 2002 had expropriated individuals' and companies' mineral rights under the Mineral Act 1991. The Constitutional Court finally decided the matter, stating that the mineral rights of individuals and companies under the Mineral Act 1991 were not expropriated.[23]

The principle "*Cuius est solum eius est usque ad coelum et ad inferos*" ["*whoever owns [the] soil, [it] is theirs all the way [up] to Heaven and [down] to Hell] attaches the ownership of the minerals to the ownership of the land underneath which the mineral is found applied from early on.*"[24] was included in common law applied in South Africa and referenced in both old and recent case law.[25]

Due to practical needs the South African courts and legislators allowed mineral rights to be registered separately and therefore to be separated from the title to land, creating a situation where there was an owner of the land and an owner of mineral rights to the minerals on and beneath the land.[26]

Those mineral rights were first described as "*the entitlement to go on the property to which they relate to search for minerals, and, if the holder finds any, to sever them and carry them away*". This "*real right*" was eventually classified as a "*quasi-servitude*".

Regarding the ownership of the mineral itself, the owner of the land would remain owner of the mineral until the mineral rights holder severs them. At the moment they become movables the ownership of the mineral passes from the land owner to the owner of the mineral right.[27] Before that, the holder of the mineral right would have a contingent right to the ownership of the mineral.[28]

---

[22] Mostert (2012).

[23] Constitutional Court, *Agri South Africa v Minister for Minerals and Energy*.

[24] Mostert (2012), p. 7.

[25] Majoni (2014), p. *23*. North Gauteng High Court South Africa (2014), para 23.

[26] North Gauteng High Court South Africa (2014), para 24.

[27] Supreme Court of South Africa Appellate Division, *Trojan Exploration Company (Pty) Ltd and Another v Rusteburg Platinum Mines Ltd and Another*.

[28] North Gauteng High Court South Africa (2014), para 29.

The mineral rights holder would be able to grant to any third party the right to prospect for or to mine the relevant mineral, e.g. by a prospecting contract or a mineral lease.[29]

Before the Minerals Act of 1991 the rights to prospect and mine were vested with the state. *Mostert* summarizes: "*The philosophy of state control over minerals during the period 1964 to 1990 resulted in a system whereby the state, in which the right to mine was vested, conferred rights to mine and prospect to mineral rights holders.*"[30]

Section 5(1) of the Minerals Act 1991, one of the last legislative acts of the Apartheid regime, stated that the right "*to enter upon (...) the land (...) to prospect and mine for such mineral (...) and to dispose thereof vested in the holder of mineral rights*". The Mining Act of 1991 was based upon a policy of privatization and deregulation, attempting to alter the regulation in regards to mineral rights that had previously been developed.[31]

Considering the dawn of the end of the Apartheid regime, this policy of privatization and deregulation was perceived by many as "*an attempt to keep assets in the hands of the white minority*" (which held nearly all mineral rights titles in Apartheid South Africa).[32]

What had been restored remained in question: one view was that the Act of 1991 restored previously existing common law mining rights.[33] The Supreme Court of Appeals did not come to the same conclusion, but found that the 1991 Act did confer on the holder of mineral rights "*the exclusive right to exploit them [the minerals]. (...) The state could no longer, as it had been entitled to under the 1967 act, grant a prospecting these in respect of unexploited mineral deposit against the will of the owner of the land or the holder of the mineral right, subject to only the payment of rental and compensation for damages.*"[34]

The difference becomes crucial when determining the question of whether or not the MRPDA 2002 expropriated mineral rights under the 1991 Act as discussed infra.

On May 1st, 2004 the Mineral and Petroleum Resources Development Act 2002 (MPRDA 2002) came into force. According to section 3(1) of the MPRDA 2002: "*Mineral and petroleum resources are the common heritage of all the people of South Africa and the State is the custodian thereof for the benefit of all South Africans*" (see supra). The private ownership of mineral rights outlined supra and the contingent ownership of the mineral itself had disappeared.[35] The

[29] North Gauteng High Court South Africa (2014), para 28.

[30] Mostert (2012), p. 55.

[31] The Supreme Court of South Africa, *Minister of Minerals and Energy v Agri SA*, para 62.

[32] Badenhorst et al. (2014), p. 289.

[33] The Supreme Court of South Africa, *Minister of Minerals and Energy v Agri SA*, para 63.

[34] The Supreme Court of South Africa, *Minister of Minerals and Energy v Agri SA*, para 63.

[35] North Gauteng High Court South Africa (2014).

former private owner of the mineral right did not have an asset any more that would have commercial value by itself.[36]

Whether or not the provisions of the MPRDA 2002 did constitute an expropriation was the focus of a lengthy judicial debate in the case of *Agri SA v Mining Minister*.[37] The question was first decided in favour of Agri SA by the High Court of South Africa North Gauteng, Pretoria which found that an expropriation had taken place.[38]

On May 31st, 2012 the Supreme Court of Appeal of South Africa decided against Agri SA. It found that an expropriation did not take place and compensation was not to be paid to the former mineral rights owner, Agri SA.[39] Its key reasoning was that common law mining rights had long ceased to exist and the Mining Act of 1991 was therefore never able to provide for those private mineral rights to Agri SA that the MPRDA 2002 would have subsequently taken away.

MJD Wallis held that because of the fact that mineral rights could only ever be exercised with the permission of the government under the preceding laws mineral rights in South Africa, the mineral rights had long departed from a mineral right constituted under the common law principle described supra. In his reasoning the MPRDA 2002 therefore leaves the title in the hands of the private mineral rights owner, but simply manages this title differently.[40]

The Constitutional Court of South Africa was called upon by Agri SA regarding section 25(1) of the Constitution of South Africa which provides that: "*No one may be deprived of property except in terms of law of general application, and no law may permit arbitrary deprivation of property.*"[41]

With its judgment of April 18th, 2013 the Constitutional Court of South Africa upheld the judgment of the Supreme Court of Appeal of South Africa. It held that while the MPRDA 2002 did indeed deprive Agri SA of its coal rights, this deprivation did not constitute expropriation. The court decided that the state did not acquire the mineral rights (as it is only their custodian, not the owner) and therefore no expropriation could have taken place. Another argument was that the transitional arrangements of the MPRDA 2002 (that allowed former mineral rights owners to apply for prospecting and mining licenses within a year of the commencement of the MPRDA 2002) provided sufficient protection and compensation in kind—the right to apply for a mining license, even if for 1 year only.[42]

---

[36] North Gauteng High Court South Africa (2014), p. 51.

[37] North Gauteng High Court South Africa (2014), p. 51.

[38] North Gauteng High Court South Africa (2014), p. 51.

[39] North Gauteng High Court South Africa (2014), p. 51; The Supreme Court of South Africa, *Minister of Minerals and Energy v Agri SA*, p. 83.

[40] North Gauteng High Court South Africa (2014), p. 51; The Supreme Court of South Africa, *Minister of Minerals and Energy v Agri SA*, p. 83.

[41] This section of the constitution has been further elaborated by the Constitutional Court of South Africa in the case *First National Bank of SA Limited t/a Wesbank v Commissioner for the South African Revenue Services and Another*.

[42] North Gauteng High Court South Africa (2014), para 74.

As stated, the current concept of "*state custodianship*" might not yet have been fully explored, but considering the judgment of the Constitutional Court of South Africa private ownership of minerals and mineral rights is not likely to return any time soon.

4.4.3 Colombia

4.4.3.1 Current Situation

According to the Constitution of Colombia the State owns the natural resources, but private rights established with prior laws remain in existence. It furthermore details that the State's ownership of non-renewable natural resources is inalienable and non-transferable.[43] In regards to the referenced private rights a system is established that such pre-existing private rights will be considered extinguished if the holder of the private mineral title suspend the exploration or exploitation for more than twelve consecutive months, without any reasonable justification.[44]

---

[43] Article 332 of the Constitution of Colombia states: "*El Estado es propietario del subsuelo y de los recursos naturales no renovables, sin perjuicio de los derechos adquiridos y perfeccionados con arreglo a las leyes preexistentes.*"

[The State is the owner of the subsoil and of the natural, non-renewable resources, without prejudice to the rights acquired and established in accordance with prior laws.].

Article 6 of the Constitution of Colombia further states that: "*La propiedad estatal de los recursos naturales no renovables es inalienable e imprescriptible.*"

[The State's ownership of non-renewable natural resources is inalienable and non-transferable]. Transfer of the ownership of minerals or mineral rights is not possible.

[44] Article 5 of law 685 of 2001 (Mining Law 2001) states: "*Los minerales de cualquier clase y ubicación, yacentes en el suelo o el subsuelo, en cualquier estado físico natural, son de la exclusiva propiedad del Estado; (...) Quedan a salvo las situaciones jurídicas individuales, subjetivas y concretas provenientes de títulos de propiedad privada de minas perfeccionadas con arreglo a las leyes preexistentes.*"

[Minerals of any type and place, located in the soil or subsoil, in any natural physical state, are exclusively owned by the State; (...). The individual, subjective and concrete legal situations which come from titles of private mining ownership granted according to pre-existing laws are exempted.] According to article 28 Mining Law 2001 those private mineral rights are transferable, e.g. can be bequeathed.

Article 29 Mining Law 2001 determines that: "*Los derechos de propiedad de los particulares sobre el suelo y subsuelo mineros sobre las minas que hubieren sido reconocidos y conservados en los términos, condiciones y modalidades establecidas en la Ley 20 de 1969, el Decreto 2655 de 1988 y la Ley 97 de 1993, se consideraran extinguidos si los interesados suspenden la exploración explotación por más de doce meses continuos, sin causa justificada constitutiva de caso fortuito fuerza mayor.*"

[The ownership rights of private persons over the mining soil and subsoil or over mines that would have been recognized and kept in the terms, conditions and means established in Act 20 of 1969, Decree 2655 of 1988 and Act 97 of 1993, will be considered extinguished if the holder of the private mineral title suspend the exploration or exploitation for more than twelve consecutive months, without any reasonable justification of unforeseen circumstances or force majeure.].

4.4.3.2 Past Legal Developments and Future Political Trends

Colombia has had a long history of parallel state and private ownership of mineral rights. In the time of the Spanish colonization, the Spanish government practiced a combination of a system called "*regalista*" and a system called "*dominal*".[45] The "*regalista*" system recognizes mineral rights as genuine sovereign rights and any use of such minerals will be derived rights, such as a mining concession of the modern mining law.[46] The "*dominal*" system allowed private persons to acquire private mineral rights from the state and in turn, the private owner has to pay compensation.[47]

The latest changes in mining laws did not influence the system of state ownership of minerals as maintained by Act 20 of 1969, decree 2655 of 1988 and Act 97 of 1993.

References

Australian Industry Commission (2007) Mining and minerals processing in Australia report. Available online at: http://www.pc.gov.au/__data/assets/pdf_file/0020/6068/07miningv1.pdf, updated on 6/24/2007. Last checked on 2013

Badenhorst PJ, Van der Vyver E, van Heerden CN (2014) Proposed nationalization of mineral rights in South Africa. J Energy Nat Resour Law 1:1–265

Kirk LJ (2007) Owner vs. contract mining. Available online at: http://www.coffey.com/Uploads/Documents/Kirk-ovcm_20070119050121.pdf, updated on 1/19/2007. Last checked on 15 February 2014

Majoni F (2014) Mine or yours? The Supreme Court of Appeal of South Africa, Anglo Operations Ltd v Sandhurst Estates (Pty) Ltd. Available online at: www.saflii.org/za/journals/DEREBUS/2013/151.rtf. Last checked on 15 February 2014

Molina JC (2014) La Dominio Minero propiedad minera en Colombia del Estado. Available online at: http://www.revistas.unal.edu.co/index.php/revistaun/article/download/13418/14090. Last checked on 15 February 2014

Mostert H (2012) Mineral law: principles & policies in perspective, A historical perspective on the economics of the ownership of mineral rights ownership. Juta, Cape Town

North Gauteng High Court South Africa (2014) Agri SA v Mining Minister, case number [2011] ZAGPPHC 62 (ZAF)

Oxford Dictionary (2014) Definition nationalization. Available online at: www.oxforddictionaries.com/definition/english/nationalize. Last checked on 15 February 2014

Princeton (2014) Definition privatization. Available online at: http://www.princeton.edu/~starr/meaning.html. Last checked on 15 February 2014

Southalan J (2012) Mining law and policy. International perspectives. Annandale, N.S.W: Federation Press

The Government of New South Wales (2013) NSW Coal Compensation Board. Available online at: http://www.ccb.nsw.gov.au/, updated on 4/8/2013. Last checked on 15 February 2014.

Williams DV (2003) Gold, the case of mines (1568) and the Waitangi Tribunal. Aus J Leg Hist, 157. Available online at: http://www.austlii.edu.au/au/journals/AJLH/2003/11.html#fnB10. Last checked on 15 February 2014

[45] Molina (2014), p. 107.

[46] Molina (2014), p. 107.

[47] Molina (2014), p. 108.

Chapter 5
May I Mine? The Question of Mining Licenses

5.1 Introduction and Disambiguation

A foreign investor will not be able to start mining activities until the respective government has granted the necessary permission, commonly in a form of a mining license.

These governmental permissions for mining activities are referred to throughout this work as mining licenses.

Different types of mining licenses cover various phases of a mining project, such as prospecting for minerals, the exploration of minerals, the exploitation/production/mining of minerals.

Further licenses are a retention license to maintain a license while not being able to further the mining project due to economic reasons and/or an ancillary licenses for infrastructure or transport.

Some jurisdiction provide for mining licenses that encompass both the exploration and the production phases of a mining project.

The terminology for different types of mining licenses differs from jurisdiction to jurisdiction and will be explained in the beginning of the relevant chapter.

5.2 Relevance

A foreign investor is only likely to invest in a long-term mining project if he can be sure that he can commence, advance and proceed with the project without being interrupted by administrative measures. The type and conditions of the awarded mining license are therefore crucial.

R.W. Roeder, *Foreign Mining Investment Law*, DOI 10.1007/978-3-319-31217-0_5

5.3 Observation Horizon

As a foreign investor will usually only be involved from the exploration phase, this work will focus on the most relevant mining licenses—licenses for the exploration of minerals, licences for extraction of minerals, and retention licenses.

For foreign investors it is crucial whether exploration licenses are granted on a first-come-first serve basis or on the basis of a competitive application process. Such a competitive application process may include qualitative criteria such as minimum spending requirements as well as cash-bidding components, similar to an auction.

Once exploration is successful, the question arises whether or not the foreign investor will be awarded a license to extract the determined resources. Some governments provide a type of mining license that automatically encompasses both, the exploration and production phase, guaranteeing the investor security of tenure. Some governments provide priority or special consideration to the holder of the exploration license. Other governments treat the holder of the exploration license like any other applicant. The processes may also prefer national and/or Indigenous investors to foreign investors.

Another factor to be considered is how artisanal mining activities are dealt with in the respective host country, inter alia whether they are tolerated by law, or, if all mining activities need a license, thereby giving exclusivity to the mining license holder in the area.

5.4 Countries

5.4.1 Australia

5.4.1.1 Current Situation

In Queensland, Australia, mining licenses are governed by the MRA 1989. The regulatory regime broadly distinguishes between the exploration and the production phase and provides a set of licenses for each. A further license is available when the time between exploration and production becomes too long, e.g. due to a fall in commodity prices leading to a situation that does not allow for economically feasible production, and yet another license is available for ancillary projects like the transport of minerals, e.g. via conveyor belts and trains.[1]

[1] According to section 129 MRA 1989: "*During the term of an exploration permit the holder of the exploration permit and any person who acts for the purpose of carrying out any activity authorized by the exploration permit, with or by such vehicles, vessels, machinery and equipment as may be necessary or expedient for the purpose of exploring for any mineral to which the exploration permit applies, may, (...), enter any part of the area of the exploration permit that is not the surface area of a reserve; and with the consent of the owner, or the consent of the Governor in*

A mining lease according to section 235 MRA 1989 entitles its holder to enter,[2] extract and sell minerals from the license area.

Infrastructure ancillary to a mining project may require further licenses. When the land necessary for the purpose of transportation is within the area of the mining license acquired under section 235 MRA 1989 no further mining license is necessary. According to section 316 MRA 1989,[3] if the investor is planning to build for transportation purposes he may, as an alternative to applying for a mining lease under section 235 MRA 1989, apply for a mining licence that is limited to such transportation purposes.

The mineral development license according to section 181 MRA 1989 addresses a public management issue specific to the commodities industry:

Any licensing system aims at the best use of natural resources for the state. Therefore exploration licenses usually include minimum spending and relinquishment requirements to make sure that the holder of the title uses the title for exploration and not simply for speculation or resale.

On the other hand, the state acknowledges the cyclic character of the commodities industry. Production might simply not be economically feasible in a year but yield profit 5 years later. That solution is a specific retention title, the mineral development license that allows its holder to keep the license until production becomes economically feasible. A mineral development license, the retention license, furthermore allows (and indeed requires) its holder to undertake further exploration and feasibility studies.[4]

Council, any part of the area of the exploration permit that is the surface area of a reserve; for the purposes of facilitating that exploration; (...)".

According to section 235 of the MRA 1989: "*(...) during the currency of a mining lease, the holder of the mining lease and any person who acts as agent or employee of the holder (or who delivers goods or substances or provides services to the holder) for a purpose or right for which the mining lease is granted may enter and be within the area of the mining lease; and upon the surface area comprised in the mining lease; for any purpose for which the mining lease is granted or for any purpose permitted or required under the lease or by this Act; may do all such things as are permitted or required under the lease or by this Act.*"

"*Any purpose permitted or required under the lease or by this Act*" and "*to do all such things as are permitted or required under the lease or by this Act*" refers to mining activities—whereas the scope is specifically determined within each mining lease granted.

[2] See infra for further details regarding possible restriction to land access.

[3] Section 316 MRA 1989 states that: "*(...) if the investors is planning to build for transportation purposes he may over land that is not in the area of the person's lease for the transportation of something through, over or under the land by a pipeline, aerial ropeway, conveyor apparatus, transmission line or similar method of transport, or road.*"

[4] According to section 181(3) of the MRA 1989: "*Without in any way limiting the activities that the Minister may specify in a mineral development license, activities leading to the evaluation and economic development of an ore body by or on behalf of the holder may include geological, geophysical and geochemical programs and other works as are reasonably necessary to evaluate the potential for development of any mineral occurrence of possible economic potential occurring in or on the area of the mineral development license; and mining feasibility studies; (...) marketing studies;(...).*"

While most permissions to mine in Australia are issued on the basis of the mentioned mining licenses supra, it is necessary to mention that "*state agreements*" are another option to acquire a permission to mine.

State agreements are contracts between the state and the mining company that become law by enactment of parliament and can help to speed up the regulatory process and/or secure the arrangements against future regulatory change. Examples of such agreements include: The Central Queensland Coal Associates Agreement Act of 1968,[5] the Queensland Nickel Agreement Act 1970[6] and the Thiess Peabody Coal Pty. Ltd. Agreement Act of 1962.[7] State agreements are used to facilitate the implementation of large scale resource projects only. They have not been used in Australia for some time now, but may still be used if so deemed useful by the government.

An application[8] for an exploration permit or a mining lease will be conditioned to meet a "*minimum expenditure*", which refers to the minimum sum the company is determined to invest in the exploration or production. Furthermore, licenses are given with time limits for exploration and work plans have to be provided for the production phase.

5.4.1.1.1 First-Come-First-Serve vs. Competitive Applications

Concerning the question of granting licenses on a first-come-first serve basis vs. competitive application Australia in particular has decided to opt towards the latter.

A rather new development are public tenders for mining exploration licenses. This was introduced by the Mining and Other Legislation Amendment Act 2013 on March 22nd, 2013.

Whilst in Australia mining titles are generally decided upon by the merits of an application (e.g. work plans), public tenders allow for further income for the state as land that "*is potentially highly prospective*" since 2012 is in the form of a "*competitive cash bidding process*".[9] While additional income for the state budget is one reason for the introduction of competitive cash bidding tenders, it also aims to avoid activities of players in the commodity market that grab mining licenses to "*secure exploration acreage purely for speculative reasons (e.g. for the purposes of on-selling at a profit, often targeting international investors)*".[10]

---

[5] Queensland Parliament (1970).

[6] Queensland Parliament (1962).

[7] Thiess Peabody Coal Pty. Ltd. Agreement Act 1962.

[8] Queensland Government (2013).

[9] Department of Natural Resources and Mines (2013b).

[10] Department of Natural Resources and Mines (2013a), p. 4.

5.4.1.1.2 Security of Tenure

As discussed supra security of tenure refers to the process of going from an exploration license to a mining production lease. In Queensland, Australia, a holder of an exploration permit has priority over other applicants, but does not have the exclusive right to be awarded a mining lease. Whether or not the applicant enjoys priority over other applicants, the ultimate discretion of awarding a mining lease lies with the Minister.[11]

5.4.1.2 Past Legal Developments and Future Political Trends

Amongst current developments are changes in the so-called relinquishment requirements. In order to ensure that mining companies do not occupy any land longer than necessary, they are required to periodically relinquish certain amount of the land under their exploration license. While the requirement to relinquish required 50 % to be relinquished after 2 years and a further 50 % of the remainder every subsequent year, section 139 of the MRA 1989 has now been amended and from an investor perspective eased solely requiring a relinquishment of 40 % by the end of the initial 3 years and by a further 50 % of the remaining area by the end of the initial 5 years after the permit has been granted.

The state can also compulsorily acquire all or part of a mining tenement. The Mines Legislation (Streamlining) Amendment Bill 2012 was passed by the Queensland Parliament in August 2012 and received assent on August 29th, 2012 to become the Mines Legislation Streamlining Amendment Act 2012 and allows for such expropriation.[12]

This section could be used if an administrative body takes land by the relevant process for a purpose other than mining, and then compulsorily acquires the mining tenement.

As to compensation this expropriation will regularly leave the tenement holder with compensation for its expenses accrued by (pre-)mining activities only.[13]

[11] According to section 129(b) of the MRA 1989: "*During the term of an exploration permit (...) the holder of the permit may, subject to compliance with this Act, have considered for grant, in priority to all other persons, an application for the grant of a mining claim, mineral development license or mining lease for all or part of the area of the permit; (...)*".

[12] Section 48 of the Mines Legislation Streamlining Amendment Act 2012 states that: "*(...) the relevant Minister may be satisfied a mining tenement interest is incompatible with the purpose for which the land is taken if, for that purpose, it is necessary to extinguish all interests in the land, including native title rights and interests. A mining tenement interest may be wholly extinguished; or partially extinguished by excluding land from the land the subject of the interest; or prohibiting the carrying out of activities by the holder of the interest.*"

[13] According to section 48(5)(b): "*In assessing any compensation to be paid to the holder of a mining tenement interest in relation to the taking of the land, allowance cannot be made for the value of minerals known or supposed to be on or below the surface of, or mined from, the land.*"

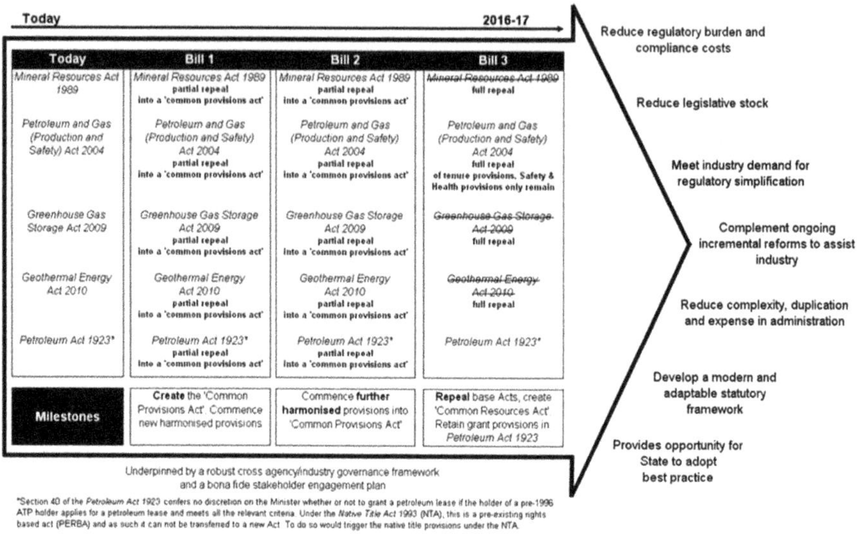

Fig. 5.1 Modernizing Queensland Resource Acts Program. *Source*: Government of Queensland, Department of Natural Resources and Mines

In addition, under the Mines Legislation Streamlining Amendment Act 2012, several functions that formerly required the consent of the Governor-in-Council, inter alia the grant of and the consolidation of mining leases and the variation of conditions can now be performed by the Minister.[14]

The Mines Legislation Streamlining Amendment Act 2012 furthermore addresses various issues regarding health and safety,[15] the coal seam gas industry[16] and the transfer of resource interests.[17] The Mines Legislation Streamlining Amendment Act 2012 was just enacted when the Queensland Government released a new plan, called the "*Modernizing Queensland Resource Acts Program*".[18] A visualization of its plan can be seen in the graphic infra (Fig. 5.1).

A corresponding industry discussion paper released in July 2013 states that: "*The Modernizing Queensland's Resources Acts (MQRA) Program is a landmark initiative that will modernize Queensland's tenures administration legislation for all resource types through the phased development of a common resources Act. This Act will provide for a unified and harmonized system of tenures administration to reduce the regulatory burden on all sectors of the Queensland resources industry, and provide an efficient, responsive and adaptable framework for the regulation of the resources sector in Queensland.*"[19]

---

[14] HWL Ebsworth (2012).

[15] HWL Ebsworth (2012).

[16] HWL Ebsworth (2012).

[17] Herbert Smith Freehills (2014).

[18] Government of Queensland (2013b).

[19] Government of Queensland (2013a), p. 1.

5.4.2 *South Africa*

5.4.2.1 Current Situation

In South Africa, mining licenses are governed by the Mineral and Petroleum Resources Development Act, No. 28 of 2002 ("***MPRDA 2002***").

The regulatory regime distinguishes between the exploration and the production phase and provides licenses for each.

A further license is available when the time between exploration and production becomes too long, e.g. due to a fall in commodity prices, leading to a situation that does not allow for economically feasible production in the near future.

According to section 3(2) of the MPRDA 2002: "*(...) As the custodian of the nation's mineral and petroleum resources, the State, acting through the Minister, may grant, issue, refuse, control, administer and manage any (...), prospecting right, (...), mining right, (...), retention permit, (...).*"

Under a prospecting right the holder may search for minerals, under the mining right he may then undertake any operation or activity for production of such mineral as detailed in the respective mining license.[20]

Furthermore, a social and labour plan is required when applying for a mining right. Regulation 46 (b) (v) of the Mineral and Petroleum Resource Development Regulation specifically requires a "*human resources development program*" for Historically Disadvantaged South Africans.

According to section 35 MPRDA 2002 in combination with sections 1 and 5 of the MPRDA 2002, the holder of a retention permit has: "*the exclusive right to be granted a mining right in respect of the retention area and mineral in question.*" The holder will have to prove on a 6 months basis that the current market situation does not allow for an economically feasible mining operation.

5.4.2.1.1 First-Come-First-Serve vs. Competitive Applications

According to section 17(1) of the MPRDA 2002 in combination with section 9(1) of the MPRDA 2002, the Minister must grant a prospecting right to the first applicant only if one applicant has applied on a particular day. According to section 9(2) of

---

[20] According to section 19 of the MPRDA 2002 in combination with sections 1 and 5 of the MPRDA 2002, the holder of a prospecting right may "(...) *intentionally search for any mineral by means of any method which disturbs the surface or subsurface of the earth, including any portion of the earth that is under the sea or under other water; or in or on any residue stockpile residue deposit, in order to establish the existence of any mineral and to determine the extent and economic value of thereof; (...).*"

According to section 25 MPRDA 2002 in combination with sections 1 and 5 of the MPRDA 2002, the holder of a mining right may: "(...) *undertake any operation or activity for the purpose of winning any mineral on, in or under the earth, water or any residue deposit, whether by underground or open working or otherwise and includes any corporation or activity incidental thereto.*"

the MPRDA 2002, "*When the Minister considers applications received on the same date he or she must give preference to applications from historically disadvantaged persons.*"

5.4.2.1.2 Certainty of Tenure

According to section 19(1)(b) of the MPRDA 2002 and under the conditions set out in section 19(2) of the MPRDA 2002, the holder of a prospecting right is entitled to apply for and be granted a mining right in respect to the mineral and prospecting area in question without discretionary power of the Minister.

5.4.2.2 Past Legal Developments and Future Political Trends

The Mineral and Petroleum Resources Development Amendment Act, No. 49 of 2008 ("***MPRDA 2008***") came into effect on June 7th, 2013 by proclamation of the President of South Africa on May 23, 2013.[21]

A key feature is that under the MPRDA 2008 it became more difficult to obtain a prospecting right or transfer from a prospecting right to a mining right, inter alia by introducing competitive elements in the process of granting the right.[22]

A detailed discussion is not relevant here as the parliament is already discussing the new MPRDA Amendment Bill 2011, which will alter the MPRDA 2002 in the form it had obtained by MPRDA 2008.

It is therefore more relevant to take a look at the new bill and the key topics of debate to be able to estimate where South Africa's mineral license system is heading.

A key question for South Africa is how to deal with the numerous applications for mineral rights, as more than 18,000 applications for mining licenses have been received by the Department of Minerals and Energy since 2004.[23]

The new online South African mineral resources administration system was launched in April 2011. By February 2012 more than 3000 prospecting rights, mining permits and mining rights were applied for by use of this new online channel.[24]

A topic of parliamentary debate is the decision whether to include competitive elements and executive discretion in the application process for mining tenures.[25]

According to the opposition in the parliament, the introduction of the Mineral and Petroleum Resources Development Amendment Bill would increase the

[21] Ramsaran (2014).

[22] Leon (2013).

[23] Government of South Africa (2009), p. 148.

[24] Government of South Africa (2012), p. 371.

[25] Leon (2013).

uncertainty for investors by introducing competitive bidding for mineral rights and further expand the discretion of the Minister, mentioning 34 instances in the mining licenses system that allow for discretion.[26]

The opposition in the parliament fears that the discretion gives a wider possibility for corruption. The government replied by stating that the discretion is to allow the Minister "*responsiveness and agility*" in dealing with complex mining questions.[27]

The heated debate over the discretion of the Minister should be seen in the light of current and past cases such as the ones of *Imperial Crown Trading*[28] and *Samber*.

A case that gives a good insight into what triggers the fears of investors and has been judged upon by the High Court of South Africa and the honourable Majiedt J. is the case of "*Doe Run Exploration SA (Pty) Ltd and Others v Minister of Minerals and Energy and Others*". The court described the circumstances: "*Doe Run has conducted extensive operations in South Africa since approximately 1995. These operations entailed prospecting activities on approximately fifteen farms in the Griqua Town area to determine whether there are viable deposits of copper, lead, zinc and silver. (…) A feasibility study was compiled and handed in to the Department of Mineral and Energy, in which 4.5 million tons ore were identified plus a further reserve of approximately 6 million tons in respect of the abovementioned minerals. Doe Run applied for a prospecting right in terms of the provisions of the Act in respect of 16 farms, but this was declined on 14 September 2005. On 15 December 2005 Doe Run again applied for prospecting rights with regard to copper, lead, zinc and silver in respect of the 16 farms on which it had been prospecting as aforementioned. On 12 October 2006 Doe Run was informed by the Second Respondent that its application had been granted in respect of 9 of the farms. Nothing was mentioned about the other 7 farms applied for.*"[29]

Only later Doe Run discovered that licenses regarding the other seven farms it had applied for had been awarded to the newly founded entity Samber 103 (Pty) Ltd.[30]

The judgment revised the decisions of the administration and, inter alia, found:

> The decision of the Deputy Director-General, Mineral Regulation, to grant a prospecting right for copper, lead and zinc, dated 14 December 2006, Protocol No 1483/2006 with Registration Number 95/2007, to Samber Trading 103 (Pty) Ltd with regard to the far Glencard 525, district Hay, Northern Cape Province, is hereby set aside and the said prospecting right I hereby declare invalid.[31]

---

[26] Democratic Alliance South Africa (2014), p. 4.

[27] Democratic Alliance South Africa (2014), p. 4.

[28] Sergeant (2014).

[29] High Court of South Africa (2008), p. 7.

[30] Sergeant (2014).

[31] High Court of South Africa (2008), p. 37.

It furthermore ordered the administration to grant one permit and process the application of Doe Run regarding other properties where permits were originally awarded to Samber 103 (Pty) Ltd. The judge commented on the processes of the administration as follows:

> It is necessary that I comment on a disturbing aspect of this case. A lamentable trend has developed in cases of this nature, i.e. concerning the issuing of rights under the Act, that very lengthy delays are experienced by applicants to have their applications finalized by the Department. The present case is no exception. These lengthy delays cannot be in the interests of the economy, where much needed investment is delayed and sometimes even lost. In the present matter a US company has already invested millions of Rands and stands ready to invest more, provided it can have finality on its applications. The extraordinary delays, alluded to in this judgment, are adverse to such foreign investment. Of further concern in this matter is that the Respondents had failed to discover the records of the various decisions, as they were called upon to do in terms of Rule 53(1). It took a contempt of court application to have same discovered. I would hope that this Court has seen the last of this disturbing trend in the present matter.[32]

Another case that in 2013 was still pending is the case of Imperial Crown Trading.[33] Imperial Crown Trading is a company that despite the lack of mining experience was awarded a mining license against Anglo American's Kumba, the largest iron ore mining company of South Africa.[34]

Not all cases that have a negative impact on the trust of investors do go to court: the four million US$ settlement between Lonmin and Keysha Investments also has the potential to disturb foreign investors trust regarding investments in South Africa.[35] The Holgoun Group Company, related to the Keysha Investment Company applied for a right over associated minerals on a portion of Lonmin mining project.

Before awarding the right on May 12th, 2010 the Department of Mineral Resources demanded Lonmin to stop mining the minerals that were by-products of its platinum group metals. Under the former Minerals Act 50 of 1991 those by-products were covered by the original Lonmin license. A change in the law when the MPRDA 2002 was introduced left the question of these kind of by-products unanswered, creating a situation where the Holgoun group company could use a legal loophole for its advantage.[36]

Regarding the question of certainty of tenure, the Secretary-General of the ANC, Gwede Mantashe stated in 2013 that mining companies "*misrepresenting*" their intentions could have their licenses revoked. This was in response to the announcement of Anglo American Platinum that it planned to halt production at its mine in Rustenburg which would endanger 14,000 jobs and seemingly contradicted agreements made with the government at the time the license was granted.[37]

---

[32] High Court of South Africa (2008), p. 37.

[33] Sergeant (2014).

[34] Sergeant (2014).

[35] McKay (2014).

[36] Brendan (2010).

[37] Sapa (2014).

In its annual report of 2011, the Department of Mineral Resources of South Africa formulated ambitious goals in the form of a vision for 2014 and a vision for 2025. The vision for 2014 aims to achieve: "*A globally competitive, sustainable and meaningfully transformed mining and minerals sector.*"[38]

The vision for 2025 states the aim to achieve to be: "*A leader in the transformation of South Africa through economic growth and sustainable development by 2025.*"[39]

Mining investors have voiced concerns whether the current policy changes will help to achieve those noble goals: "*To be able to make large capital investment decisions mining and exploration companies need certainty on what we're going to be handed. What we'd like to see is that the terms we've agreed upon remain intact, but no one can give a perfectly clear answer on what a mining or production right stemming from a current exploration or prospecting right will entail.*"[40]

The amendment bill would empower the South African Minister for Natural Resources furthermore to influence the pricing of natural resources sold from South African mining projects and to impose export permits on minerals, very much taking the key economic decisions of a foreign investor in natural resources into the Minister's hands.[41]

Considering the implications of the new bill it is likely that it will see some time in the parliamentary process as did the last bill—and further intense public discussion.[42]

5.4.3 Colombia

5.4.3.1 Current Situation

In 2013 mining licenses were again governed by the law 685 of 2001 (Mining Law 2001). The regulatory regime does not distinguish between a license for each, the exploration and production phases, but provides a single license, the mining concession.

The grant of such mining concession requires that any mining activity is "*carried out in a harmonious manner of the principles and norms of rational*

[38] Department of Mineral Resources South Africa (2011), p. 4.

[39] Department of Mineral Resources South Africa (2011), p. 4.

[40] Peyper (2014).

[41] Peyper (2014).

[42] Want (2014).

exploitation of non-renewable natural resources and of the environment" and furthermore demands a focus on sustainable development as well as economic and social benefits for the country.[43]

The Mining Law also emphasizes that the right to explore and exploit the mines of State's ownership can only be given by the State itself[44] and by terms provided in the mining concession granted.[45]

5.4.3.1.1 First-Come-First-Serve vs. Competitive Applications

If all legal requirements, such as the technical, operative and environmental obligations set forth in article 59 of the Mining Law 2001 are met, the Agencia Nacional de Minería will decide upon the applications on a first come first serve basis.

---

[43] According to article 1, the Mining Law 2001 aims to "*(...) fomentar la exploración técnica y la explotación de los recursos mineros de propiedad estatal y privada"; and: "(...) se realice en forma armónica con los principios y normas de explotación racional de los recursos naturales no renovables y del ambiente, dentro de un concepto integral de desarrollo sostenible y del fortalecimiento económico y social del país.*"

[(...) promote the technical exploration and exploitation of the mineral resources of State and private ownership; and: (...)see that its use is carried out in a harmonious manner of the principles and norms of rational exploitation of non-renewable natural resources and of the environment, within the integral concept of sustainable development and economic and social strengthening of the country.]

[44] According to article 14 of the Mining Law 2001: "*(...) únicamente se podrá constituir, declarar y probar el derecho a explorar y explotar minas de propiedad estatal, mediante el contrato de concesión minera, debidamente otorgado e inscrito en el Registro Minero Nacional*".

[(...) the right to explore and exploit the mines of State's ownership can only be constituted, declared or proved by means of a contract of mining concession, duly awarded and registered at the National Mining Register].

[45] Article 14 in combination with Article 45 of the Mining Law 2001 states: "*El contrato de concesión minera es el que se celebra entre el Estado y un particular para efectuar, por cuenta y riesgo de este, los estudios, trabajos y obras de exploración de minerales de propiedad estatal que puedan encontrarse dentro de una zona determinada y para explotarlos en los términos y condiciones establecidos en este Código (...).*"

[The contract of mining concession is that which it is agreed upon between the State and an individual to carry out, on his account and at his own risk, the studies, works and installations of exploration of minerals of State's ownership that can be found within a determined area and to exploit in the terms and conditions established in this Code.]

The scope of the mining concession under the Mining Law 2001 includes: "*(...) las fases de exploración técnica, explotación económica, beneficio de los minerales por cuenta y riesgo del concesionario y el cierre o abandono de los trabajos y obras correspondientes.*"

[(...) the stages of technical exploration, economic exploitation, beneficiation of minerals at the concessionaire's own account and risk and the closing or abandonment of the corresponding works and installations.]

5.4.3.1.2 Security of Tenure

As the mining concession encompasses both the exploration license and production phases, the process of transferring an exploration license into a mining license (on paper) is non-existent. The time between exploration and mining can be prolonged by applying for a deferral according to article 74 of the Mining Law 2001, which is similar to a retention license outlined infra.

5.4.3.2 Past Legal Developments and Future Political Trends

Before February 9th, 2001 mining licenses were regulated by Act 20 of 1969, decree 2655 of 1988 and Act 97 of 1993. These laws still govern some mining licenses issued before February 9th, 2001.[46] These old license regimes required the investor to acquire different licenses for exploration and production.

From 2001 until 2010, mining was governed by Mining Law 2001. On February 9th 2013 the Colombian Parliament passed the law 1382 of 2010.

With its judgement from May 11th, 2011 the Constitutional Court of Colombia declared the Mining Law 2010 unconstitutional, but for a time of 2 years postponed most of the effects of the judgment.[47]

In its reasoning it found the law: "*Inexequible por exigencia de la realización de una consulta previa a las comunidades indígenas y afrodescendientes*".

[Unconstitutional for the deficiency of the law to properly address the constitutional right of prior consultation for Indigenous groups and people with African heritage].[48]

The Colombian government did not use the time that the Constitutional Court had given it to enact a new and constitutional law. After the 2 years, by May 11th, 2013 the former Mining Law 2001 came back into force yet again.

The government quickly issued decrees 933, 934 and 935 on May 9th, 2013—just 2 days before the 2 years period ended.

Decree 933 deals with the formalization of artisanal/traditional mining as well as technical and environmental aspects, such as the protection of certain forests and wetlands.

Decree 934 specifies reasons for rejection of certain applications on the basis of an analysis of the supporting financial statements. It also details the procedure for electronically submitted applications.

---

[46] Law Business Research Ltd (2014), p. 2. The key passage reads: "(. . .) inexequible la Ley 1382 de 2010 (. . .)", but deferred: "(. . .) los efectos de la inexequibilidad declarada por el término de dos años, de conformidad con lo expuesto en la parte motiva de esta sentencia."

[Law 1382 from 2010 unconstitutional, but for a time of 2 years postponed the effect of the judgment except for certain interim measures outlined in the judgment].

[47] Corte Constitucional de Colombia (2011).

[48] Corte Constitucional de Colombia (2011), p. 1.

Decree 935 regulates extensions of existing contracts, limiting the discretion of the regulatory body to grant extensions in cases where the applicant does not comply with legal, technical or economic conditions.

The unconstitutional Mining Law 2010 would have amended article 31 Mining Law 2001 by a tender process in addition to the principle of "*first come first served*" established by the Mining Law 2001.[49]

The possibility to allow for a tender process has now already been reintroduced in the law 1440 of 2011, "*El plan nacional de desarrollo 2010-2014*"[50] [The national development plan 2010-2014], which touches upon some specific questions of the Mining Law of 2001, but does not replace it. The tender process is similar to the one outlined supra in the Mining Law 2010 and includes minimum payments other than royalties necessary.

These provisions not only include the best technical, economic, social and environmental standards in the screening process, but also focus on the financial contribution to the state budget that a mining concession applicant will have to make.

On January 30th, 2012 resolution number 180102 regarding article 108 law 1450 (Strategic Minerals) determined what minerals and areas are considered strategic and can fall under this tender process.[51]

Regarding the security of tenure, the Mining Law 2010 included a provision establishing the need to renegotiate the terms of mining licenses after the exploration phase is over. As the Mining Law 2010 was declared unconstitutional the requirement is currently not in force.

Decree 943 of May 14, 2013, outlined supra, only requires concessionaires to demonstrate economic and technical benefit for the nation before a renewal is granted, but does not speak of renegotiations of mining licences already granted.[52]

---

[49] Article 31 Mining Law 2001 as proposed would have stated: "*La Autoridad Minera también podrá delimitar otras áreas especiales que se encuentren libres, sobre las cuales, de conformidad con la información geológica existente, se puede adelantar un proyecto minero de gran importancia para el país, con el objeto de otorgarlas en contrato de concesión a través de un proceso de selección objetiva, a quien ofrezca mejores condiciones técnicas, económicas, sociales y ambientales para el aprovechamiento del recurso.*"

[The Mining Authority may also define other special areas that are free, on which, in accordance with existing geological information, a mining project of great importance for the country can be advanced, in order to grant the concession agreement through an objective selection process, based upon who offers the best technical, economic, social and environmental conditions for the use of the resource.]

[50] Government of Colombia 2011, *Plan Nacional de Desarrollo*. Regarding the tender process it requests: "*(...) Lo anterior con el fin de que estas áreas sean otorgadas en contrato de concesión especial a través de un proceso de selección objetiva, en el cual la autoridad minera establecerá en los términos de referencia, las contraprestaciones económicas mínimas distintas de las regalías, que los interesados deben ofrecer.*"

[This is to ensure that these areas are granted by special concession through a strict selection process, in which the mining authority will establish in the terms of reference the minimum payments other than royalties, which the applicants must offer.]

[51] USGS (2012).

[52] Law Business Research Ltd (2014), p. 5.

Nevertheless one case was observed where the Government of Colombia forced BHP Billiton Cerromatoso Iron into a renegotiation process. This leaves some amount of uncertainty for foreign investors.[53]

Another key topic of debate in Colombia is the question of legalization of artisanal/traditional mining activities. Colombia has a high percentage of traditional miners that produce their livelihood from artisanal mining. In nearly all cases they do not possess a mining license. The Mining Law of 2001 states that generally illicit explorations and exploitation of mining deposits constitute a criminal offense, but differentiates between illicit mining and occasional/artisanal mining, whereas the latter is not considered illicit. What is to be considered occasional mining is further detailed, but in general it can be said that any kind of artisanal mining/occasional mining that only profits the miner and his/her family will not be considered illicit.[54]

With regard to artisanal/traditional mining the law 1440 of 2011, "*El plan nacional de desarrollo 2010-2014*" [The national development plan 2010-2014] states that it shall be prohibited to use substantive mechanical equipment if such is not registered in the National Mining Registry for occasional/artisanal Mining.[55]

---

[53] Beltrán (2013).

[54] The general rule in article 159 of the Mining Law of 2001 is that: "*La exploración y explotación ilícita de yacimientos mineros, constitutivo del delito contemplado en el artículo 244 del Código Penal (...).*"

[Illicit exploration and exploitation of mining deposits constitutes a criminal offense according to Article 244 of the Penal Code of Colombia].

The Mining Law of 2001 differentiates between "*ilícit*" [illicit] mining and "*occasional*" [occasional] mining. According to article 152 of the Mining Law 2001: "*La extracción ocasional y transitoria de minerales industriales a cielo abierto, que realicen los propietarios de la superficie, en cantidades pequeñas y a poca profundidad y por medios manuales, no requerirá de concesión del Estado.*"

[The occasional and transitory extraction of industrial minerals by open pit mining—that is carried out by the owners of the surface in small amounts, not much depth and by manual work—will not require of a concession of the State.] and is therefore not to be considered illicit. Occasional activities are restricted as the extracted minerals may only: "*(...) tener como destino el consumo de los mismos propietarios, en obras y reparaciones de sus viviendas e instalaciones, previa autorización del dueño del predio. Todo otro destino industrial o comercial que le den a los minerales extraídos, al amparo de este artículo, les está prohibido.*" [(...) be used by the owners in works and repairs of their homes and installations, [by] previous authorization of the owner of the properties. Any other industrial or commercial destination given to the extracted minerals, covered by this Article, is prohibited.] According to article 155 small scale gold panning is also permitted.

Regarding criminal prosecution the Mining Law 2001 states that: "*Hasta tanto la Autoridad Minera no resuelva las solicitudes de legalización (...), ni a proseguirles las acciones penales señaladas en los artículos 159 y 160 de este Código.*"

[Until the Mining Authority resolves the legalization processes (...) it shall not proceed for criminal actions provided for in Articles 159 and 160 of this Code [the Mining Law 2001].

[55] According to the mining the law 1440 of 2011, "El plan nacional de desarrollo 2010–2014 "*(...) se prohibe en todo el territorio nacional, la utilización de dragas, minidragas, retroexcavadoras y demás equipos mecánicos en las actividades mineras sin título minero inscrito en el Registro Minero Nacional.*"

[Since the enactment of this law, is prohibited throughout the country, to use dredges, diggers, backhoes and other mechanical equipment in mining not registered in the National Mining Registry].

The discussion that considers occasional/artisanal Mining is yet ongoing in Colombia. The trend seems to point towards a more strict approach in the future, also in consideration of the environmental pollution caused by certain types of occasional/artisanal mining activities.[56]

References

Beltrán H (2013) Government could extend Cerro Matoso negotiations. BNamericas, 9/24/2013. Available online at: http://www.bnamericas.com/news/mining/government-could-extend-cerro-matoso-negotiations/322065018. Last checked on 15 February 2014

Brendan R. (2010) Lonmin the latest victim of the DMR. MiningMX, 8/6/2010. Available online at: http://www.miningmx.com/news/platinum_group_metals/lonmin-the-latest-victim-of-the-dmr.htm. Last checked on 15 February 2014

Corte Constitucional (2011) Reforma al Codigo de Minas – Consulta previa de medidas legislativas a las comunidades étnicas, judgment of 05 November 2011. Reference: C-366/11. Available online at: http://www.corteconstitucional.gov.co/relatoria/2011/c-366-11.htm. Last checked on 15 February 2014

Democratic Alliance South Africa (2014) Press Conference Document_MPRDA Bill. Available online at: https://docs.google.com/file/d/0B_-slGu8-FTxWlduUWdhZWtDaEU/edit?pli=1. Last checked on 15 February 2014

Department of Mineral Resources South Africa (2011) Annual Report 2010/2011. Available online at: http://www.info.gov.za/view/DownloadFileAction?id=177944. Last checked on 15 February 2014

Department of Natural Resources and Mines (2013a) Competitive cash bidding project probity report. Available online at: http://mines.industry.qld.gov.au/assets/mines-pdf/ccbp-probity-report-may-2013.pdf, updated on 5/21/2013. Last checked on 15 February 2014.

Department of Natural Resources and Mines (2013b) Competitive tendering. Edited by Queensland Government. Available online at: http://mines.industry.qld.gov.au/mining/competitive-tendering.htm, updated on 8/2/2013. Last checked on 15 February 2014

Government of Queensland (2013a) Modernizing Queensland's resources acts program – discussion paper. Available online at: http://mines.industry.qld.gov.au/assets/legislation-pdf/mqra-dealings-discussion-paper.pdf, updated on 8/16/2013. last checked on 15 February 2014

Government of Queensland (2013b) Modernizing Queensland resource acts program. Available online at: http://mines.industry.qld.gov.au/mining/modernising-qld-resource-acts-program.htm, updated on 9/6/2013. Last checked on 15 February 2014

Government of South Africa (2009) Pocket guide to South Africa 2008/2009: minerals and mining. Available online at: http://www.gcis.gov.za/sites/www.gcis.gov.za/files/docs/resourcecentre/pocketguide/2008/015_minerals.pdf, updated on 1/11/2013. Last checked on 15 February 2014

Government of South Africa (2012) SA yearbook mineral resources. Available online at: http://www.gcis.gov.za/sites/www.gcis.gov.za/files/docs/resourcecentre/yearbook/2011/21_Mineral%20resources.pdf, updated on 1/11/2013. Last checked on 15 February 2014

High Court (2008) Doe run exploration SA (Pty) Ltd and Others v Minister of Minerals and Energy and Others, Judgment of 8 February 2008. References: (499/07) [2008] ZANCHC 3. Available online at: http://www.saflii.org/za/cases/ZANCHC/2008/3.pdf. Last checked on 15 February 2014

[56] Schmidt (2015).

HWL Ebsworth (2012) In brief: Mines Legislation (Streamlining) Amendment Act 2012. Available online at: http://www.hwlebsworth.com.au/latest-news-a-publications/publications/energy-and-resources/item/726-mines-legislation-amendment-act-2012.html. Last checked on 15 February 2014

Law Business Research Ltd (2014) Colombia - Mining - Reference - Latin Lawyer. Available online at: http://www.cardenasycardenas.com/archivos/52.M2013%20-%20Colombia%20%282%29.pdf http://www.lbresearch.com. Last checked on 15 February 2014

Leon P (2013) Confusion over new mining laws. Available online at: http://www.moneyweb.co.za/moneyweb-safm-market-update/r-1300. Last checked on 15 February 2014

McKay D (2014) Lonmin, Holgoun deal is in bad faith. Available online at: http://www.miningmx.com/page/opinion/columnists/1425774-Lonmin-Holgoun-deal-is-in-bad-faith#.UhTXbj9GKDs. Last checked on 15 February 2014

Peyper L (2014) Mining law changes to send investors scuttling. Available online at: http://www.miningmx.com/page/news/markets/1629216-Mining-law-changes-to-send-investors-scuttling#.UhPD9G1GKDs. Last checked on 15 February 2014

Queensland Government (2013) Minerals tenure types and forms. Available online at: http://mines.industry.qld.gov.au/mining/minerals-tenures.htm, updated on 8/9/2013. Last checked on 15 February 2014

Queensland Parliament (1962) Thiess Peabody Coal Pty. Ltd. Agreement Act 1962. Available online at: http://www.legislation.qld.gov.au/LEGISLTN/CURRENT/T/ThiePCoalAgrA62.pdf. Last checked on 15 February 2014

Queensland Parliament (1970) Queensland Nickel Agreement Act 1970. Available online at: http://www.legislation.qld.gov.au/LEGISLTN/CURRENT/Q/QldNickelAgrA70.pdf. Last checked on 15 February 2014

Ramsaran A (2014) Mineral and Petroleum Resources Development Amendment Act (49/2008): Commencement (Gazette 36512, Proc 14). In Polity.org.za. Available online at: http://www.polity.org.za/article/mineral-and-petroleum-resources-development-amendment-act-492008-commencement-gazette-36512-proc-14-2013-05-31. Last checked on 15 February 2014

Sapa (2014): Mining licences can be revoked – Mantashe. Mining Weekly. Available online at: http://www.miningweekly.com/article/mining-licences-can-be-revoked-mantashe-2013-01-18. Last checked on 15 February 2014

Schmidt CW (2015) Quicksilver and gold: mercury pollution from artisanal and small-scale gold mining. Available online at: http://ehp.niehs.nih.gov/120-a424/. Last on checked 22 March 2015

Sergeant B (2014) The history behind the Imperial Crown Trading Saga. In Mineweb.com Mineweb. Available online at: http://www.mineweb.com/mineweb/content/en/mineweb-political-economy?oid=113805&sn=Detail. Last checked on 15 February 2014

Herbert Smith Freehills (2014) Streamlining Queensland's mining and petroleum compliance regulations. Available online at: http://www.herbertsmithfreehills.com/insights/legal-briefings/streamlining-queenslands-mining-and-petroleum-compliance-regulations. Last checked on 15 February 2014

USGS (2012) The Mineral Industry of Colombia in 2011. Available online at: http://minerals.usgs.gov/minerals/pubs/country/2011/myb3-2011-co.pdf, updated on 10/15/2012. Last checked on 15 February 2014

Want M (2014) Amendments to the South African mining law – a controversy in the making, Lexology. In: Fasken Martineau DuMoulin LLP (ed) Available online at: http://www.lexology.com/library/detail.aspx?g=e690fb1f-11bc-40ca-a3b0-ee7336743e4d. Last checked on 15 February 2014

Chapter 6
May I Enter? The Question of Land Access

6.1 Introduction

For the purpose of this work land access refers to the legal framework for foreign investors to enter on the land of a third party to conduct activities necessary to realize a mining project. This may include activities such as transport, drilling and establishing and using production facilities. If applicable for the respective country, the question of land access may also include the relationship of the foreign investor with Indigenous, Tribal or Indian-/Afro-Colombian titleholders and local governments and their respective planning authorities.

6.2 Relevance

While geophysical, gravity, electromagnetic and magnetic field surveys might be conducted airborne and by remote sensing, nearly all other mining activities require access to land.

As described supra, the ownership of the land, the ownership of the mineral, the ownership of the respective mineral right and the ownership of the mining license may fall apart. For a foreign investor this creates the question whether and by what process he may enter the land.

Land use and access to land are crucial and often disputed issues for the mining industry. Reasons behind this are factors inherent with mining activities: restriction of potential other economic productivity such as agriculture, environment related complications and the possible disruption of community life, both on the area of the mining lease itself and in adjacent properties.[1]

[1] Bakheit (2005), p. 1.

R.W. Roeder, *Foreign Mining Investment Law*, DOI 10.1007/978-3-319-31217-0_6

6.3 Observation Horizon

Issues of land access for the foreign investor may arise in regards to the owner of the land, Indigenous, Tribal and Indian land title holders and the local governments—or with several of these parties.

In each of the relationships outlined supra the state government may decide to allow the foreign investor to enter upon the land simply on the basis of the mining license.

The state government may also chose to demand the foreign investor to inform, consult or negotiate with the owner of the land, Indigenous, Tribal or Indian land title holders and local governments or several of these parties. The state may provide support for the negotiation by means of administrative guidance, alternative dispute resolution mechanisms or litigation. The state may also decide to establish a veto power for a third party.

The state may finally require the foreign investor to pay compensation for access to land, based on the value of the mineral resources in the subsoil or alternatively the disturbance of the original use of the land caused by the mining activities on the land.

The State is furthermore entitled and required to make a decision in the public interest regarding whether mining activities should be given precedence over other forms of land use and thereby decide what is to be considered the best use of land.[2]

6.4 Countries

6.4.1 *Australia*

Land in Queensland, Australia consists of Crown land and private land. Crown land refers to land owned by the Commonwealth of Australia or the state.[3] When the land over which the mining license is granted is Crown land, the conditions for entry depend on the category of the land concerned. In state parks, national parks and wilderness areas mining activities generally cannot be conducted.

In conservation reserves and regional parks exploration and mining is restricted. Here a mining license and a land access permit are likely to include more restrictions regarding the type and scope of the mining activities conducted. The agreement from the relevant government department, until 1990 the Land Administration Commission and now the Department of Environment and Heritage Protection is required to realize a mining project.[4]

[2] Bakheit (2005), p. 3.

[3] Department of Natural Resources and Mines (2014).

[4] Department of Natural Resources and Mines (2014).

Land without a special status has no additional restrictions on exploration and mining, hence the usual steps necessary to acquire a mining license suffice.[5]

Regarding the relationship of a foreign investor and third parties, a distinction has to be made between private landowners, native titleholders and local authorities:

6.4.1.1 The Relationship of the Foreign Investor with the Owner of the Land

6.4.1.1.1 Current Situation

If the investor does not own the land, then ownership of the minerals (vested within the State), the license to mine (vested with the investor) and the ownership of the land (third party) falls apart.

As both—exploration and production—force the investor to access the land of a third party to various degrees, the legislation in Queensland provides for a detailed framework of the relationship between the investor and the owner of the land. For the holder of a production tenement, e.g. a mining lease, land access rights follow from the mining lease itself. For the holder of an expiration tenement, e.g. exploration permit and/or a mineral development license the following framework applies:

If the land is privately owned, access to it is governed by the schedule 1 of the MRA 1989. The MRA stipulates that the access to the land will have to take place in accordance with the Land Access Code 2010.[6] The mining license might include further obligations and rules.

Schedule 1 of the MRA 1989 [Access and compensation provisions for exploration permits and mineral development licences] is the primary source of legal obligation, whereas the Land Access Code 2010[7] provides further guidance. An example is the interplay between section 10 of schedule 1 of the MRA 1989 and section 5 of the Land Access Code.

An example of the interplay between the MRA and the Land Access Code would be the MRA stating that an investor must not enter private land before a conduct and compensation agreement is concluded with the owner of the land. The Land Access Code then details that such investor shall make early contact with the landholder

---

[5] A detailed guide on land management in Queensland, Australia can be found at: Queensland Government (2013).

[6] According to section 777 of the MRA 1989 it is determined that: "*If a condition of a mining tenement is inconsistent with a mandatory provision of the land access code, the mandatory provision prevails to the extent of the inconsistency.*"

[7] Department of Employment (2010b).

and arrange to inspect the property well in advance of any planned commencement of activities.[8]

Land access for the purpose of exploration that comprises only preliminary activities requires only an entry notice, whereas advanced activities that are likely to have a significant impact on a landholder's business land use require a compensation agreement to be in place before an entry notice can be given.[9] Whilst the bottom line of such compensation agreements in most cases is financial compensation for land access, legally the compensation is not based upon any rights to the minerals by the private landowner derived from ownership of land. It rather is a payment for damage to the surface of the land and restrictions to the full use of the land by the owner—results that usually occur when undertaking minerals exploration.

Provided that the process under the MRA 1989 is followed, landowners will not be able to prevent the entry of mining companies to their land for exploration, but the process guarantees that their situation is duly considered and compensation for the disturbance of land is being paid for.[10]

6.4.1.1.2 Past Legal Developments and Future Political Trends

When the Queensland government introduced the new land access framework discussed supra it committed itself to a review after 12 months. This review, culminating in the report of the land access review panel, also known as the "*Watson*" Report referring to the review panel's chair Dr David Watson, made a list of 12 recommendations to modify the current legal framework.[11] Considering the high profile of the members of the review panel, it is likely that at least some if not most of the recommendations will be implemented in some form.

The recommendations with the highest potential for strong impact in the near future are that the Government is to[12]:

- (. . .) notify all landholders covered by a tenure or authority at the time of grant in order to ensure all parties are informed that a resource tenure process has commenced and what that means.

---

[8] Section 10 of schedule 1 of the MRA 1989 states that: "*A person must not enter private land in an exploration tenement's area to carry out an advanced activity for the tenement (the relevant activity) unless each eligible claimant for the land is a party to an appropriate conduct and compensation agreement.*"

According to section 5 of the Land Access Code the holder of the mining license "*(. . .) shall make early contact the landholder and arrange to visit and inspect the property well in advance of any planned commencement of authorized activities.*"

[9] Department of Employment (2010a).

[10] Department of Employment (2010a).

[11] Land Access Review Panel (2012).

[12] Land Access Review Panel (2012), p. 20.

- (. . .) establish an independent panel to determine disputes arising in negotiating a Conduct and Compensation Agreements (CCA) in order to provide parties with a simpler and faster way to facilitate a definitive resolution of land access negotiations.
- (. . .) appoint an independent third party or organization to clarify what are 'reasonable and necessary professional costs to negotiate a CCA', initially by establishing a database of legal and other professional fees in order to establish the range of professional fees being paid by resource companies in relation to negotiation of CCAs and to use this information to give guidance.
- (. . .) work with the resource and agricultural sectors to develop 'standard Conduct and Compensation Agreements' by industry for coal, CSG and minerals in order to create standard CCAs that reflect the diversity of the resource sector and the land areas in which it operates.
- (. . .) introduce a way for parties to opt-out of the requirement to sign a CCA for advanced activities in order to simplify the process for two willing parties who do not wish to sign a formal agreement.
- (. . .) review the scope of 'compensable effects' in order to ensure the meaning of 'compensable effects' clearly articulates what a landholder can be compensated for [this could include e.g. the cost for the time to negotiate an agreement].
- (. . .) review the Land Access Framework in 3 years in order to ensure the land access arrangements are functioning properly and review the implementation of the recommendations in this report.

Nevertheless, sometimes the details remaining outside the report are more important that the ones within: Before the report was published, there was a strong movement from landowner organizations for the establishment of a veto or similar right to stop unwanted access to private land by the respective landowners.[13] This was not considered as a recommendation. Therefore, it is unlikely that we shall see a landowners' veto against mining companies' access to private land anytime soon.

6.4.1.2 The Relationship of the Foreign Investor with Indigenous Australians

6.4.1.2.1 Current Situation

Furthermore, Indigenous Australians might have a claim to the land for which the investor is seeking a mining license. If a group of Indigenous Australians is recognized as the traditional owners of the land, they are awarded native title to the land.

Native Title ownership and ownership of the land might be in the hands of the same group of Indigenous Australians, but more often than not native titleholders

[13] Lock the Gate Alliance (2013).

and landowners will be two groups of people a foreign investor will have to deal with.

Native Title is a form of customary title, recognized and protected by the Native Title Act of 1993.[14] It does not extend to the ownership of mineral resources, but entitles the Native Title group to: "*(...) possession, occupation, use and enjoyment of "their" land.*".[15] Native titles claimants may apply to the Federal Court to determine their claim to such native title. Procedurally a special National Native Title Tribunal was established which aids the Federal Court in determining Native Title and Compensation issues.[16]

Once native title has been recognized, mining activities may only be conducted if the mining lease is granted under an expedited procedure according to section 32 Native Title Act 1993 or after the negotiation of a land use agreement under the "*Right to Negotiate*" ("***RTN***") according to section 31 Native Title Act 1993 was agreed upon between the parties or decided upon by court. Another (voluntary) agreement found in this context are *Indigenous Land Use Agreements* ("***ILUA***"). If substantive impact on the indigenous community is unlikely an expedited process may be established.[17] Finally, an ILUA is a "*voluntary agreement between Aboriginal groups and others about the use and management of land and waters*". [18]

The negotiation process or a possible arbitral decision according to section 31 Native Title Act 1993 is supported by the Native Title Tribunal, which is "*(...) an impartial, independent administrative agency*".[19] The Tribunal came into operation in January 1994 after it was established by the Native Title Act 1993.[20] According to section 108 Native Title Act 1993 the Native Title Tribunal inter alia: "*(...) has the functions of providing assistance, mediating or conducting*

[14] Details on the history and content of native title can be found at: Koppenol, President Land and Resource Tribunal (2011).

[15] Year Book Australia (1995).

[16] According to section 13 Native Title Act 1993 native titles claimants may: "*(...) apply to the Federal Court (...) for a determination of native title in relation to an area for which there is no approved determination of native title; (...).*" According to section 107 Native Title Act 1993: "*A National Native Title Tribunal is established*".

[17] According to section 32 Native Title Act 1993 in connection with section 237 Native Title Act 1993 an expedited procedure can be established, if: "*(...) the act is not likely to interfere directly with the carrying on of the community or social activities of the persons who are the holders (...) of native title in relation to the land or waters concerned; and the act is not likely to interfere with areas or sites of particular significance, in accordance with their traditions, to the persons who are the holders (...) of the native title in relation to the land or waters concerned; and the act is not likely to involve major disturbance to any land or waters concerned or create rights whose exercise is likely to involve major disturbance to any land or waters concerned.*" According to section 32 Native Title Act 1993 the native title holder may object to such expedited procedure.

[18] A detailed outline of the process can be found at: Native Title Tribunal (2014).

[19] National Native Title Tribunal (2014).

[20] National Native Title Tribunal 2014).

a review (...)." to support the negotiation process. Judicial review of the decisions by the Native Title Tribunal may be requested.[21]

Expedited process or not: a key effect of the *Native Title Act 1993* outlined supra therefore is the ability of Indigenous Australians to have a claim to native title. Thus a mining company wishing to operate in the area in question will have to negotiate with Indigenous Australians in the so called "*native title negotiations*" in order to gain access. Those mandatory negotiations have in turn led to numerous voluntary ILUAs being concluded, governing all areas of the interaction between mining companies and Indigenous Australians.

6.4.1.2.2 Past Developments and Future Political Trends

To understand the development and status quo of the native title system it is crucial to be aware of the *Mabo Case*.[22] When reference is made to the "Mabo Case" it is usually referred to the decision *Mabo and Others v Queensland (No.2)*.

The prior decision *Mabo v Queensland (No. 1)*[23] declared invalid an attempt of the Queensland Government to retrospectively abolish any possible native title rights with the Queensland Coast Islands Declaratory Act—and thereby taking the basis of the decision *Mabo and Others v Queensland (No.2)*.

Already in 1982 Eddie Mabo and further plaintiffs demanded to have their traditional land rights recognized by the High Court of Australia. Their claim derived from the constant living of the Meriam people in the area, with special reference to their self-governance from past to present. On June 3rd, 1992 the High Court of Australia overruled the preexisting legal notion of "*terra nullius*" in *Mabo v Queensland*.[24] The High Court ruled instead that the Meriam people were entitled to: "*possession, occupation, use and enjoyment of 'their land' (most of the Murray Islands)*".[25]

This decision led to the *Native Title Act of 1993* and after the case *Wik people vs. Queensland*[26] to the *Native Title Amendment Act 1998*. Analysis of the *Native Title Act 1993* shows that it did start a paradigmatic shift in the thinking not only of the mining industry in Australia.[27]

---

[21] According to section 81 Native Title Act 1993 the Native Title Tribunal "*(...) has jurisdiction to hear and determine applications filed in the Federal Court that relate to native title and that jurisdiction is exclusive of the jurisdiction of all other courts except the High Court.*"

[22] High Court of Australia (1992).

[23] High Court of Australia (1988).

[24] "*Terra Nullius*" in this context referred to the notion that Australia was not inhabited upon the arrival of the British Crown.

[25] Year Book Australia (1995).

[26] High Court of Australia (1996); High Court of Australia *1996, The Thayorre People v The State of Queensland & Ors.*

[27] Year Book Australia (1995).

The Prime Minister commented on the Native Title Bill by addressing the Australian parliament: "*... as a nation, we take a major step towards a new and better relationship between Aboriginal and non-Aboriginal Australians....*"[28]

Through the native title negotiations it has become a common feature of the native title agreements to include *comprehensive agreements* that on the one hand include financial compensation (the legislative requirement) or private royalties, but on the other hand also address other matters that impact the relationship between Indigenous Australians and mining companies.

Many comprehensive agreements are confidential. Therefore the full extent of agreements between mining companies and Indigenous Australians on training, employment, ownership and management participation within native title agreements cannot be determined. A publicly available agreement is the "*Argyle Diamond Mine Participation Agreement: Management Plan Agreement.*"[29]

The Argyle Diamond Mine Participation Agreement: Management Plan Agreement ("***ADMPAMPA***") sets out the rules by which the relationship between traditional owners and Argyle Diamonds regarding the Argyle mine site will be governed. The Argyle Diamond Mine Participation Agreement: Management Plan Agreement works in conjunction with the Argyle Diamond Mine Indigenous Land Use Agreement.[30]

The section of the ADMPAMPA that concerns training and employment sets up principles and specific duties for all parties and explains those principles and duties in legal and plain English.[31]

In section 2.2 (a) of the ADMPAMPA, Argyle sets out the goal to hire local Indigenous people to an extent that by commencement of the underground operations they will represent at least 40 % of the workforce at the mine. In section 2.2 (b) of the ADMPAMPA, Argyle furthermore agrees to review its recruitment and training practices and discuss all matters with an established relationship committee if those goals are not met.

The Argyle Diamond Mine Participation Agreement: Management Plan Agreement is one of many. The number of agreements that refer to training and employment within the "*Agreements, Treaties and Negotiated Settlements with Indigenous Peoples in Settler States database*" is substantial and growing.[32] "*The Agreements, Treaties and Negotiated Settlements with Indigenous Peoples in Settler States: their role and relevance for Indigenous and other Australians [project]*" began in March 2002. It was conducted as an Australian Research Council Linkage Project. The original aim of the project was more narrow and focused on examining treaty and agreement-making with Indigenous Australians as well as the nature of the cultural,

[28] Year Book Australia (1995).

[29] Details can be found at: ATNS, p. 101.

[30] ATNS (2014b), p. 101.

[31] ATNS (2014b), p. 102.

[32] ATNS (2014a).

social and legal rights encompassed by past, present and potential agreements and treaties.[33] The project now also includes agreements between traditional owners and mining companies.

6.4.1.3 The Relationship of the Foreign Investor with the Local Government

The influence of local governments regarding the planning relevant for mining projects in Queensland, Australia has its legal grounding in the Sustainable Planning Act 2009.

According to section 77 of the Sustainable Planning Act 2009, local governments may influence the use of the land in their respective municipalities via the following local planning instruments: "*a planning scheme; a temporary local planning instrument and a planning scheme policy.*"

The relationship between the MRA 1989 and the Sustainable Planning Act 2009 is described in section 4A of the MRA 1989 and states that the Planning Act does not apply to activities covered by the MRA 1989. The MRA 1989 and mining licenses granted under the MRA 1989 therefore prevail over the Sustainable Planning Act 2009, leaving no room for inconsistency. Another option for local governments to exercise influence is an "*objector*" to the grant of a mining lease by outlining why the grant would be adverse to the local interests. It may also block permits for infrastructure necessary for the realization of mining projects that lay outside the area of the mining lease under the MRA 1989—and are therefore governed by Sustainable Planning Act 2009 only.

6.4.2 South Africa

According to section 48 MPRDA 2002 no reconnaissance permission, prospecting right, mining right or mining permit may be issued in respect of land comprising a residential area; any public road, railway or cemetery; any land being used for public or government purposes or reserved in terms of any other law [e.g. national parks according to the National Parks Act 1976] and areas identified by the Minister by notice in the Gazette in terms of section 49 MPRDA 2002, e.g. military zones.

In considering the relationship of a foreign investor to third parties on all other areas of land, a distinction must be made between private land owners, tribal title holders and local municipalities.

---

[33] ATNS (2014a).

6.4.2.1 The Relationship of the Foreign Investor with the Owner of the Land

6.4.2.1.1 Current Situation

According to the MPRDA no investor may prospect or mine without "*notifying and consulting with the land owner*". To prospect or mine the investor will have to document the result of such consultation and provide such documentation to the authorities, specifically the Regional Manager designated by the Department of Mineral Resources.[34]

Where the holder of the prospecting right or mining right is then prevented from conducting necessary mining activities the Regional Manager is to be notified.[35]

The Regional Manager in turn—according to section 54(2) of the MRPDA 2002—will contact and inform the land owner about the legal procedure and analyse the situation.

If the Regional Manager finds that "*the [land] owner or occupier has suffered or is likely to suffer loss or damage as a result of the reconnaissance, prospecting or mining operations*" then according to section 54(3) of the MRPDA 2002 he must request the parties concerned "*to endeavour to reach an agreement for the payment of compensation for such loss or damage*".

If the parties fail to reach an agreement, compensation will be determined by arbitration or the courts according to 54(4) of the MRPDA 2002.

If the Regional Manager determines that further negotiations affect the objects of the Act he may recommend to the Minister to expropriate the land according to section 55 of the MRPDA 2002 or stop further activities by the mineral license holder. An example could be section 2(g) of the MRPDA 2002 regarding security of tenure or section 2(f) of the MRPDA 2002 regarding the promotion of equitable access to the nation's mineral and petroleum resources to all the people of South Africa.

---

[34] According to section 5(4) of the MPRDA 2002 (4) "*No person may prospect for or remove, mine, conduct technical co-operation operations, reconnaissance operations, explore for and produce any mineral or petroleum or commence with any work incidental thereto on any area without (...) notifying and consulting with the land owner or lawful occupier of the land in question.*" For both a prospecting right (according to section 16(4)(b) of the MPRDA 2002) and a mining right (according to section 27(5)(b) of the MPRDA 2002) the investor will need "*to notify in writing and consult with the land owner and lawful occupier and any other affected parties and submit the result of the said consultation within 30 days from the date of the notice* [of acceptance of the application by the regional manager]".

According to section 1 of the MPRDA 2002 the Regional Manager "*(...) means the officer designated by the Director-General [of the Department of Mineral Resources] (...) as regional manager for a specified region*".

[35] According to section 54(1) of the MRPDA 2002 "[the holder of the mineral license] *is prevented from commencing or conducting any reconnaissance, prospecting or mining operations because the owner or the lawful occupier of the land in question refuses to allow such holder to enter the land; places unreasonable demands in return for access to the land; or cannot be found in order to apply for access* [as a next step he is to notify the relevant Regional Manager]".

6.4.2.1.2 Past Legal Developments and Future Political Trends

The case *Hudson v. Mann and another*[36] determines the overall precedence of mineral rights over other use of the land and at the same time established that those rights to be exercised *civiliter modo* (in a manner least disturbing to other use of the land).

The Minerals Act 1991 stated in section 5(1) the mineral rights holder's right "*to enter upon relevant land (...), together with such persons, plant or equipment as may be required for the purposes of prospecting and mining (...) and to dispose thereof.*"

Prior to the MRPDA the landowner was only able to force the owner of the mineral license into negotiation if the Minister deemed so necessary.[37]

Compared to the MPRDA 2002, the Minerals Act 1991 was favourable in both wording and substance for a foreign investor by making the Minister's opinion necessary for the land owner or occupier to proceed to claim compensation and making such determination by the Minister final.[38] The doctrine that mining activities will in general prevail over other uses of land has been maintained under the MPRDA 2002,[39] but as shown, it has been altered to empower the land owner by removing the requirement for Minister's consent before the mining

---

[36] High Court of South Africa (1950).

[37] According to sections 41 and 42 of the Minerals Act 1991: *"(...) the Minister is satisfied, after considering any written representations submitted to him (...) and after such investigations as the Minister may deem necessary that such owner has suffered or is likely to suffer damage as a result of disturbance or subsidence of land caused by mining operations or operations in connection therewith; or any obstruction established on land by any person entitled to mine on such land and who mines or intends to mine thereon for any mineral; and that the owner has made all reasonable efforts to negotiate a settlement with the other person for the payment of compensation for the damage (...)*[the Minister shall] *shall, (...) in writing direct such other person to negotiate a settlement with such owner for the payment of compensation for such damage.*"

Section 42(3) of the Minerals Act 1991 outlines the procedure when an agreement in such a negotiation could not be reached as follows: "*(If the parties...) are unable to agree on the purchase price of such land, or if such person and such owner, after a direction from the Minister, are unable to negotiate a settlement for (...) such (...) compensation shall be determined by arbitration in accordance with the Arbitration Act 1965 (Act 42 of 1965), or by any competent court if such owner prefers the last-mentioned procedure.*"

[38] Section 42(3) Minerals Act 1991 also excluded further future claims by stating that: "*(If the owner) has notified the Minister or the Director-General (to force the owner of the mineral license into negotiation and was rejected), or if a settlement resulting from a direction (...) has been negotiated, or if compensation has been determined by arbitration or by any competent court (...) neither such owner nor any subsequent owner of such land, nor any person who has or may acquire any interest in such land, shall, while the person (the mineral license holder) or his successor in title is entitled to mine on such land for the mineral concerned, be entitled to apply to any court for (...) a settlement (...) or an arbitration award or order of court (...) and thereby preventing the last-mentioned person or his nominee from commencing or continuing on such land with the mining of such mineral or operations in connection therewith.*"

[39] Bakheit (2005), p. 14.

license holder can enter into formal negotiations and/arbitration to determine compensation.

With the end of segregation, the relationship between foreign investors and e.g. HDSA in the homelands was included in the general relationship between foreign investors and private owners of the land.

Post-Apartheid land reforms, mainly aimed to transfer white ownership of land to black ownership will require foreign investors to carefully study who the actual owner of land is and take into account restitution claims.[40]

6.4.2.2 The Relationship of the Foreign Investor with Historically Disadvantaged South Africans/Tribal Authorities

6.4.2.2.1 Current Situation

Laws on specific areas of living for certain groups have been abolished. Special rules for entering land where the population is white or black or collared therefore do not exist anymore. The homeland policy was abolished. Specific rules on land access to areas with predominantly HDSAs ceased to exist.

Specific rules for tribes, e.g. ownership of land by the tribal authority rather than individuals still exist.[41] De iure those negotiations are governed by the same land access rules as for negotiating with any other land owner. De facto, the negotiation will have to address the various interests within the tribe,[42] and are often covered by comprehensive agreements. One such agreement, the Royal Bafokeng Nation and Impala Platinum Joint Venture Agreement is outlined infra in Sect. 6.4.2.2.2.

6.4.2.2.2 Past Legal Developments and Future Political Trends

The history of tribal land is closely connected with the history of the Apartheid regime and the rules governing the segregated system.[43] One of the pillars of the Apartheid regime was the homeland policy. After the end of the Apartheid regime the homeland regime seized to exist, and some of the land was transferred to local tribal authorities.

Comprehensive agreements, also referred to as tribal agreements in South Africa, are agreements between mining companies and local citizens.[44] Such agreements can cover various topics, e.g. royalty payments and/or agreements

---

[40] Woodhouse (2012), p. 848.

[41] Sapa (2012).

[42] Claassens (2013).

[43] Smith (2013).

[44] Cooperative Governance - Tribal Affairs (2014).

regarding local employment and training and the establishment of a joint venture for the joint exploration for minerals.

A well-documented comprehensive agreement is the agreement between Impala Platinum and the Royal Bafokeng Nation, the "*Royal Bafokeng Nation and Impala Platinum Joint Venture Agreement*".[45] The Royal Bafokeng Nation is the owner of the land within the platinum deposit is located.[46]

The agreement, signed in April 2007 included a provision of a 13.4 % ownership of Impala Platinum to the Royal Bafokeng Nation and a 49 % participation in Impala Refining Services Limited. The deal also includes royalty payments and a commitment by Impala Platinum to contribute the equal of over $AUD 18 million to the Impala Bafokeng Trust for community development. According to the agreement the Royal Bafokeng Nation is allowed to nominate the deputy chairperson and two out of ten board members of Impala Refining Services Limited.

A specific challenge for the South African mining industry is the substantial number of migrant workers in South Africa. Migrant workers are especially relevant in the gold mining sector. Some claim that the majority of the workers in most gold mining projects are migrant workers, mostly from the Eastern Cape or countries such as Mozambique or Lesoto.[47] Considering the diversity and the fluctuation of the migrant workers there is the danger that agreements with migrant workers have to be renegotiated again and again.

There are now demands to transfer the tribal ownership to private ownership of the members of the tribes.[48] Indigenous land rights have been and will continue to be a crucial topic for foreign investors in South Africa.[49]

6.4.2.3 The Relationship of the Foreign Investor with the Local Government

6.4.2.3.1 Current Situation

Another issue is the relationship between the Department of Mineral Resources and licenses granted under the MPRDA 2002 on the one side and local municipalities and their planning authority under local planning laws, e.g. the Land Use Planning Ordinance 15 of 1985 ("***LUPO***") on the other. LUPO is governed by the local administration and is applicable side to side with the MPRDA 2002. The necessity to deal with various governmental agencies can lead to time consuming and expensive administrative processes, and create legal uncertainty for investors. To address those issues a discussion in South Africa is currently under the way,

[45] ATNS (2014c).

[46] Capps (2013).

[47] South African History Online (2013).

[48] Sapa (2012).

[49] Moster and Fitzpatrick (2014).

regarding the development of an intergovernmental system that would allow for a one stop shop approach. This would give more legal certainty to landowners, mining license holders and local governments alike.[50]

6.4.2.3.2 Past Legal Developments and Future Political Trends

In the case of *Maccsand (Pty) Ltd v City of Cape Town*[51] Macsand had been issued a mining permit under section 27 of the MPRDA 2002 by the Department of Mineral Resources. After it started to mine, it was stopped by the city of Cape Town that had obtained an interdicting and restraining order that halted the mining activities based on LUPO.

LUPO allows a municipality to zone (declare) parts of its territory for specific purposes. In this particular case the city of Cape Town did not zone an area for which Macsand had been issued a mining permit under section 27 of the MPRDA 2002 for mining activities.

The High Court of the Western Cape, "*the court a quo*", the Supreme Court of Appeal and finally the Constitutional Court dismissed challenges against an interdicting and restraining order which halted the mining activities. It declared LUPO applicable side by side with the MPRDA 2002. The reasoning has been described in detail elsewhere.[52] For a foreign investor this means that it will have to deal not only with the Department of Mineral Resources and the MPRDA 2002, but also with the municipal administration and the effects of LUPO.

6.4.3 Colombia

The Mining Law 2001 of Colombia outlines the land access regime for different types of land and distinguishes between free areas where mining is allowed under the license regime outlined infra, special reserves, national security areas, Indigenous areas and areas of restricted mining where additional conditions apply.[53] There are also areas excluded from any mining activity.

---

[50] Olivier et al. (2013), p. 562.

[51] Constitutional Court of South Africa (2012); Olivier et al. (2013), p. 562.

[52] Olivier et al. (2013), pp. 540–561.

[53] Articles 31–38 of the Mining Law 2001 references: "*areas libres*" [free areas] mining is allowed under the license regime outlined infra, in "*reservas especiales*" [special reserves], "*zonas de seguridad nacional*" [national security areas] and "*zonas de mineria restringída*" [areas of restricted mining] additional conditions must be met to be granted a mining licenses. In "*zonas excluibles de la mineria*" [areas excluded from mining] no mining will be allowed. In "*zonas indigenas*" special rules apply.

6.4.3.1 The Relationship of the Foreign Investor with the Owner of the Land

Regarding the relationship to third parties with land rights the Mining Law 2001 gives the mining concession holder the right to impose on third parties' properties with the necessary activities for the realization of the mining project as determined in the mining concession.[54] The mining concession holder however will have to agree (rather than only to consult) with the owner or holder on the corresponding compensation. Such compensation however does not take into account the value of the mineral wealth, but rather the economic value of the current use of the land.[55]

---

[54] Article 15 of the Mining Law 2001 states that the mining concession holder may: "*(...) a gravar los predios de terceros con las servidumbres necesarias para el ejercicio eficiente de dichas actividades.*"

[(...) impose on third parties' properties with necessary easements/servitudes for an efficient exercise of such activities.]

Those easements are further specified in articles 166–185 Mining Law 2001. Access to land is considered such an easement and is more specifically outlined in article 177 Mining Law 2001: "*Habrá servidumbre de uso de terrenos. El interesado acordara con el dueño o poseedor el plazo y la correspondiente retribución. Se entenderá que esta servidumbre comprende el derecho a construir e instalar todas las obras y servicios propios de la exploración, construcción, montaje, extracción, acopio y beneficio de los minerales y del ejercicio de las demás servidumbres.*"

[The use of lands will have its own easement. The interested party has to agree with the owner or holder on the time limit and the corresponding compensation. It will be understood that this easement includes the right to build and install all works and services corresponding to exploration, construction, erection, exploitation, ore storage, ore dressing and to the exercise of all other servitudes or easements.]

[55] According to article 184 of the Mining Law 2001 compensation should take into account the following guidelines: "*En la fijación de las indemnizaciones y del monto de la caución a que esta obligado el minero par causa del establecimiento y uso de las servidumbres, serán de observancia par los interesados, los peritos y las autoridades, las siguientes reglas y criterios:*

- *Para la estimación del valar comercial del terreno, se tendrán en cuenta sus condiciones objetivo as de ubicación, calidad y destino normal y ordinario y no las características y posibles rendimientos del proyecto minero, la potencial abundancia o riqueza del subsuelo del mismo o la capacidad económica a de los concesionarios;*
- *La ocupación parcial del terreno solo dará lugar al reconocimiento y pago de la indemnización en cuantía proporcional al uso de la parte afectada, a menos que dicha ocupación afecte el valar y el uso de las zonas no afectadas; (...)*"

[The assignment of the compensations and the amount of the bail that the miner is committed to pay due to the establishment and use of servitudes and easements, should be observed by the interested parties, the appraisers and authorities, by following rules and principles:

- For the estimation of commercial value of the land, its objective conditions of location, quality, normal and ordinary destination, will be taken in account and not the characteristics and possible output of the mining project, the potential abundance or wealth of the subsoil of such land, and the economic capacity of the concessionaires.
- The partial occupation of the land will give way to an acknowledgement and payment of a compensation in a proportional amount to the use of the affected part, unless such occupation affects the value and use of areas not affected. (...)]

If such an agreement is not being reached, the mining concession holder can have the question of access and compensation determined by a court or may seek an expropriation of the land in question.[56]

Articles 186–193 outline the detailed procedure for expropriation. It is estimated that this procedure usually takes about 1 year.[57]

This is a clear sign of how the government of Colombia has determined for their nation that mining is the best use of land in the Colombian public interest.

6.4.3.2 The Relationship of the Foreign Investor with Indian-/Afro-Colombians

The rights of the Indian and Afro-Colombian population lead to two alterations in land access for mining activities. The modifications apply to both, acquiring the mining license and the way mining is to be conducted in the respective area.

6.4.3.2.1 Mining Concession

The government identifies specific Indian mining zones in which exploration and exploitation of the mining soil and subsoil will focus on protection and participation of Indian communities and groups. The Indian communities and groups are further protected as every proposal of private persons to explore and exploit minerals within Indian mining zones will have to be solved with the participation of representatives of the respective Indian communities and are subject to their right

[56] Article 13 of the Mining Law 2001 establishes the ground for expropriation of land for the purpose of mining activities by stating: "*(...), declarase de utilidad pública e interés social la industria minera en todas sus ramas y fases. Por tanto podrán decretarse a su favor, a solicitud de parte interesada y por los procedimientos establecidos en este Codigo, las expropiaciones de la propiedad de los bienes inmuebles y demás derechos constituidos sobre los mismos, que sean necesarios para su ejercicio y eficiente desarrollo.*"

[(...), the mining industry in all its branches and stages, hereby is declared of public service and social interest. Therefore, at request of the interested party and by the established procedures in this Code, expropriations of property of assets and all other rights constituted on them, that might be necessary for exercise and efficient development, can be decreed in its favour.]

[57] Cárdenas et al. (2012), p. 179.

of privilege.[58] Such participation may take place in the form of joint-ventures of the Indian communities with third parties.[59]

For foreign investors this means that they cannot be awarded the mining concession in an Indian Colombian area, but they can establish contracts with Indian Colombians that provide a similar legal environment. Articles 131–136 of the Mining Law 2001 outline a similar procedure for mining areas of Afro-Colombian Communities.

6.4.3.2.2 Mining Conduct

When an area has been specifically declared an Indian or Afro-Colombian mining zone according to article 121 Mining Law 2001 the mining activities are to be carried out in a manner that does not affect cultural, social and economic values of communities.[60]

A similar obligation to take special care of the cultural integrity of the local communities is established for Afro-Colombian communities in article 131 of the Mining Law 2001.

---

[58] According to article 122 of the Mining Law 2001: "*La autoridad minera sefialara y delimitara, con base en estudios técnicos y sociales, dentro de los territorios indígenas, zonas mineras indígenas en las cuales la exploración y explotación del suelo y subsuelo mineros deberán ajustarse a las disposiciones especiales del presente Capitulo sobre protección y participación de las comunidades y grupos indígenas asentados en dichos territorios. Toda propuesta de particulares para explorar y explotar minerales dentro de las zonas mineras indígenas será resuelta con la participación de los representantes de las respectivas comunidades indígenas y sin perjuicio del derecho de prelación que se consagra en el artículo 124 de este Código.*"

[Based on technical and social studies the mining authority will indicate and delimit within the Indian Territory, Indian mining zones in which exploration and exploitation of the mining soil and subsoil should be adjusted to special dispositions of the present article on protection and participation of Indian communities and groups established in such territories.

Every proposal of private persons to explore and exploit minerals within Indian mining zones will be solved with the participation of representatives of the respective Indian communities and subject to their right of privilege consecrated in Article 124 of this Code.]

[59] According to article 126 of the Mining Law 2001: "*Las comunidades grupos indígenas que gocen de una concesión dentro de la zona minera indígena, podrán contratar la totalidad o parte de las obras y trabajos correspondientes, con personas ajenas a ellos.*"

[The communities or Indian groups that possess a concession within the Indian mining zone, can make contracts regarding all or part of the corresponding works and installations, with non-Indian people.]

[60] Article 121 Mining Law 2001 states: "*Todo explorador o explotador de minas esta en la obligación de realizar sus actividades de manera que no vayan en desmedro de los valores culturales, sociales y económicos de las comunidades y grupos étnicos ocupantes real y tradicionalmente del área objeto de las concesiones o de títulos de propiedad privada del subsuelo.*"

[Every mining explorer or exploiter is in the obligation to carry out its activities in a manner that does not affect cultural, social and economic values of communities or ethnic groups, real and traditionally occupants of the area object of concessions or of titles of soil's private ownership.]

6.4.3.3 The Relationship of the Foreign Investor with the Local Government

6.4.3.3.1 Current Situation

In Colombia national Mining Law prevails over municipal planning law with the exception of mining activities that take place in the inner city limits. It is especially noteworthy that municipalities are restricted to include areas in their local planning schemes that are permanently excluded from mining activities.[61]

6.4.3.3.2 Past Legal Developments and Future Political Trends

The history of the power of local government in Colombia and municipal planning laws has been described elsewhere.[62] There were no legal disputes challenging the relationship between the Mining Code and municipal planning laws, but a major report on the future of mining[63] and other authors[64] demand more power for local governments in the planning process.

References

ATNS. About us (2014a) Available online at: http://www.atns.net.au/page.asp?PageID=2. Last checked on 15 February 2014

ATNS. Argyle Diamond Mine Participation Agreement: Management Plan Agreement (2014b) Available online at: http://www.atns.net.au/agreement.asp?EntityID=2592. Last checked on 15 February 2014

ATNS. Royal Bafokeng Nation and Impala Platinum Joint Venture Agreement (2014c) Available online at: http://www.atns.net.au/agreement.asp?EntityID=4124. Last checked on 15 February 2014

[61] According to article 37 of the Mining Law 2001: "*Con excepción de las facultades de las autoridades nacionales y regionales que se señalan en los artículos 34 y 35 anteriores, ninguna autoridad regional, seccional o local podrá establecer zonas del territorio que queden permanente o transitoriamente excluidas de la minería. Esta prohibicion comprende los planes de ordenamiento territorial (...).*"

[With the exception of faculties of the national or regional authorities mentioned in the previous Articles 34 and 35, no regional, sectional or local authority can establish areas that remain permanently or transitorily excluded from mining activity. This prohibition covers plans of territorial ordinance (...).] As articles 34 Mining Law 2001 and 35 Mining Law 2001 from a municipal point of view only refer to the protection of land within its city limits it can be established that in Colombia, the national Mining Law prevails over municipal planning law.

[62] Details on the Local planning laws can be found at: Vitta (2013).

[63] Salamanca (2013), p. 51.

[64] Summers and Useche (2013).

Bakheit T (2005) Mining & land access issues in African mineral laws. The Centre for Energy, Petroleum and Mineral Law and Policy, Annual Review (9)
Capps G (2013) Capps Rustenburg minerals. Available online at: http://www.landdivided2013.org.za/sites/default/files/Capps%20Rustenburg%20minerals.pdf, updated on 5/23/2013. Last checked on 15 February 2014
Cárdenas BP, Bejarano D, Guerra D (2012) Colombia. In: Sutcliffe S (ed) Mining law: jurisdictional comparisons. Thomson Reuters, London pp 175–190
Claassens (2013) Traditional leadership. Available online at: http://www.landdivided2013.org.za/sites/default/files/Claassens%20traditional%20leadership.pdf, updated on 5/23/2013. Last checked on 28 September 2013
Constitutional Court (2012) Maccsand (Pty) Ltd v City of Cape Town and Others, Judgment of 12 April 2012. References: (CCT103/11) (CC) [2012] ZACC 7; 2012 (4) SA 181 (CC); 2012 (7) BCLR 690 (CC). Available online at: http://www.saflii.org/za/cases/ZACC/2012/7.html. Last checked on 15 February 2014
Cooperative Governance - Tribal Affairs. About Us (2014) Available online at: http://www.cogta.gov.za/cgta/index.php/component/content/article/172-about-us/46-about-us.html. Last checked on 15 February 2014
Department of Employment, Economic Development and Innovation (2010a) Guide to Queensland's new land access laws. Edited by Economic Development and Innovation Department of Employment. Available online at: http://mines.industry.qld.gov.au/assets/land-tenure-pdf/6184_landaccesslaws_guide_print.pdf. Last checked on 15 February 2014
Department of Employment, Economic Development and Innovation (2010b) Land Access Code. Edited by Economic Development and Innovation Department of Employment. Available online at: http://mines.industry.qld.gov.au/assets/land-tenure-pdf/land_access_code_nov2010.pdf. Last checked on 15 February 2014
Department of Natural Resources and Mines. Crown-land (2014) Available online at: http://www.nrm.qld.gov.au/museum/surveying_history/crown-land.html. Last checked on 15 February 2014
High Court (1950) *Hudson v. Mann and another*, References: 950(4) SA 485(T) at 488 E-F, key passage cross referenced in: Trojan Exploration Company Proprietary Ltd. and Another v Rustenburg Platinum Mines Ltd. and Others, Judgment of 31 May 1996 in para 8. References: (609/94) [1996] ZASCA 74; 1996 (4) SA 499 (SCA); [1996] 4 All SA 121 (A). Available online at: http://www.saflii.org/za/cases/ZASCA/1996/74.html. Last checked on 15 February 2014
High Court of Australia (1996) Wik Peoples v Queensland ("Pastoral Leases case"), Judgment of 23 December 1996. References: [1996] HCA 40; (1996) 187 CLR 1; (1996) 141 ALR 129; (1996) 71 ALJR 173. Available online at: http://www.austlii.edu.au/cgi-bin/sinodisp/au/cases/cth/HCA/1996/40.html?query=Wik. Last checked on 15 February 2014
High Court of Australia (1988) *Mabo v Queensland (No 1)*, Judgment of 8 December 1988. References: [1988] HCA 69; (1989) 166 CLR 186. Available online at: http://www.austlii.edu.au/au/cases/cth/high_ct/166clr186.html. Last checked on 15 February 2014
High Court of Australia (1992) *Mabo v Queensland (No 2)* ("*Mabo case*"), Judgment of 3 June 1992. References: [1992] HCA 23; (1992) 175 CLR 1. Available online at: http://www.austlii.edu.au/au/cases/cth/HCA/1992/23.html. Last checked on 15 February 2014
Koppenol GJ, President Land and Resource Tribunal (2011) Evolution of native title. Available online at: http://www.landcourt.qld.gov.au/documents/speeches/Evolution%20of%20Native%20Title.pdf, updated on 1/17/2011. Last checked on 15 February 2014
Land Access Review Panel (2012) Land Access Review Panel report. Available online at: http://mines.industry.qld.gov.au/assets/native-title-pdf/Land_Access_Review_Panel_report.pdf, updated on 12/7/2012. Last checked on 15 February 2014
Lock the Gate Alliance (2013) Lock the gate alliance. Available online at: http://www.lockthegate.org.au/, updated on 1/23/2013. Last checked on 15 February 2014

Moster H, Fitzpatrick P (2014) Law Against Law: Indigenous Rights and the Richtersveld Cases. Available online at: http://www2.warwick.ac.uk/fac/soc/law/elj/lgd/2004_2/mostertfitzpatrick/. Last checked on 15 February 2014

National Native Title Tribunal (2014) About the tribunal. Available online at: http://www.nntt.gov.au/au/Pages/Tribunaloverview.aspx. Last checked on 15 February 2014

Native Title Tribunal (2014) Steps to an indigenous land use agreement. Available online at: http://www.nntt.gov.au/news-and-communications/publications/documents/booklets/ilua_steps.pdf. Last checked on 15 February 2014

Olivier NJJ, Williams C, Badenhorst PJ (2013) Maccsand (Pty) Ltd v City of Cape Town 2012 (4) SA 181 (CC). Potch Elekt regs 15(5). doi:10.4314/pelj.v15i5.15

Queensland Government (2013) Queensland land title practice manual. Available online at: http://www.nrm.qld.gov.au/property/titles/pdf/ltpm.pdf, updated on 7/11/2013. Last checked on 15 February 2014

Salamanca LJG (2013) Conflictividad minera y ordenamiento ambiental y territorial en Colombia. Estudio de la Contraloría General de la República.: Magazín Massiris: Geografía, ordenamiento territorial y desarrollo territorial sostenible. Available online at: http://www.massiris.com/2013/05/conflictividad-minera-y-ordenamiento.html. Last checked on 15 February 2014

Sapa (2012) Transfer tribal land, 7/25/2012. Available online at: http://www.news24.com/SouthAfrica/News/Transfer-tribal-land-Agri-SA-20120725. Last checked on 15 February 2014

Smith H (2013) Smith Mining and land law. Available online at: http://www.landdivided2013.org.za/sites/default/files/Smith%20Mining%20and%20land%20law.pdf, updated on 23 May 2013. Checked on 28 September 2013

South African History Online (2013) The glitter of gold. Available online at: http://www.sahistory.org.za/archive/glitter-gold, updated on 9/28/2013. Last checked on 15 February 2014

Summers R, Useche C (2013) Post-conflict planning in Colombia. In Planning, 5/22/2013. Available online at: http://www.planningresource.co.uk/news/1183559/Post-conflict-planning-Colombia/. Last checked on 15 February 2014

Vitta JFR (2013) Land planning in Colombia. UNHABITAT. Available online at: http://www.urbangateway.org/sites/default/ugfiles/land_readjustment_experience_in_colombia.pdf, updated on 2/26/2013. Last checked on 15 February 2014

Woodhouse P (2012) Reforming land and water rights in South Africa. Dev Change 43 (4):847–868. doi:10.1111/j.1467-7660.2012.01784.x

Year Book Australia (1995) The Mabo case and the native title act. Edited by The Australian Bureau of Statistics. Available online at: http://www.abs.gov.au/Ausstats/abs@.nsf/Previousproducts/1301.0Feature%20Article21995. Last checked on 15 February 2014

Chapter 7
Performance Requirements

7.1 Introduction and Disambiguation

In this work "*performance requirements*" refers to obligations imposed by the host state on the investor to run its business in a certain manner. In the resource industry, this can include: expenditure requirements to make sure the investor actually undertakes mining activities and does not use the mining license for speculative purposes; requirements to hire local and/or Indigenous personnel; requirements to purchase local supplies for the realization of the mining project; and/or requirements to hire local businesses for services.[1] This work will focus on performance requirements that directly or indirectly force a foreign investor to hire local/Indigenous personnel.

7.2 Relevance

Foreign investors, as any other business entity, aim to reduce costs. Furthermore mining projects require specific technical expertise, especially in terms of the engineering and management.

On the one hand, foreign investors that act on global scale have an interest to hire staff from global labour market, purchase supplies from the global market with the best quality to cost ratio and hire services from the global market that they deem to be best suitable for the project. Performance requirements and interests of a foreign investor therefore collide and may strongly impact on the profitability of a project.

On the other hand, local and Indigenous communities voice valid concerns about being exploited when a foreign investor arrives on site with its own personnel and suppliers, leaving the local/indigenous population with the detriments and risks of

[1] Dolzer and Schreuer (2008), p. 82.

R.W. Roeder, *Foreign Mining Investment Law*, DOI 10.1007/978-3-319-31217-0_7

the mining operation, but no jobs and therefore no immediate economic advantage.[2] Protests resulting from such a perceived setback have the potential to halt mining projects or even cause them to fail.[3]

7.3 Observation Horizon

The government may choose to establish local requirements regarding hiring of local/Indigenous workers. This performance requirement may be absolute, allowing only local/Indigenous workers to participate in the mining operation, it may also require a certain percentage of local/Indigenous workers, or it allows the foreign investor to freely chose his employees.

Notwithstanding direct legal obligations, land access legislation may also establish pressure to hire local/Indigenous workers. Further indirect measures may include a restrictive visa regime for foreign workers, preferential procurement policies and the requirement to establish local production capacities.

7.4 Countries

7.4.1 Australia

7.4.1.1 Current Situation

There is no specific binding legislation in Australia that obliges mining companies to hire or train Indigenous Australians.

Indigenous Australian employment in the mining industry is still a crucial topic to address for foreign investors in Australia. Its importance derives from the fact that most of the mining projects in Queensland, Australia are in land that overlaps with or is in close proximity to land in respect of which Indigenous Australians have rights and interests, by way of native title claims or rights.

Furthermore it is a historical commitment of the Commonwealth of Australia to provide equal opportunities for all Australians—which applies to national and international investors alike. It is also important to notice that the impact of mining operations, specifically on Indigenous Australians, is a highly politicised topic in Australia.[4]

[2] Sutherland (2012), p. 17.

[3] Suter (1997), p. 278.

[4] Coronado and Fallon (2010), p. 666.

When taking into account the current unemployment rate of over 50 % among those identifying themselves as Indigenous Australians, the potential for conflict in the realm of Indigenous employment in the mining industry becomes obvious.[5]

The political context outlined supra leads to a situation that could be called a de facto performance requirement: it has become so usual to hire local/Indigenous Australians that not doing so could anger the local/indigenous population and potentially disturb the smooth progression of the project.[6]

A legislated performance requirement is a preferential procurement policy that alters laws to allow for preferential procurement towards Indigenous enterprises and aims to maximize Indigenous employment and business opportunities.[7] This preferential procurement policy was part of the *Indigenous Economic Development Strategy*[8] and was implemented on July 1st, 2011. It does not constitute an obligation to preferentially procure, but solely alters laws to allow for preferential procurement against competition law barriers.

The establishment of a performance requirement can also be achieved indirectly by opening-up or narrowing down visa requirements for specialized skilled personnel necessary in the mining industry. An investor might want to bring its own personnel for a mining project. By limiting the available visas and by introducing time limits on those visas a government can force a mining company to hire local personnel to realize its projects. In Australia the relevant visa class is the visa 457 which "*allows skilled workers to come to Australia and work for an approved business for up to four years.*"[9] A discussion paper of the Ministerial Advisory Council on Skilled Immigration in respect of the purpose of the 457 visa states that businesses are to sponsor a skilled overseas worker only if they cannot find an appropriately skilled Australian citizen.[10] For a foreign investor this means that it must take special care when applying for a visa to make clear to the authorities that a special skillset—e.g. not simply a "*mining engineer*" is needed, in order to avoid (trained) worker's visa application being rejected.

In 2012 the application process for the visa and the time limit of 4 years left uncertainty for foreign investors whether or not they would be able to hire and keep trained and skilled foreign workers. Considering the long timeframe of mining projects, a 4 year limit can be considered a hindrance.

Taking into account the acknowledgment in the discussion paper mentioned supra that the visa program has been growing strongly and reached the 100,000 mark for the first time in September 2012 further political discussion and possible changes are likely to create uncertainty for investors in the years to come.[11]

---

[5] Australian Government Productivity Commission (2014).

[6] Validakis (2014).

[7] Australian Government-Department of Education (2014).

[8] Australian Government (2014).

[9] Government of Australia (2014).

[10] Ministerial Advisory Council on Skilled Immigration (2014), p. 2.

[11] Ministerial Advisory Council on Skilled Immigration (2014), p. 2.

7.4.1.2 Past Legal Developments and Future Political Trends

The *Mabo Case*[12] outlined supra led to a new form of interaction between Indigenous Australians and mining companies. Whilst fundamentally focused on land use, the interaction established communication channels and opened negotiations.[13] Native title agreements now increasingly include provisions on Indigenous employment in the mining workforce besides the required financial compensation for the use of land by the mining company. This was also an impulse for mining companies to develop Indigenous employment programs.

Indigenous employment has been and remains common in the Australian mining industry to a growing extent.[14] Up to the last mining boom starting in the 1990s, Indigenous employment in the mining industry was a rather rare occurrence. Now changes are clearly visible and are documented as such[15]:

A study released by the Australian Bureau of Statistics in 2006 showed that the number of employees with Indigenous background has increased by nearly 80 % between 2001 and 2006. That rise was also comparatively higher than the rise of workers in the mining industry in general.[16] In addition, Indigenous employment in the mining industry rose to an overall participation of 2.3 %, which also broadly represents the ratio of the indigenous population in relation to the Australian population overall.[17]

It has been argued that this figure should be challenged on the grounds that after comparing the relative numbers of Indigenous employees on mining sites with the percentage of the indigenous population in mining areas the picture becomes less positive. [18]

Considering the fly in and fly out arrangements with non-Indigenous Australians this argument cannot stand. In the mining industry, more than in most other industries, local employment is greatly expanded by a national and international workforce.

There are also a small but increasing number of enterprises owned by Indigenous Australians that participate in or provide services to the mining industry.[19] The example of the Foxleigh Coal Mine in Central Queensland where *Indigenous Business Australia* invested on behalf of Indigenous Australians is an illustration of this change.[20]

---

[12] High Court of Australia, *Mabo and Others v Queensland.*

[13] Brereton and Parmenter (2008), p. 67.

[14] Brereton and Parmenter (2008), p. 67.

[15] Tiplady and Barclay (2007).

[16] Brereton and Parmenter (2008), p. 70.

[17] Brereton and Parmenter (2008), p. 70.

[18] Brereton and Parmenter (2008), p. 70.

[19] Brereton and Parmenter (2008), p. 70.

[20] Australian Government (2014).

This development is a part of a bigger picture change in Australia: in her lectures entitled "*Changing the Paradigm*: *Mining Companies, Native Title and Aboriginal Australians*", delivered as part of the Boyer Lectures, *Langton* looks past the numbers and discusses what she calls "*quiet revolution*".[21] She refers to the appearance of an Indigenous Australian middle class in Australia largely carried by the impact of the mining industry on Indigenous Australians.

Whilst not a generally legislated performance requirement and distinct of the issue of Indigenous employment, another recent development is the establishment of an obligation to build a production site close to a mining project. In the Aurukun Bauxite project in Western Cape York (North Queensland) the tender terms[22] included a "*development requirement*" to build a production site, in this case an alumina refinery, close to the mining project.[23]

Considering these developments it is unlikely that an investor will have to expect further legislated performance requirements regarding the employment of local/ indigenous population in the near future. The practical pressure to expand Indigenous employment in the mining industry is nevertheless likely to remain or even increase.

7.4.2 South Africa

7.4.2.1 Current Situation

Legislation that specifically deals with the participation in management and employment of HDSA are inter alia: the Constitution of South Africa of 1996, the Broad-based Black Economic Empowerment Act 53 of 2003 ("***B-BBEE Act 2003***"), the Preferential Procurement Framework Act No. 5 of 2000 and the MPRDA 2002.

The *B-BBEEA 2003* and the corresponding provisions in the MPRDA 2002 the Mining Charta 2002 and the Mining Charta 2010 cannot be fully understood without at least a brief overview of the unique history of black empowerment in South Africa.[24] Therefore a brief historical introduction shall already be included at this point; past legal developments and future political trends will be featured infra.

The pre-1994 period was governed by the Apartheid system. The Apartheid system was a government system based on discrimination and racial segregation that was established in 1948. It was abolished only in 1994. During the Apartheid regime, a minority of whites dominated a black and coloured majority. In the

---

[21] Langton (2014).

[22] McDonald (2014).

[23] Taylor (2013).

[24] A detailed account of the history and challenges of Black Economic Empowerment in South Africa can be found at: Ponte et al. (2007).

crucial mining sector, this included measures such as blacks and coloureds not being allowed to hold a mining license or titles to land. Over time this led to a situation where the black and coloured population would lack financial resources, education and job opportunities.[25]

In the early 1990s, soon to be President Nelson Mandela negotiated terms of change with the outgoing Apartheid government.[26] One of the key agreements was that after the change in power there would not be a massive nationalization, but instead a form of slower redistribution of wealth.[27]

Shortly after the beginning of the presidency of Nelson Mandela in 1994 the government implemented its reconstruction and development program. This program did not achieve the full outcome and was then replaced by a program that soon became known as Black Economic Empowerment.[28]

It became clear that the Black Economic Empowerment program only benefited a few. Instead of alleviating South African poverty on a broad scale it only created a new "*black elite*" that replaced or supplemented the white elite already in place.[29]

This finally let to the mentioned Broad-Based Black Economic Empowerment approach. One of its cornerstones was to not only shift the ownership patterns, e.g. black shareholding, but to also empower black employees and to foster black management participation and black human resource development.[30]

7.4.2.1.1 The Broad-Based Black Economic Empowerment Act 53 of 2003

Before the historic background described and according to its preamble the B-BBEE Act 2003 aims to *increase broad-based and effective participation of black people in the economy and a more equitable income distribution* amongst the citizens of South Africa, specifically it shall:

- "*increase the number of black people that manage, own and control enterprises and productive assets*;
- *facilitate ownership and management of enterprises and production assets by communities, workers, cooperatives and other collective enterprises*;
- *foster human resource and skills development*;
- *achieve equitable representation in all occupational categories and levels in the workforce*:
- *foster preferential procurement*; *and*
- *foster investment in enterprises that are owned or managed by black people*."

---

[25] Ramlall (2012), p. 285.

[26] South African History Online (2014).

[27] Smith (2010).

[28] Ramlall (2012), p. 274.

[29] Ramlall (2012), p. 274.

[30] Ramlall (2012), p. 274.

The Act is accompanied by a verification and certificate system that shows the Broad-Based Black Economic Empowerment ("***B-BBEE***") performance of companies. Companies may choose to be measured using the Generic Scorecard or their individual sector scorecards.[31]

The B-BBEE status—the extent to which a company complies with the goals of the *B-BBEE Act 2003*—can then not only be used by customers, but also by government, e.g. to decide whether to award a mining license or in public procurement.[32]

Furthermore, section 12 of the *B-BBEE Act 2003* requires the government to draft a Charter to support the transformation of specific sectors according to the aims of the constitution.

The *B-BBEE Act 2003* does not require companies to be compliant, but a non-B-BBEE compliant company will be disadvantaged in public tenders according to the Preferential Procurement Policy Framework Act No. 5 of 2000. The disadvantage is also likely to extend to private contractual relationships, as other companies can increase their B-BBEE rating by contracting with B-BBEE complying companies.

7.4.2.1.2 MPRDA 2002

Another key piece of legislation influencing performance requirements is the MPRDA 2002 (introduced supra in Sect. 5.4.1.1).

The MRPDA 2002 was to a large extent a result of the acknowledgment that equitable access to ownership, management and employment of previously disadvantaged people in the resource industry had not been achieved in the first years after the end of the Apartheid.[33]

It links the grant of a mining license with the requirement to provide a social and labour plan.[34]

A social and labour plan is therefore already required at the time of the application for a mining right. Regulation 46(b)(v) of the Mineral and Petroleum Resource Development Regulation specifically requires a "*human resources development program*" which includes the mine's plan to achieve a participation of 40 % of HDSAs in the management of the mine within 5 years from the granting of the mining right.

---

[31] Kloppers and du Plessis (2008), p. 98.

[32] Kloppers and du Plessis (2008), p. 99.

[33] Mostert (2012), p. 78.

[34] According to section 23(1) of the MRPDA 2002: "(. . .) *the Minister must grant a mining right if—(. . .) the applicant has provided financially and otherwise for the prescribed social and labour plan*".

7.4.2.1.3 Mining Charter 2002

The Broad-Based Socio-Economic Empowerment Charter for the South African Mining Industry ("***Mining Charter 2002***"), required by the BEE Act and the MRPDA Act, was developed by the Department of Minerals and Energy with input from the South African Chamber of Mines, the National Union of Mineworkers and the South African Development Association and signed on October 11th, 2002.[35] As such, it stands somewhere between legislation, government policy and a CSR policy.

Its goal is to "*create an industry that will proudly reflect the promise of a non-racial South Africa*"[36] and to "*provide a framework for progressing the empowerment of historically disadvantaged South Africans in The Mining and Minerals Industry*".[37]

7.4.2.1.3.1 Employment Equity

Regarding the equity of employees, the Mining Charter specifically requires companies to establish targets of at least 40 % for HDSAs employment equity.[38]

7.4.2.1.3.2 Human Resource Development

Regarding the employment of HDSAs, the Mining Charter has different requirements for different stakeholders. It requires all stakeholders including foreign investors to support the Development of Human Resources by[39]:

- "*developing a skills development strategy that includes audits,*
- *providing scholarships,*
- *providing* "*on the job*" *training of mine workers,*
- *offering employees the opportunity to become functionally literate and numerate, and*
- *by providing career paths with the opportunity to progress to a higher level.*"(...) *in order to increase participation and ownership by HDSAs in the mining industry, mining companies agree:*
- *to achieve 26 % HDSA ownership of the mining industry assets in 10 years by each mining company; and*
- *that where a company has achieved HDSA participation in excess of any set target in a particular operation then such excess maybe utilized to offset any shortfall in its other operations.*"

[35] Kloppers and du Plessis (2008), p. 107.

[36] Government of South Africa (2004), p. 1.

[37] Government of South Africa (2004), p. 2.

[38] Government of South Africa (2004), p. 4.

[39] Government of South Africa (2004), p. 4.

7.4.2.1.3.3 Enforcement

While setting and publishing targets and achievements on an annual basis was required by the Mining Charter 2002, direct enforcement mechanisms were lacking.

While not specifically outlined as enforcement mechanism in the Mining Charter 2002, preferential procurement for HDSA companies could be seen as an indirect self-enforcement mechanism. Preferential procurement for HDSA companies, legislated in the Preferential Procurement Framework Act No. 5 of 2000, refers to the increase in companies' B-BBEE ratings when they deal with other companies that have a high B-BBEE rating.

Another "*enforcement mechanism*" can be seen in the scorecards that measure the compliance level of mining companies against the goals of the Mining Charter. Mining companies are required to indicate their level of compliance on their webpage and in their annual report, and will be able to display a higher B-BBEE rating when complying with the Mining Charter.[40]

7.4.2.1.4 Mining Charter 2010

The Amendment of the Broad-Based Socio-Economic Empowerment Charter for the South African mining and minerals industry of 2010 (the Mining Charter 2010) reaffirms the employment equity, human resource development and 26 % B-BBEE ownership goals.

It differs from the Mining Charter 2002 by establishing an explicit enforcement mechanism.[41]

This results in the possibility of punitive measures under section 99 of the MPRDA 2002, e.g. the revocation of a mining license.[42]

7.4.2.2 Past Legal Developments and Future Political Trends

There are only very few litigated cases that directly address the need for companies to employ historically disadvantaged South Africans. In *Fuel Retailers Association of Southern Africa v Director General Environmental Management, Department of Agriculture, Conservation and Environment, Mpumalanga Province & Others*[43] the Constitutional Court addressed the question: "*of the nature and scope of the obligations of environmental authorities when they make decisions that may affect*

[40] Kloppers and du Plessis (2008), p. 108.

[41] According to section 3 of the Mining Charter 2010: "*Non-Compliance with the provisions of the charter and the MRPDA shall render the mining company in breach of the MRPDA and subject to the provisions of section 47 read in conjunction with section 98 and 99 of the Act.*"

[42] Government of South Africa (2011), p. 6; Seccombe (2010).

[43] Constitutional Court of South Africa, *Fuel Retailers Association of Southern Africa v Director General Environmental Management.*

the environment, in particular, the interaction between socio-economic development and the protection of the environment." and found that: "*...the nature and the scope of the obligation to consider the impact of the proposed development on socio-economic conditions must be determined in the light of the concept of sustainable development and the principle of integration of socio-economic development and the protection of the environment.*"

Thereby the court obligated the administration to take into account socioeconomic development. Even if one could argue that this would include the employment of HDSA, the court did not go on to establish an obligation for mining companies.

From a speech of President Zuma it can be taken that: "*While black people constitute 87 % of the economically active population, their representation is clearly nowhere near this percentage in both executive and non-executive directorship positions.*"[44] A survey conducted in 2010 shortly before the speech shows that 91 % of all CEO positions of companies listed at the Johannesburg Stock Exchange ("***JSE***") where held by whites.[45] In 2013 it was revealed that more than 75 % of private companies were not B-BBEE compliant.[46]

This was in line with the statement of the Minister of Natural Resources in the 2011 annual report. The Minister explained that "*a comprehensive assessment of the outcomes of the Mining Charter as reported in our previous annual report revealed a lack of compliance by the mining industry with the implementation of the objectives outlined therein. To overcome the inadequacies, the Mining Charter was subsequently amended and gazetted late last year.*"[47]

Considering the highly politicized discussion on this topic, it is likely that the in future foreign investors in the mining sector will face even stronger performance requirements in South Africa.

7.4.3 Colombia

7.4.3.1 Current Situation

The Mining Law 2001 gives the mining authority the power to appoint a minimum percentage of workers originated from the respective region that should be hired and to check this performance requirement on a periodical basis.[48]

---

[44] Fin 24 (2010).

[45] Ramlall (2012), p. 277.

[46] Ramlall (2012), p. 277.

[47] Department of Mineral Resources South Africa (2011), p. 18.

[48] Article 254 of the Mining Law 2001 states: "*En los trabajos mineros y ambientales del concesionario de minas la autoridad minera, oídos los interesados, sefialara los porcentajes mínimos de trabajadores oriundos de la respectiva región y domiciliados en el área de influencia*

Indians and Afro-Colombians have a special status in the Colombian mining landscape. The Mining Law 2001 gives them preferences ("(...) *they should be preferable be associated to* (...) *its works and installations* (...)").[49]

7.4.3.2 Past Legal Developments and Future Political Trends

The performance requirement in this regards used to be much stricter. According to the former Labour Code a foreign investor was to hire not less than 90 % of Colombians as staff and not less than 80 % of Colombians as managers and qualified personnel.[50]

This requirement was however already modified in a way that would allow wide discretion by the government in the case of specifically qualified foreign workers which would often be the case for specialized mining activities.[51] The government regularly made use of this power.[52]

---

de los proyectos que deberán ser contratados. Periodicamente estos porcentajes seran revisables."

[In the mining and environmental works of the mining concessionaire, once the interested parties have been heard, the mining authority will appoint the minimum percentages of workers originated from the respective region and domiciled in the area of influence of the projects that should be hired. Periodically, these percentages will be checked.]

[49] Regarding Indian or Afro-Colombian mining zones article 128 of the Mining Law 2001 states: "*En caso de que personas ajenas a la comunidad o grupo indígena obtengan título para explorar y explotar dentro de las zonas mineras indígenas,* (...), *deberán vincular preferentemente a dicha comunidad o grupo, a sus trabajos y obras y capacitar a sus miembros* (...)."

[Where people alien to the community or Indian group obtain a title in order to explore and exploit within the Indian mining zones, (...), they should be preferable be associated to such community or group, to its works and installations and [make sure] to train its members (...).]

[50] According to former article 74 of the Código substantive de trabajo [Labour Code] it was stated that: "*Todo empleador que tenga a su servicio más de diez (10) trabajadores debe ocupar colombianos en proporción no inferior al noventa por ciento (90 %) del personal de trabajadores ordinarios y no menos del ochenta por ciento (80 %) del personal calificado o de especialistas o de dirección o confianza. Los trabajadores nacionales que desempeñen iguales funciones que los extranjeros, en una misma empresa o establecimiento, tienen derecho a exigir remuneración y condiciones iguales.*"

[Any employer who employs more than ten (10) workers has to hire not less than ninety percent (90 %) of Colombian workers as staff and not less than eighty percent (80 %) of Colombian workers as qualified personnel and management. Domestic workers who perform the same duties as foreigners, in the same company or establishment, are entitled to equal pay and conditions.]

[51] Article 75 of the Código substantive de trabajo stated: "*El Ministerio del Trabajo puede disminuir la proporción anterior: a) Cuando se trate de personal estrictamente técnico e indispensable, y sólo por el tiempo necesario para preparar personal colombiano; y b) Cuando se trate de inmigraciones promovidas o fomentadas por el gobierno.* (...)".

[The Ministry of Labour may decrease the previous ratio: a) In the case of strictly technical and indispensable personnel, and only for the time necessary to prepare Colombian personnel, and b) In the case of immigrant workers promoted or encouraged by the government. (...)].

[52] Gomez (2001), p. 42.

Both articles were repealed by Article 65 of Law 1429 of 2010 (Labour law amendment), and a general performance requirement for hiring of local personnel ceased to exist.

Regarding the hiring requirement of Indian/Afro-Colombian workers in their respective mining zones, details were specified in resolution 18 0666 of 2010 that determined minimum quotas.[53]

Since 2012 the requirements were not applied by the government any more, hence there were no legislated local hiring requirements in place besides the discretion given to the mining authorities outlined supra.[54]

References

Australian Government Productivity Commission, Overcoming Indigenous Disadvantage: Key Indicators 2011 (2014) Available online at: http://www.pc.gov.au/gsp/Indigenous/key-indicators-2011. Last checked on 15 February 2014

Australian Government-Department of Education, Employment and workplace relations: indigenous opportunities policy (2014) Available online at: http://deewr.gov.au/background-Indigenous-opportunities-policy. Last checked on 15 February 2014

Australian Government, Indigenous business Australia (2014) Available online at: http://www.iba.gov.au/. Last checked on 15 February 2014

Brereton D, Parmenter J (2008) Indigenous employment in the Australian mining industry. J Energy Nat Resour Law 26:66–90

Cárdenas BP, Bejarano D, Guerra D (2012) Colombia. In Sutcliffe S (ed) Mining law: jurisdictional comparisons. Thomson Reuters, pp 175–190

Coronado G, Fallon W (2010) Giving with one hand. On the mining sector's treatment of Indigenous stakeholders in the name of CSR. Int J Sociol Soc Policy 30:666–682

Department of Mineral Resources South Africa (2011) Annual Report 2010/2011. Available online at: http://www.info.gov.za/view/DownloadFileAction?id=177944. Last checked on 15 February 2014

Dolzer R, Schreuer C (2008) Principles of international investment law. Oxford University Press, Oxford/New York

Fin 24 (2010) Survey: 91% of SA CEOs white. In Fin 24, 3/3/2010. Available online at: http://www.fin24.com/Business/Survey-91-of-SA-CEOs-white-20100302. Last checked on 15 February 2014

Gomez J (2001) Foreign direct investment in Colombia. LLM Theses and Essays, paper 14. In Digital Commons @ Georgia Law, LLM Theses and Essays 2001. Available online at: http://digitalcommons.law.uga.edu/cgi/viewcontent.cgi?article=1017&context=stu_llm. Last checked on 15 February 2014

Government of Australia, Temporary work (skilled) visa (subclass 457) (2014) Available online at: http://www.immi.gov.au/skilled/skilled-workers/sbs/. Last checked on 15 February 2014

Government of South Africa (2004) South African Mining Charta - broad-based socio-economic empowerment charter for the South African mining industry. Available online at: http://www.cidafund.co.za/charters/miningCharter.pdf. Last checked on 15 February 2014

[53] Cárdenas et al. (2012), p. 185.

[54] Law Business Research Ltd (2014).

Government of South Africa (2011) Amendment of the mining charter BBSEEC, September 2010. Available online at: http://www.bullion.org.za/MediaReleases/Downloads/Amended_of_BBSEE_Charter.pdf. Last checked on 15 February 2014

Kloppers H, du Plessis W (2008) Corporate social responsibility, legislative reforms and mining in South Africa. J Energy Nat Resour Law 26:91–119

Langton M (2014) The quiet revolution: indigenous people and the resources boom. In: 2012 Boyer Lectures. Available online at: http://www.abc.net.au/radionational/programs/boyerlectures/2012-boyer-lectures/4305696. Last checked on 15 February 2014

Law Business Research Ltd (2014) http://www.lbresearch.com: Latin Lawyer. Available online at: http://latinlawyer.com/reference/topics/46/jurisdictions/8/colombia/. Last checked on 15 February 2014

McDonald C (2014) Aurukun Project - Queensland government. In: Government of Queensland. Available online at: http://www.dsdip.qld.gov.au/development-planning/aurukun-project.html. Last checked on 15 February 2014.

Ministerial Advisory Council on Skilled Immigration (2014) Discussion paper on strengthening the integrity of the subclass 457 program. Edited by Government of Australia. Available online at: http://www.minister.immi.gov.au/media/bo/2013/bo202339.htm. Last checked on 15 February 2014

Mostert H (2012) Mineral law. Principles & policies in perspective. Juta, Cape Town

Ponte S, Roberts S, van Sittert L (2007) 'Black economic empowerment', business and the state in South Africa. Dev Chang 38(5):933–955. doi:10.1111/j.1467-7660.2007.00440.x

Ramlall S (2012) Corporate social responsibility in post-Apartheid South Africa. Soc Responsibility J 8(2):270–288. doi:10.1108/17471111211234888

Seccombe A (2010) South Africa: new mines charter to speed pace of change. In allAfrica.com, 9/14/2010. Available online at: http://allafrica.com/stories/201009140934.html. Last checked on 15 February 2014

Smith AD (2010) Why FW de Klerk let Nelson Mandela out of prison. In The Guardian/The Observer, 1/31/2010. Available online at: http://www.guardian.co.uk/world/2010/jan/31/nelson-mandela-de-klerk-apartheid. Last checked on 15 February 2014

South African History Online (2014) The freedom struggle in Cape Town. In: South African History Online. Available online at: http://www.sahistory.org.za/topic/negotiations-and-transition. Last checked on 15 February 2014

Suter K (1997) Mercenaries, mines and mistakes. World Today 53(11)

Sutherland J (2012) Hipsters need not to apply. Can Bus 85(19):17–18

Taylor C (2013) Queensland retenders Aurukun. In MyResources.com, 8/8/2013. Available online at: http://www.myresources.com.au/publications/oil-a-gas-bulletin/news/3945-queensland-retenders-aurukun. Last checked on 15 February 2014

Tiplady T, Barclay MA (2007) Indigenous employment in the Australian minerals industry. Centre for Social Responsibility in Mining, University of Queensland, Brisbane

Validakis V (2014) Protestors line up to stop Whitehaven's Maules Creek mine. In Australian Mining. Available online at: http://www.miningaustralia.com.au/news/protestors-line-up-to-stop-whitehaven-s-maules-cre. Last checked on 15 February 2014

Chapter 8
Distribution of Profits

8.1 Introduction and Disambiguation

The distribution of profits refers to the question of what share the state takes of the profits of the foreign investor. This is generally determined by the question to what extend the state imposes taxes,[1] royalties and fees[2] on the foreign investor.

Royalties are a common terminology in mining laws around the world and have been defined as "(...) *an instrument that provides the owners of mineral resources* (...) *with compensation for the depletion of their non-renewable resources by the mining companies*."[3]

8.2 Relevance

Unlike other foreign investments, foreign investment in depletable natural resources such as minerals may only generate wealth once. The question of how to distribute this wealth is therefore crucial both for a foreign investor and the host state.

[1] Taxes have been defined as: *"Öffentliche Abgaben, die ein Gemeinwesen kraft Zwangsgewalt in einseitig festgesetzter Höhe und (anders als bei Gebühren und Beiträgen) ohne Gewährung einer Gegenleistung von natürlichen und juristischen Personen seines Gebietsbereichs erhebt."* [Public charges levied unilaterally by a community in virtue of coercive power on natural and legal persons in its jurisdiction—and—unlike fees, without the granting of a specific consideration [quid pro quo].] in Gabler Wirtschaftslexikon, *Stichwort*: *Steuern*.

[2] Fees have been defined as: *"Abgaben, die als Entgelt für eine spezielle Gegenleistung einer Behörde oder öffentlichen Anstalt erhoben wird."* [Charges levied of an administrative body or a public institution for a specific consideration [quid pro quo]] in Gabler Wirtschaftslexikon, *Gabler Wirtschaftslexikon*: *Stichwort Gebühr*.

[3] ASA (2014).

R.W. Roeder, *Foreign Mining Investment Law*, DOI 10.1007/978-3-319-31217-0_8

While it is also possible for a national investor to create profits from a mining project in a host state and then take the profits abroad, for a foreign investor this will be the rule and expectation. The host state therefore has a limited time window only to take a part of the profits from the mining project.

8.3 Observation Horizon

The work does not undertake to provide a detailed analysis of the international and national tax environment for mining projects, but will highlight the most relevant taxes, royalties and fees only.[4]

The question for this work is whether or not and to what extent corporate income taxes are levied on mining projects and whether or not there are special taxes, e.g. windfall taxes, that only apply to mining projects.

While technically only the taxes will be based on the actual profit of a foreign investor, royalties (often based on value and tonnage of the mineral produced) and fees (often fixed sums, e.g. mineral license rents) also impact the profit margin of a foreign investor. Hence these types of revenues of the host state will also be taken into account. Marginal taxes and fees will be named, but not analysed in depth.

The work will furthermore ask whether the tax regime provides for a stable tax environment that ensures planning certainty for investors, or whether taxes, royalties and fees are frequently changed, causing planning uncertainty.

Whilst acknowledging that double tax agreements or other international tax law considerations may further impact on the profit of a foreign investor the work will focus on the share of the profit the host state takes from the foreign investor.

8.4 Countries

8.4.1 Australia

8.4.1.1 Current Situation

Participation in the profit derived from the exploration of natural resources is a crucial factor in Australia's national development. Both the Government of the Commonwealth and the state governments benefit from mining profits through the imposition of taxes, royalties and stamp duties.

[4] A global overview can be found at: Ernst & Young Global Limited (2014).

8.4.1.1.1 Corporate Income Tax

Both resident and non-resident companies have to pay corporate income tax at a rate of 30 %.

The corporate income tax rate applies to both resident and non-resident companies. A resident company is liable to corporate income tax on its worldwide income and capital gains. A non-resident company is liable to corporate income tax on its Australian sourced income only.

If a double taxation agreement is in place a non-resident company will only be taxed on its income directly generated by its local subsidiary.[5]

8.4.1.1.2 Minerals Resource Rent Tax

Starting July 1st, 2012 a new national taxation regime was applied to iron ore, coal and coal seam gas as incident of coal mining—the Minerals Resource Rent Tax ("***MRRT***").[6]

The MRRT, administered under the Minerals Resources Rent Tax Act 2012, applies a tax rate of 30 % to mining project interests. When taking into account that mining expenditures and a MRRT allowance are deductible, the effective tax rate becomes 22.5 %. Miners with profits less than 50 million $AUD are exempt. Together with other tax breaks the exceptions led to the MRRT being a far less efficient tax instrument than hoped for by the Commonwealth Government.[7]

8.4.1.1.3 Royalties

Royalties are payments to the state government for rights to extract natural resources. Royalties are payable pursuant to section 320 of the MRA 1989 and, in case of petroleum, pursuant to section of the 590 Petroleum and Gas (Production and Safety) Act 2004 ("***PGSA***").

In 2013 the royalty rates for minerals were set in schedule 4 MRR and differ from mineral to mineral, e.g. for coal there is a variable royalty based on the price per tonne of coal of 7 % of the value up to and including $100. For a value over $100 and up to and including $150 per tonne the royalty is 7 % for the first $100 and for the remainder 12.5 %. For a value past $150 it is 7 % for the first $100, 12.5 % for the next $50 and for the remainder 15 %.[8]

---

[5] Ashurst (2014).

[6] Australian Taxation Office (2014).

[7] Newmatilda (2014).

[8] Office of State Revenue (2014).

8.4.1.1.4 Mining Specific Surface Fee

The mining license holder must pay the state a rent for the area of the mining lease. Differential rates of rent are determined form time to time for exploration and production licenses.[9]

8.4.1.1.5 Stamp Duty

Stamp duty, or transfer duty as it is called in Queensland, Australia is a state charge levied on the transfer of assets, such as an interest in a resource project or the purchase of an interest in an entity that itself holds a resource project. Dutiable transfers include the transfer of an interest in a joint venture, the purchase of an interest in a partnership as well as the acquisition of an interest in a trust. The rate of duty payable depends on the value of the transaction and is between 1.5 and 5.75 % of the greater of the unencumbered value of the assets concerned and the consideration.[10]

8.4.1.1.6 Further Taxes and Tax Incentives

Further non-mining specific taxes that a foreign investor might encounter include capital gains tax and the goods and services tax.

Another expense to be paid relates to project carbon emissions. Commencing July 1st, 2012 the Australian carbon pricing scheme imposes a fixed price on carbon emissions and is then turned into a market regulated price scheme by July 1st, 2015. This regime is especially relevant for open pit mining operations.[11]

8.4.1.2 Past Legal Developments and Future Political Trends

Australian states have taxed mining activities ever since the first gold rush in the 1850s. At the time the Victorian government changed between charging miners monthly lump sum license fees (comparable to today's licensing fees), demanding export duty and demanding a percentage of the value of production (comparable to today's royalties).[12] The question of taxation has been a constant part of discussion ever since the "*Eureka Stockade*" events around December 3rd, 1854.[13]

---

[9] Government of Queensland (2014).

[10] Queensland Government (2014).

[11] PKF (2013), p. 17.

[12] La Croix (1992), p. 216.

[13] La Croix (1992), p. 214.

A constant development are the cuts in Australia's corporate income tax rate that decreased from 49 % in the mid-80s to 30 % since 2001. Australia always tried to provide an internationally competitive corporate income tax environment. Currently Australia is discussing a further cut of company income tax from 30 to 29 %.[14]

The most important development of the last decade was the development of the Mineral Resource Rent Tax ("***MRRT***"). The MRRT, or "*Resource Super Profits Tax* ('***RSPT***')" as its first draft was called, was originally planned to expand to all minerals and to not include the several tax breaks it now does.[15] A strong lobby engagement paid off for the mining industry, leaving only the "*skeleton*" of the ***MRRT*** in place.[16]

The MRRT was further undermined by the behaviour of the states. As royalties paid to the states are creditable against the liability deriving from the MRRT, the income of the Commonwealth depends on the royalty rates of the states that used their discretion and raised royalties in response to the MRRT.

The behaviour of the states (acting against the interest of the Commonwealth) can only be understood by factoring in the importance of the federal system and the comparably decentralized localization of power in the political system in Australia. The states consider income from the minerals as being within their discretion and some opposed to the MRRT.[17]

Mining royalties are quickly adapted to changing commodity prices.

In 2012 the coal royalty, based on the price per tonne of coal was still at 7 % of the value for a price up to $200 per tonne and 10 % of the value for prices that exceeded $200 per tonne.[18] The legislation facilitates frequent changes by setting the royalty rates in a schedule of the MRR rather than in the MRA 1989.

The Fiscal Repair Amendment Act 2012 included exploration permits in the scope of stamp duty. Farm in agreements are excluded[19] and the Commissioner for State Revenue issued *Public Ruling DA000.12.1* ("*Transfer duty - Exemption for farm-in transactions in the resources sector*") *that confirms this* exclusion.[20]

Considering the perceived "*mining crisis*"[21] Queensland, Australia is unlikely to see a strong increase in taxes, royalties or stamp duty in the near future. There is some concern about the absence of a sovereign wealth fund comparable to the one of Norway. If those concerns become the general opinion further tax raises might be discussed. This situation leads to further legal uncertainty for foreign investors.

---

[14] Institute of chartered Accountants Australia (2014).

[15] Ernst & Young (2013).

[16] Maher and Kelly (2014).

[17] AAP (2013).

[18] Office of State Revenue (2014).

[19] Utz (2014).

[20] Utz (2014).

[21] PwC PricewaterhouseCoopers Australia (2013).

8.4.2 *South Africa*

8.4.2.1 Current Situation

According to section 3(2) of the MPRDA 2002, the state: "*As the custodian of the nation's mineral and petroleum resources,* (...), *acting through the Minister, may*— (...) *in consultation with the Minister of Finance, determine and levy, any fee or consideration payable in terms of any relevant Act of Parliament*."

The government of South Africa has used the legal grounding and issued the following taxes and royalties:

8.4.2.1.1 Corporate Income Tax

Any company which is either managed or incorporated in South Africa is considered a resident for tax purposes. Resident companies are taxed at a flat rate of 28 %. In addition, from April 1st, 2012, branches of foreign companies which are effectively managed in South Africa will also be taxed at 28 %.[22]

South Africa taxes the mining industry through a specific mining corporate tax that differs from the generally applied flat rate corporate tax. The mining corporate tax uses a formula allowing the mining company to partly deduct costs for shaft sinking and mine equipment expenditure.[23]

8.4.2.1.2 Windfall Tax

No windfall taxes are applied specifically to mining revenues.

8.4.2.1.3 Mining-Specific Surface Fee

No mining specific surface fee applies.

8.4.2.1.4 Royalties

In 2008 a specific royalty regime, governed by the Mineral and Petroleum Resource Royalty Act, No. 28 of 2008 was introduced.

According to section 2 of the Mineral and Petroleum Resources Royalties Act 2008 any "*person that wins or recovers a mineral resource from within the Republic*" is required to pay royalties for the benefit of the National Revenue Fund.

[22] Government of South Africa (2014), p. 147.

[23] Webber Wentzel (2013).

According to section 4(1) of the Mineral and Petroleum Resources Royalties Act 2008, for refined minerals the royalty rate is calculated as follows: "*0.5* + [*earnings before interest and taxes*/ (*gross sales in respect of refined mineral resources x 12.5*)] *x 100*". The rate shall not exceed 5 %.

According to section 4(2)) of the Mineral and Petroleum Resources Royalties Act 2008, for unrefined minerals the royalty rate is calculated as follows: "*0.5* + [*earnings before interest and taxes*/ (*gross sales in respect of unrefined mineral resources x 9*)] *x 100*". The rate shall not exceed 7 %.

The royalties become payable when the mineral is transferred, where transfer is defined as "*the disposal, the export, the consumption, theft, destruction or loss of the mineral resource*" according to section 1 of the Mineral and Petroleum Resources Royalties Act 2008.

Royalties paid are considered to be an expense incurred in the production of income by the mineral extractor and as such are deductible in terms of section 11 (a) of the South African Income Tax Act.[24]

8.4.2.1.5 Transfer Duty

Transfer duty, governed by the Transfer Duty Act no. 40 of 1949, is calculated on the basis of the value of the property in question. Depending on the value of the transaction, the transfer duty is between 3 and 8 %.[25]

8.4.2.1.6 Further Taxes and Tax Incentives

Further taxes include capital gains tax and dividend tax. Fees, e.g. registration fees are marginal.

Net capital gain, financial gain that derives from the disposal of assets, is taxed by the capital gains tax, a special form of income tax. The rate of this tax is 33 % (effective tax rate 13.3 %) for individuals and at 66.6 % (effective tax rate 26.7 %) for companies. This will most likely only be relevant for foreign investors in the natural resources sector when divesting real estate used for a mining operation.[26]

The dividend withholding tax which came into effect on April 1, 2012 is a 15 % tax on dividends from shares of all resident companies and those non-resident companies listed on the Johannesburg Stock Exchange. It replaced the Secondary Tax on Companies (STC), a 10 % tax previously added to the corporate tax.[27]

[24] ASA (2014).

[25] Government of South Africa (2014), p. 147.

[26] Government of South Africa (2014), p. 159.

[27] Government of South Africa (2014), p. 160.

Through the amended Income Tax Act 1962, governed by the Industrial Development Corporation of South Africa, investments in the development of small and medium scale mining projects are supported.

8.4.2.2 Past Legal Developments and Future Political Trends

The latest development important from a foreign investor's standpoint was that from April 1st, 2012 branches of foreign companies which are effectively managed from the outset are also taxed at 28 %. Prior to April 2012 those companies were being taxed at a higher rate of 33 %.[28]

A "*resource rental tax*" is being discussed with the ANC supporting the idea of a 50 % windfall tax that is to kick in after the investor has made a "*reasonable return*". What constitutes a "*reasonable return*" in the opinion of the ANC has not been stated though.[29] The discussion came immediately after the ANC rejected the idea of nationalization of the mining industry in 2012.[30]

Before the MPRDA 2002, South Africa did not collect royalties for the state. The Mining Law 1991 was generally viewed as providing for private mineral rights. This prohibited the state from collecting royalties for its own use as the royalties would be *ius usus fructus*, they would belong to the owner as yield of the private mineral right.

With the MPRDA 2002 the old regime changed. As the custodian of its mineral resources, the government of South Africa is entitled and through the Mineral and Petroleum Resource Royalties Act 2008 obliged to ensure that any person that wins or recovers a mineral resource from within the Republic pays royalties for the benefit of the National Revenue Fund.

South Africa has used its tax regime to provide incentives for foreign investment. Through the amended Income Tax Act 1962, governed by the Industrial Development Corporation of South Africa, investment in the development of small and medium scale mining projects is supported. Incentives include listing of assets on the South African stock exchanges, loans and (quasi-)equity participation in the mining projects.[31]

Also after Apartheid, taxes, royalties and stamp duties are still used in a large scale as a political way to incentivize or decelerate investments and project development. The rare earth project at Steenkampskraal and its operator Great Western Minerals Group Ltd.[32] for example profit from a government waiver of royalty payments, which in this case would amount to about 6 % of gross revenue.[33]

---

[28] Government of South Africa (2014), p. 159.

[29] Reuters (2012).

[30] Reuters (2012).

[31] Webber Wentzel (2013), p. 86.

[32] Great Western Minerals Group Ltd. (2014).

[33] Royalties Rates (2006).

There is a discussion on empowering the South African Minister for Natural Resources to influence the pricing of natural resources sold from South African mining projects and to impose export permits on minerals.[34] The idea has already triggered strong criticism,[35] but also received support.[36]

This discussion has to be seen in the context of the current energy crisis in South Africa. The regulation of pricing and the imposition of export permits aim to provide the South Africa state-owned energy provider, Eskom with cheap coal for its energy production. Eskom currently purchases coal at about 20 % of the export price and fears a lack of coal supply.[37]

8.4.3 Colombia

8.4.3.1 Current Situation

8.4.3.1.1 Corporate Income Tax

According to the Colombian Tax Code a 25 % rate of corporate tax applies to entities that accrue their income through branches or permanent establishments of foreign companies, whereas for all other entities the corporate tax rate is 33 %.[38]

The additional annual income tax ("***CREE***") came into force January 1st, 2013 and levies an additional 9 % income tax for income during 2013, 2014 and 2015 and an additional 8 % of income hereafter, but excludes income derived by foreign companies that fall under the 25 % tax rate outlined supra.[39]

---

[34] Lorimer (2014).

[35] Lorimer (2014).

[36] Ruffini (2014).

[37] Ruffini (2014).

[38] According to article 240 of the Estatuto Tributario [Colombian Tax Code]: "(. . .), *la tarifa sobre la renta gravable de las sociedades anónimas, de las sociedades limitadas y de los demás* (. . .) *que obtengan sus rentas a través de sucursales o de establecimientos permanentes, es del veinticinco por ciento (25%).*

(. . .), *las rentas obtenidas por las sociedades y entidades extranjeras, que no sean atribuibles a una sucursal o establecimiento permanente de dichas sociedades o entidades extrajeras, estarán sometidas a la tarifa del treinta y tres (33%).*"

[(. . .), the rate on the taxable income of corporations, limited partnerships and other entities (. . .) that get their income through branches or permanent establishments is twenty-five percent (25%).

(. . .), income derived by foreign companies and organizations, which are not attributable to a branch or permanent establishment of such companies or foreign entities, are subject to the rate of thirty-three percent (33%).]

[39] PKF (2013), p. 82.

8.4.3.1.2 Windfall Tax

No windfall taxes are applied specifically to mining revenues.

8.4.3.1.3 Royalties

Colombia levies Royalties on every exploitation of non-renewable natural resources in state ownership.[40]

The royalty rates are currently set at a percentage of the value of the tonnage in combination with a reference price set by the Energy Mining Planning Unity.[41]

In the case of private ownership the foreign investor is to pay no less than 0.4 % of the value of the production in currency or in kind.[42]

8.4.3.1.4 Stamp Duty

According to Article 319 of the Colombian Tax Code a financial transaction fee of 0.4 % applies to financial transactions between the tax payer's accounts.

According to Article 319 of the Colombian Tax Code stamp duty, or stamp tax as it is called in Colombia is to be paid for the official acknowledgment/registration of documents, e.g. contracts. The standard rate is 1.5 % of the value of the contract.

---

[40] Article 227 of the Mining Law 2001 states: "(...), *toda explotación de recursos naturales no renovables de propiedad estatal genera una regalía como contraprestación obligatoria. Esta consiste en un porcentaje, fijo o progresivo, del producto bruto explotado objeto del título minero y sus subproductos, calculado medido al borde o en boca de mina, pagadero en dinero o en especie. También causara regalía la captación de minerales provenientes de medios o fuentes naturales que técnicamente se consideren minas.*"

[(...) every exploitation of non-renewable natural resources in state ownership generates royalties as a compulsory counter-benefit. This consists of a percentage, fixed or progressive, of the exploited gross product, on the product of the mining title, and its sub-products, calculated or measured on the mine head, payable in currency or in kind. (...).]

[41] Cárdenas et al. (2012), p. 187.

[42] Article 227 of the Mining Law 2001 in so far states: "*En el caso de propietarios privados del subsuelo, estos pagaran no menos del 0.4% del valor de la producción calculado o medido al borde o en boca de mina, pagadero en dinero o en especie.*"

[In the case of private owners of the subsoil, those should pay no less than 0.4% of the value of the production calculated or measured on the mine head, payable in currency or in kind.]

8.4.3.1.5 Surface Fee

Colombia applies a surface fee for the use of the land.[43]

The surface fee is stipulated at one daily minimum salary per hectare and per annum for areas up to 2000 ha and up to three daily minimum salaries per hectare per annum for areas larger than 5000 ha.[44] In 2013 the minimum wage in Colombia was about 11 $US a day.[45]

8.4.3.1.6 Further Taxes and Tax Incentives

Other taxes that an investor might encounter in Colombia are value added tax, net worth tax, municipality tax and property tax.

Colombia has a net worth tax that applies to both foreign investors and local investors alike. The tax rate depends on the net worth of the investor[46]:

- If the net worth is equal or higher than one billion Colombian pesos a rate of 1 % applies.
- If the net worth is equal or higher than three billion Colombian pesos a rate of 3 % applies.
- If the net worth is higher than five billion Colombian pesos a rate of 6 % applies.

Municipal taxes apply for carrying out commercial activities within the municipal jurisdiction in question. Revenues from exports of minerals are excluded. The amount paid for royalties will be subtracted from the amount of the municipal tax.[47]

Furthermore, property tax ranging from 0.1 to 0.16 % applies.[48]

---

[43] According to article 230 of the Mining Law 2001: "*Los canones superficiarios sobre la totalidad del area de las concesiones durante la exploracion,* (...), *son compatibles con la regalía y constituyen una contraprestación que se cobrara por la entidad contratante sin consideraci6n a quien tenga la propiedad o posesión de los terrenos de ubicación del contrato.* (...)"

[The surface fees on the total area of concessions during the exploration, the erection and construction (...), are compatible with the royalty and constitute a price that will be collected by the contracting agency without taking into consideration who has the property or possesses the lands of the contract. (...)].

[44] Law Business Research Ltd (2014), p. 3.

[45] Jiménez (2014).

[46] Cárdenas et al. (2012), p. 188.

[47] Cárdenas et al. (2012), p. 188.

[48] Gomez (2014), p. 54.

There is also a tax incentive scheme in place for foreign investors investing in the Colombian mining sector that introduce a flat tax rate of 15 % for those who use the so called "*Zona Francas*" [Free Zones].[49]

8.4.3.2 Past Legal Developments and Future Political Trends

Past taxes included the remittance tax regime that taxed any transfer of capital from any income, including paid dividends. The remittance tax regime rate was reduced over time in the 1990s and has now been abolished.[50]

On February 9th, 2010 the Columbian parliament passed the law 1382 of 2010. It is structured as an amendment to the law 685 of 2001. As the former was declared unconstitutional, the amount of service fees to be paid depends on the date when the concession was granted. For those granted before February 9th, 2010 and after May 12th, 2013 the surface fee is outlined supra. For concession agreements granted between February 9th, 2010 and May 12th, 2013 the surface fee is determined on the duration of the title. The surface fee is stipulated at one daily minimum salary per hectare per annum for the first 5 years and will then increase by one-quarter of a minimum daily wage per hectare per year biannually.[51]

References

AAP (2013) Royalty impact on MRRT reviewed: Gillard. The Sydney Morning Herold, 26 March 2013. Available online at: http://news.smh.com.au/breaking-news-national/royalty-impact-on-mrrt-reviewed-gillard-20130326-2gs2p.html. Last checked on 15 February 2014

ASA (2014) Getting to the bottom of South Africa's new mining royalties. Available online at: http://www.accountancysa.org.za/resources/ShowItemArticle.asp?ArticleId=1932&Issue=1091. Last checked on 15 February 2014

Ashurst (2014) Mining in Australia – an introduction for investors. Available online at: www.ashurst.com/doc.aspx?id_Content=8821. Last checked on 15 February 2014

Australian Taxation Office (2014) Minerals resource rent tax. Edited by Australian Taxation Office. Available online at: http://www.ato.gov.au/Business/Minerals-resource-rent-tax/. Last checked on 15 February 2014

Cárdenas, BP, Bejarano D, Guerra D (2012) Colombia. In: Sutcliffe S (ed) Mining law: jurisdictional comparisons. Thomson Reuters, London pp 175–190

Ernst & Young (2013) July 2010 Australia's proposed Minerals Resource Rent Tax. Available online at: http://www.ey.com/Publication/vwLUAssets/Proposed_Mineral_Resources_Rent_

[49] According to article 240 (1) of the Colombian Tax Code: *"Fíjase a partir del 1 de enero de 2007, en un quince por ciento (15%) la tarifa única del impuesto sobre la renta gravable, de las personas jurídicas que sean usuarios de Zona Franca."*

[Beginning with January 1st, 2007 a flat rate of fifteen percent (15%) tax is applied on taxable income of legal persons who use the free zones]; Cárdenas et al. (2012), p. 189.

[50] Gomez (2014), p. 52.

[51] Law Business Research Ltd (2014), p. 3.

Tax/$FILE/Proposed_Mineral_Resource_Rent_Tax.pdf, updated on 8/9/2013. Last checked on 15 February 2014

Ernst & Young Global Limited (2014) Worldwide Corporate Tax Guide. Available online at: http://www.ey.com/GL/en/Services/Tax/Worldwide-Corporate-Tax-Guide—Country-list. Checked on 2/10/2014

Gomez J (2014) Foreign Direct Investment in Colombia. LLM Theses and Essays, paper 14. In Digital Commons @ Georgia Law, LLM Theses and Essays 2001. Available online at: http://digitalcommons.law.uga.edu/cgi/viewcontent.cgi?article=1017&context=stu_llm. Last checked on 15 February 2014

Government of Queensland (2014) Mineral tenure rents. Available online at: http://mines.industry.qld.gov.au/mining/rental-rates-mining.htm. Last checked on 15 February 2014

Government of South Africa (2014) South Africa's Investor Handbook. Available online at: http://www.thedti.gov.za/DownloadFileAction?id=742. Last checked on 15 February 2014

Great Western Minerals Group Ltd. (2014) About us. Available online at: http://www.gwmg.ca/index.cfm?ReportID=203280. Last checked on 15 February 2014

Institute of chartered Accountants Australia (2014) Corporate tax rate to change. Available online at: http://www.charteredaccountants.com.au/Industry-Topics/Reporting/News-and-guidance-on-regulatory-matters/News-and-updates/Corporate-tax-rate-to-change.aspx. Last checked on 15 February 2014

Jiménez FA (2012) En $22.800 mensuales se ajustó el mínimo. El Colombiano 29.12.2012. Available online at: http://www.elcolombiano.com/BancoConocimiento/E/en_$22800_mensuales_se_ajusto_el_minimo/en_$22800_mensuales_se_ajusto_el_minimo.asp. Last checked on 15 February 2014

La Croix SJ (1992) Property rights and institutional change during Australia's gold rush. Explor Econ Hist 29(2):204–227. doi:10.1016/0014-4983(92)90011-K

Law Business Research Ltd (2014) http://www.lbresearch.com: Colombia - Mining - Reference - Latin Lawyer. Available online at: http://www.cardenasycardenas.com/archivos/52.M2013%20-%20Colombia%20%282%29.pdf. Last checked on 15 February 2014

Lorimer J (2014) Politicsweb – MPRDA Amendment Bill will cost thousands of mining jobs – James Lorimer – FEATURES. Available online at: http://www.politicsweb.co.za/politicsweb/view/politicsweb/en/page71619?oid=398573&sn=Marketingweb+detail&utm_source=twitterfeed&utm_medium=twitter. Last checked on 15 February 2014

Maher S, Kelly J (2014) Miners strike out against MRRT with advertising campaign. The Australian. Available online at: http://www.theaustralian.com.au/national-affairs/in-depth/miners-strike-out-against-mrrt-with-advertising-campaign/story-fnb56a2t-1226325344456. Last checked on 15 February 2014

Newmatilda (2014) Why the mining tax won't pay the bills. Available online at: https://newmatilda.com/2013/02/12/why-mining-tax-wont-pay-bills. Last checked on 15 February 2014

Office of State Revenue (2014) Royalty rates. Available online at: https://www.osr.qld.gov.au/royalties/rates.shtml. Last checked on 15 February 2014

PKF (2013) Worldwide Tax Guide. Available online at: http://www.pkf.com/media/1956673/worldwide%20pkf%20tax%20guide%202013.pdf, updated on 7/30/2013. Last checked on 15 February 2014

PwC PricewaterhouseCoopers Australia (2013) Mine 2013: A Confidence Crisis - Review of global trends in the mining industry. Edited by PricewaterhouseCoopers. Available online at: http://www.pwc.com.au/industry/energy-utilities-mining/publications/mine-a-confidence-crisis.htm, updated on 8/5/2013. Last checked on 15 February 2014

Queensland Government (2014) Office of State revenue: Rates of duty. Available online at: https://www.osr.qld.gov.au/duties/about-duties/rates-of-duty.shtml. Last checked on 15 February 2014

Royalties Rates (2006) South Africa's draft mining royalties rates. Africa Res Bull Econ 43 (10):17164A. doi:10.1111/j.1467-6346.2006.00584.x

Reuters (2012) South Africa's ANC supports windfall tax on miners. Reuters, 12/19/2012. Available online at: http://uk.reuters.com/article/2012/12/19/uk-safrica-anc-idUKBRE8BI0G920121219. Last checked on 15 February 2014

Ruffini A (2014) Coal compact necessary for SA's electricity sector. Esi Africa. Available online at: http://www.esi-africa.com/node/16677. Last checked on 15 February 2014
Utz C (2014) New farm-in exemption for the mining sector has a sting in the tail – Energy and Natural Resources – Australia. Available online at: http://www.mondaq.com/australia/x/252260/Mining/New+farmin+exemption+for+the+mining+sector+has+a+sting+in+the+tail. Last checked on 15 February 2014
Webber Wentzel (2013) Mining law toolkit. Available online at: http://www.webberwentzel.com/wwb/action/media/downloadFile?media_fileid=7909, updated on 4/25/2013. Last checked on 15 February 2014

Chapter 9
Repatriation of Foreign Investments

9.1 Introduction and Disambiguation

Repatriation of foreign investment refers to the ability of the foreign investor to remove its investments and profits made from the host country where the mining project is realized. Repatriation of foreign investments therefore refers to the ability of the foreign investor to return those profits to the home jurisdiction of the foreign investor or to invest them in another jurisdiction.

9.2 Relevance

It has been said: "*The main objective of all foreign investment is to make profits and to repatriate those profits to the home state.*"[1] While not all foreign investments made are indeed being repatriated, the ability to repatriate profits made of foreign investments—and the invested assets themselves—is conditio-sine-qua-non. It is a worst-case scenario for a foreign investor to have its assets and profits locked in one jurisdiction while it has to service loans or pay up on obligations in another jurisdiction.[2]

9.3 Observation Horizon

This question will analyse whether and to what extent the government of a host state has chosen to allow the repatriation of foreign investments fully, partly, or not at all.

---

[1] Sornarajah (2010), p. 207.

[2] Sornarajah (2010), p. 207.

R.W. Roeder, *Foreign Mining Investment Law*, DOI 10.1007/978-3-319-31217-0_9

Repatriation of foreign investment may be regulated directly by a foreign exchange regime. It may furthermore be regulated indirectly by means of price controls of the minerals extracted by the foreign investor or by requiring permits for the export of such minerals. Free repatriation of foreign investments may further be hindered by controls or prohibitions of the transfer of shares in the corporate entity used to realize the mining project.

9.4 Countries

9.4.1 Australia

9.4.1.1 Current Situation

While the admission of foreign investments is governed by a stringent regime, the repatriation of foreign investments or profits derived therefrom is currently not limited by a specific regime. The Banking Regulations 1959 currently do not limit the repatriation of foreign investments at this point of time.

The Banking Act of 1959 does however give the Governor-General the right to implement regulations at any time that he considers it "(. . .) *expedient to do so for purposes related to foreign exchange or the foreign exchange resources of Australia.*"[3] This power has not been used in recent decades, but yet the possibility exists and would not require further parliamentary approval.

Under the Australian withholding tax regime, payments of dividends, interest and royalties paid to non-residents fall under the tax withholding regime. Generally 10 % for interest and 30 % for dividends and royalties must be held back unless an international agreement applies. "*Fully franked*" dividends, dividends paid from revenue after tax, are excluded from the withholding tax regime.[4] While levied at the time of the money leaving the country, withholding tax is not a means of hindering repatriation of profits or an additional tax for foreigners, but rather a system aiming to secure tax claims are paid before profits are taken out of the country.[5]

[3] According to section 39 of the Banking Act of 1959: "*Where the Governor-General considers it expedient to do so for purposes related to foreign exchange or the foreign exchange resources of Australia; the protection of the currency or the protection of the public credit or revenue of Australia;* (. . .) *the Governor General may make regulations,* (. . .)."

[4] Australian Taxation Office (2014).

[5] Australian Taxation Office (2014).

9.4.1.2 Past Legal Developments and Future Political Trends

All the same the regulations are still in place and could be used again if the Governor General at any time: "(...) *considers it expedient to do so* (...).".[6] Even in the time of the international economic crisis this was not discussed as a serious option though. Australia is therefore unlikely to see such an option executed in the near future.

9.4.2 *South Africa*

On behalf of the Minister of Finance, the South African Reserve Bank is responsible for the administration of exchange controls in South Africa.[7] The South African Reserve Bank was established by section 9 of the Currency and Banking Act, No 31 of 1920 and is governed by the amended South African Reserve Bank Act, No 90 of 1989. Exchange control is governed by the amended Exchange Control Regulations 1961, last amended January 14th, 2011.

Regarding the repatriation of foreign investment (income from foreign assets invested in South Africa by non-residents) the South African Reserve Bank states that:

- "*Any income earned on the [foreign direct] investment may be transferred abroad.*"[8]
- "*Should a non-resident disinvest from this country, the local sale or redemption proceeds of non-resident owned assets in South Africa would be regarded as freely transferable.*"[9]

9.4.3 *Colombia*

9.4.3.1 Current Situation

Foreign investment must be registered with the Central Bank of Colombia to allow repatriation of capital and profits. When the foreign investment is registered, the repatriation of capital and profits (also in the form of dividends) is permitted without restriction.[10]

[6] PWC (2013), p. 4.

[7] South African Reserve Bank (2014).

[8] South African Reserve Bank (2014).

[9] South African Reserve Bank (2014).

[10] Deloitte & Touche (2014).

Companies in Columbia selling products in foreign currencies generally have to repatriate the amount gained in foreign currencies in Colombian pesos. Branches or affiliate offices of foreign companies active in the energy sector and/or undertaking mining activities regarding coal, ferronickel or uranium are exempt from this requirement, but instead have to exchange into Colombian pesos all funds necessary to pay for mining activities in Colombia.[11]

Dividends, when accompanied by valid financial documentation, can be paid out to national and foreign investors in foreign currency without restriction.[12]

9.4.3.2 Past Legal Developments and Future Political Trends

Decree 444 of 1967 further established the requirement to register profits with the Exchange Office to ensure that any profits were being repatriated.

As of January 10th, 2012 the Colombian government also requires that minerals only be sold by holders of a valid mining concession and trade agents registered under the "*single trader registration*".[13] Officially this is not aimed at restricting the repatriation of foreign investment, but is rather to ensure due payment of taxes and royalties and to restrict illegal mining activities.

Also in general, foreign exchange controls have been reduced in Colombia in the last few decades. Some of the remaining tasks, inter alia the registration of the repatriation of capital and profits, were delegated to banks as authorized foreign exchange intermediaries.[14]

References

Australian Taxation Office, PAYG withholding|Australian Taxation Office (2014) Available online at: http://www.ato.gov.au/Business/PAYG-withholding/. Last checked on 15 February 2014

Cárdenas BP, Bejarano D, Guerra D (2012) Colombia. In: Sutcliffe S (ed) Mining law: jurisdictional comparisons. Thomson Reuters, London pp 175–190

Deloitte & Touche (2014) Foreign investment and exchange controls in Colombia - finance and banking. Colombia. Available online at: http://www.mondaq.com/x/2823/Foreign+Investment+And+Exchange+Controls+In+Colombia. Last checked on 15 February 2014

Law Business Research Ltd (2014) http://www.lbresearch.com: Colombia - mining - reference - Latin lawyer. Available online at: http://www.cardenasycardenas.com/archivos/52.M2013%20-%20Colombia%20%282%29.pdf. Last checked on 15 February 2014

PWC (2013) Doing business in Australia - business guide. Available online at: http://www.pwc.com.au/legal/assets/GuideBusiness2011.pdf, updated on 3/18/2013. Last checked on 15 February 2014

[11] Law Business Research Ltd (2014), p. 1.

[12] Law Business Research Ltd (2014), p. 1.

[13] Cárdenas et al. (2012), p. 185.

[14] Deloitte & Touche (2014).

Sornarajah M (2010) The international law on foreign investment, 3rd edn. Cambridge University Press, Cambridge/New York

South African Reserve Bank (2014) Financial surveillance and exchange controls. Available online at: http://www.resbank.co.za/RegulationAndSupervision/FinancialSurveillanceAndExchangeControl/Pages/Financial%20Surveillance%20and%20Exchange%20Control-Home.aspx. Last checked on 15 February 2014

Chapter 10
Conflict Resolution

10.1 Introduction and Disambiguation

In this work conflict resolution refers to the legal framework for the resolution of disputes between the foreign investor and the host state, land owners and Indigenous Australians/Tribal authorities and Indian-/Afro-Colombians that may occur in the lifecycle of a mining project.

10.2 Relevance

Mining projects, whether realized by surface or underground mining, have a high potential for conflict between the foreign investor and the various stakeholders mentioned supra.

On the one hand the foreign investor will be concerned about the security and profitability of its long term capital investments. As legal stability is crucial for investment decisions in long-term projects,[1] the foreign investor will be concerned about impacts of changes in the regulatory framework and a possible bias of the courts of the host state.

On the other hand the government of the host state, the local government, land owners and Indigenous Australians/Tribal authorities and Indian-/Afro-Colombians will be concerned about the social, economic and environmental impact of the mining activities.

The government of the host state will not be willing to cede any aspect of its sovereignty when guaranteeing legal stability and will want to rely on domestic courts rather than international arbitrators.[2]

---

[1] Pereira (2013), p. 252.

[2] Silva (2012), p. 5.

R.W. Roeder, *Foreign Mining Investment Law*, DOI 10.1007/978-3-319-31217-0_10

10.3 Observation Horizon

This indicator will analyse dispute resolution mechanisms established to solve disputes related to mining investment between the foreign investor and the host state. This work distinguishes between "*national*" and "*international*" dispute resolution mechanisms.

"*National*" dispute resolution mechanisms refer to dispute resolution mechanisms solely established by and conducted in and under the auspices of the host state.

"*International*" dispute resolution refers to dispute resolution mechanisms established inter alia by international organizations, such as the International Centre for Settlement of Investment Disputes ("***ICSID***") or international arbitration bodies or any kind of hybrid dispute resolution mechanisms.

In terms of national dispute resolution mechanisms this work will examine whether mining related conflicts are determined by a court system specialized on mining related conflicts or by the general judiciary of the host state. The same will be examined regarding disputes with Indigenous Australians/Tribal Authorities and Indian-/Afro-Colombians.

This work will further examine whether either administrative review processes or alternative dispute resolution mechanisms are available to settle mining investment related disputes.

In terms of international dispute resolution mechanisms this work will focus on international recourses, such as ICSID/international arbitration. It will also investigate whether or not international investments are protected by bilateral investment treaties. This work will not provide a review of general foreign investment law or bilateral investment treaties, as this research has been undertaken thoroughly in the last decades.[3]

This work will furthermore examine whether or not the host state is willing to enter into legal stability contracts with foreign investors.

[3] For a detailed review of foreign investment law see: Sornarajah (2010); Dolzer and Schreuer (2008).

10.4 Countries

10.4.1 Australia

10.4.1.1 National Conflict Resolution Mechanisms

10.4.1.1.1 Current Situation

Australia acknowledges the specifics of mining related conflicts and besides the more broad jurisdiction of the Land Court system established specific Native Title Tribunals which are commonly addressed in mining conflicts.

The Land Court has the jurisdiction over mining related conflicts, specifically over conflicts "*arising in relation to prospecting, exploration or mining or to any permit, claim, license or lease granted or issued under* [*the MRA 1989*]"[4] and land access conflicts in relation to mining activities.[5]

The Land Court is not uniquely designed for mining conflicts though and does also have jurisdiction over a wide range of different issues.[6] It does however focusses on land use issues and the rules of evidence support solving conflicts in unequal power positions of the parties as the Land Court is not bound by the general rules of evidence and may inform itself in "*the way it considers appropriate*"—which can be helpful if certain parties to an dispute, e.g. Native Australians, are unfamiliar with Western concepts of dispute resolution.[7]

This allows the Land Court to be flexible in the way it deals with concerns raised by various non-legally trained stakeholders.

---

[4] According to section 5(1) of the Land Court Act 2000: "*The Land Court has the jurisdiction given to it under this Act or another Act* (. . .)". In combination with section 363 of the MRA 1989 the Land Court has substantive jurisdiction to "(. . .) *hear and determine actions, suits and proceedings arising in relation to prospecting, exploration or mining or to any permit, claim, license or lease granted or issued under this Act* [*MRA 1989*] (. . .)".

[5] According to section 363 (2)(e) of the MRA 1989 this includes disputes on land access as "(. . .) *any matter arising between applicants or holders in relation to prospecting, exploring or mining, or arising between applicants or holders and owners of land in relation to prospecting, exploring or mining*."

[6] Howard and McWhinney (2014).

[7] According to section 7(a) of the Land Court Act 2000: "*The Land Court has, for exercising jurisdiction conferred under this Act or another Act, all the powers of the Supreme Court* (. . .)".

According to section 7 of the Land Court Act 2000: "*In the exercise of its jurisdiction, the Land Court is not bound by the rules of evidence and may inform itself in the way it considers appropriate; and must act according to equity, good conscience and the substantial merits of the case without regard to legal technicalities and forms or the practice of other courts*."

The flexibility is also reflected in the importance of Alternative Dispute Resolution mechanisms. Further details can be found in the Land Court Rules 2000 and the Land Court Regulations 2010.[8] Appeals may be directed to the Land Appeal Court, which on a general level finally determines the matter.[9]

The jurisdiction for matters regarding native title (see supra) lies with the Federal Court.

According to section 213(2) of the Native Title Act 1993 the jurisdiction for matters regarding native title lies with the Federal Court.

Specifically, the Federal Court has jurisdiction over native title determination applications and is responsible for their mediation. The Federal Court hears and determines compensation applications, claim registration applications and applications to remove agreements from the Register of Indigenous Land Use Agreements.[10]

According to section 108 of the Native Title Act of 1993 a Native Title Tribunal will assist the Federal Court. Most cases will be referred to the Native Title Tribunal in the first instance.[11]

The Land Court also has jurisdiction in cases under the Aboriginal Cultural Heritage Act 2003 regarding the approval of cultural heritage management plans, but not native title determination or disputes.[12]

A traditional judiciary system is also in place in Australia, but does not have the jurisdiction over mining licenses and land access issues other than on appeal from those courts.[13]

Mining conflicts that touch upon Constitutional rights fall in the jurisdiction of the High Court of Australia.[14]

---

[8] According to section 37 of the Land Court Act 2010: "*The Civil Proceedings Act 2011, part 6 (the ADR [Alternative Dispute Resolution] provisions) applies to proceedings started under this Act.*"

According to section 39 of the Civil Proceedings Act 2011: "*An ADR process is a process of mediation or case appraisal under which the parties are helped to achieve an early, inexpensive settlement or resolution of their dispute. In this part, an ADR process includes all the steps involved in an ADR process, including pre-mediation and post-mediation sessions; and a case appraisal session; and joint sessions; and private sessions;* (...)"

[9] According to section 64 of the Land Court Act 2010: "*A party to a proceeding in the Land Court may appeal to the Land Appeal Court against all or part of the decision of the Land Court.*" *According to section 71(2) Land Court Act 2010*: "*Subject to part 4, every decision of the Land Appeal Court is final and conclusive.*"

[10] Federal Court of Australia (2014).

[11] Federal Court of Australia (2014). Overlapping issues are discussed in section 32E of the Land Court Act 2000: "(...) *under the Commonwealth Native Title Act a claimant or body corporate objects to the doing of an act; and the State is required to ensure that the objection to the doing of the act is heard by an independent person or body. The Land Court in its cultural heritage division has jurisdiction to hear the objection.*"

[12] Howard and McWhinney (2014).

[13] A detailed review with three case study examples can be found at: Federal Court of Australia's Indigenous Dispute Resolution & Conflict Management Case Study Project 2013, *Case Studies in Indigenous Dispute Resolution & Conflict Management in Australia.*

[14] High Court of Australia (2014).

10.4.1.1.2 Past Legal Developments and Future Political Trends

The Gold Fields Act of 1855 of New South Wales[15] introduced a system of local courts that were established by the government, but its nine members were elected by the miners themselves; the government only appointed one of them to serve as the chairman.[16] Those local courts could be seen as a predecessor to today's Land Court in Queensland. The Land Court as such was established in 1884 as the Land Board,[17] but with a focus on jurisdiction over leases, valuations, rentals and compensation issues.[18]

The Land Court was conferred with the jurisdiction of the Land and Resources Tribunal regarding mining issues in 1997,[19] which itself had replaced the Queensland Mining Wardens Court.[20]

Presently, major changes to the outlined current Land Court system (outlined supra) are not in sight.

10.4.1.2 Specific Foreign Investor: Host State Conflict Resolution Mechanisms

10.4.1.2.1 Current Situation

Conflicts arising out of foreign investment in mining projects in Australia that fall under the scope of a bilateral investment treaty with a provision on investor-state arbitration can fall under the jurisdiction of an international arbitration tribunal such as the International Centre for the Settlement of Investment Disputes (ICSID).

Australia signed the ICSID convention on March 24th, 1975. With deposition on May 2nd, 1991 the convention entered into force for Australia on June 1st, 1991.[21]

Investor-state arbitration agreements referring to ICSID are a regular feature in Australian bilateral investment treaties and they are also used by Australian companies abroad.[22] Australia has given full effect to the enforcement of ICSID arbitral decisions.[23]

---

[15] Queensland became a separate state in 1859; in 1855 the area that is now Queensland was a part of New South Wales. For a detailed history of Queensland see: Queensland Government (2014).

[16] La Croix (1992), p. 215.

[17] Government of Queensland (2014).

[18] Howard and McWhinney (2014).

[19] King, Deputy President Land and Resource Tribunal (2011).

[20] Howard and McWhinney (2014).

[21] ICSID (2013).

[22] Clapham (2013).

[23] Buckley (1993), p. 94.

10.4.1.2.2 Past Legal Developments and Future Political Trends

In 1990 the Australian Parliament passed the ICSID Implementation Act of 1990 in order to fulfil "*Australia's obligations under the Convention on the Settlement of Investment Disputes between States and Nationals of Other States*", according to the long title of the ICSID Implementation Act 1990. The Attorney-General praised the implementation of the ICSID convention as a "*great benefit to Australia*" as it "*not only further enhances Australia's claim as a centre for international arbitration, but Australian investors abroad will be able to have recourse to a respected, convenient and well-known method of dispute settlement.*"[24]

Two decades later, in April 2011 the then incumbent Australian government announced that it will no longer include in its investment treaties clauses that refer disputes between foreign investors and the Commonwealth of Australia or states to an international arbitration body. Conflicts that arise will be heard by Australian domestic courts instead.[25] The explanatory statement reads as follows:

> The Gillard Government supports the principle of national treatment – that foreign and domestic businesses are treated equally under the law. However, the Government does not support provisions that would confer greater legal rights on foreign businesses than those available to domestic businesses. Nor will the Government support provisions that would constrain the ability of Australian governments to make laws on social, environmental and economic matters in circumstances where those laws do not discriminate between domestic and foreign businesses. The Government has not and will not accept provisions that limit its capacity to put health warnings or plain packaging requirements on tobacco products or its ability to continue the Pharmaceutical Benefits Scheme. In the past, Australian Governments have sought the inclusion of investor-state dispute resolution procedures in trade agreements with developing countries at the behest of Australian businesses. The Gillard Government will discontinue this practice.[26]

This change in policy has been challenged,[27] but also came as no surprise to commentators observing the discussions in Australia.[28] One key issue was the heralded investment dispute with Philip Morris Asia that is challenging the plain packaging legislation under the 1993 agreement between the Government of Australia and the Government of Hong Kong for the Promotion and Protection of Investments.[29] Also, the government of Australia was afraid that an investor would be able to challenge the Australian Pharmaceutical Benefits Scheme,[30] a system introduced by the Australian government to subsidize the cost of prescription medicines.[31] Considering these issues which in the opinion of the Government of

[24] Commonwealth Law Bulletin (2014).

[25] Trakman (2012b), p. 83.

[26] Government of Australia (2011), p. 14.

[27] JDSupra (2014).

[28] Kurtz (2012), p. 6.

[29] Government of Australia - Attorney-General's Department (2014).

[30] Trakman (2012a), p. 958.

[31] Department of Health and Ageing (2014).

Australia are crucial to the wellbeing of Australians it is unlikely Australia will move back towards more openness to the idea of international arbitration of conflicts with foreign investors any time soon.

10.4.2 South Africa

10.4.2.1 National Conflict Resolution Mechanisms

South Africa does not have a specific mining related judicial conflict resolution system in place. Before mining conflicts are referred to the general judiciary the MRPDA 2002 requires an obligatory administrative review process.[32]

The court of first instance is the Magistrate's Court for claims with a value of up to 100,000 South African Rand (district division) and 300,000 South African Rand (regional division). Claims with a value above these thresholds will be heard by the High Court.[33]

According to section 166(e) of the Constitution of South Africa, the parliament has the power to establish or recognize specialized courts: "(. . .) *any other court established in terms of an Act of Parliament, including any court of a status similar to either the High Courts or the Magistrates' Courts.*" It has used this power e.g. for a specialized Labour Court according to the Labour Relations Act, No 66 of 1995 and the Competition Tribunal according to section 41 of the Competition Act 15 2000.[34]

The Parliament has not exercised its power to establish a specialized court for mining/energy or land access matters. Therefore land access matters—both with tribal land owners and any other land owners—will be heard before a Magistrate's Court or a High Court in the first instance, depending of the value of compensation in question.

According to section 168(3) of the Constitution of South Africa, the Supreme Court of Appeal "(. . .) *is the highest court of appeal except in constitutional matters, and may decide only appeals; issues connected with appeals; and any other matter that may be referred to it in circumstances defined by an Act of Parliament.*"

---

[32] According to section 96(3) of the MRPDA 2002: "(. . .)*any person whose rights or legitimate expectations have been materially and adversely affected or who is aggrieved by any administrative decision in terms of this Act may appeal* (. . .) *to the Director-General* (. . .) *or the Minister* (. . .)." The "*may*" has to be read as a "*must*" as according to section 96(3) of the MRPDA 2002: "No person may apply to the court for the review of an administrative decision contemplated in subsection (1) until that person has exhausted his or her remedies in terms of that subsection."

Section 96(4) of the MRPDA 2002 refers to sections 6, 7(1) and 8 of the Promotion of Administrative Justice Act 2000 (Act No. 3 of 2000) which in turn determines the competent courts via section 1 of the Promotion of Administrative Justice Act 2000.

[33] Paleker (2011), p. 364.

[34] Paleker (2011), p. 361.

The Constitutional Court of South Africa is according to section 167(2) of the Constitution of South Africa "(...) *the highest court in all constitutional matters,*" but "*may decide only constitutional matters, and issues connected with decisions on constitutional matters*". An application from another court is possible according to section 167(6) of the Constitution of South Africa if the merits touch upon constitutional matters.

Alternative Dispute Resolution mechanisms are available within the South African justice system.[35] Their use is not obligatory or specifically encouraged for mining license or land access disputes.

There is also a vast traditional justice system. Their relationship to the justice system described supra is a topic of debate. Those traditional justice systems do not apply to mining licenses or land access.[36]

10.4.2.2 Specific Foreign Investor: Host State Conflict Resolution Mechanisms

10.4.2.2.1 Current Situation

While South Africa has not signed the ICSID convention, since the end of Apartheid it has negotiated over 40 bilateral investment treaties, 20 of which have entered into force.[37] These bilateral investment treaties provide for investor-state arbitration, e.g. before ICSID and under the United Nations Commission on International Trade Law Arbitration rules ("***UNCITRAL***").[38]

10.4.2.2.2 Past Legal Developments and Future Political Trends

During the Apartheid regime, South Africa did not enter into bilateral investment treaties.[39]

Starting with the bilateral investment treaty between South Africa and the United Kingdom which was signed on September 20th, 1994, in the time immediately past the end of Apartheid, between 1994 and 1998, South Africa concluded 15 bilateral investment treaties, mostly with European countries and some more in the years following 1998.[40] It has been said that South Africa entered into them in a hurry to quickly stimulate foreign investment.[41]

[35] Joubert (2014).

[36] South African Government News Agency (2014).

[37] Peterson (2006), p. 4.

[38] UNCTAD (2012), p. 6.

[39] Peterson (2006), p. 6.

[40] Department of Trade and Industry South Africa (2013), p. 2.

[41] Green (2012).

On the basis of those bilateral investment treaties, South Africa has been challenged before the ICSID panel, inter alia under a bilateral investment treaty between Italy and South Africa and Belgium[42]: the case *Piero Foresti, Laura de Carli and others v. Republic of South Africa*[43] concerned a granite mining operation.

The two key issues at hand were a challenge to jurisdiction in that South Africa argued that under South African common law, mineral rights could not be an asset of the investor and therefore should not be considered investments under the bilateral investment treaty, and the question whether Black Economic Empowerment measures could amount to expropriation as defined under the treaties. In this particular case the claimant withdrew from the claim leaving the judges with the decisions on costs only.[44] They awarded the costs against the claimant, which can be seen as an indicator that the judges were inclined to uphold the legality of the South African measures under the bilateral investment treaty. The case certainly added to notion that bilateral investment treaties could have a severe impact on Black Economic Empowerment in South Africa.[45]

Based on similar experience between 2007 and 2010, the South African government had all "*first-generation*" [concluded immediately after the end of Apartheid] bilateral investment treaties concluded by South Africa after the end of Apartheid reviewed.[46] The review found "*The relationship between bilateral investment treaties and foreign investments* [is] *ambiguous* (...) *And that bilateral investment treaties pose risks and limitations on the ability of the government to pursue its constitutional based transformation agenda* [Black Economic Empowerment]".[47]

As a result of this review the cabinet decided[48]:

- to develop a new Investment Act to codify and clarify typical bilateral investment treaty-provisions into domestic law;
- to terminate the first-generation bilateral investment treaties and offer partners the opportunity to renegotiate them;
- to only enter into bilateral investment treaties that include investor-state arbitration agreements in cases of "*of compelling economic and political circumstances*",[49] e.g. if the potential treaty partner was a capital exporting country[50]; and
- to develop a new model bilateral investment treaty.

---

[42] Collins (2010).

[43] ICSID (2010).

[44] Collins (2010).

[45] Tayob (2009).

[46] Department of Trade and Industry South Africa (2012).

[47] Department of Trade and Industry South Africa (2012).

[48] Department of Trade and Industry South Africa (2013), p. 8.

[49] Woolfrey (2014).

[50] Trakman (2012b), p. 83.

The latest developments have seen South Africa terminate its bilateral investment treaties with both Belgium and Luxembourg.[51] This caused concern among business leaders, specifically in the European Union.[52]

Considering the decisions of the cabinet outlined supra, further terminations are likely, leaving foreign investors with legal uncertainty until the new planned foreign investment law and bilateral investment treaties are in place.[53]

10.4.3 Colombia

10.4.3.1 National Conflict Resolution Mechanisms

10.4.3.1.1 Current Situation

Colombia does not have a specific mining related judicial conflict resolution system in place and has split jurisdiction for the various mining related conflicts. Conflicts regarding mining concessions fall under the jurisdiction of the Administrative Courts,[54] under the Civil Courts if they are land access matters[55] and under the

[51] Green (2012).

[52] Marais (2012).

[53] Langalanga (2014).

[54] Article 293 of the Mining Law 2001 states: "*De las acciones referentes a los contratos de concesión que tengan por objeto la exploración y explotación de minas, conocerán, en primera instancia, los tribunales administrativos con jurisdicción en el lugar de su celebración.*"

[The proceedings referring to concession contracts relating to the exploration and exploitation of the mines fall under the jurisdiction of the administrative courts with jurisdiction in the place where the mining activities are undertaken.]

[55] Land access conflicts are governed by the procedure outlined in article 285 of the Mining Law 2001, that establishes first an administrative procedure and then the jurisdiction of the civil court system: "*Cuando por motivo del ejercicio de las servidumbres legales, necesarias para el uso y beneficio de las obras y trabajos mineros, el propietario o poseedor de los terrenos sirvientes pidiere ante el alcalde se fije una caución al minero en los términos del artículo 184 de este Código, se ordenara que por un perito se estime su monto dentro del término de treinta (30) días. Una vez rendido el dictamen, el alcalde señalara dicha caución en los cinco (5) días siguientes. La decisión será apelable ante el Gobernador en el efecto devolutivo y solo se concederá si el interesado constituye provisionalmente tal garantía, en la cuantía fijada por el alcalde. La cuantía de la caución, una vez en firme, podrá ser revisada por el juez* [*civil*] *del lugar de ubicación de los predios de acuerdo con las reglas generales de* (...)."

[When due to the exercise of the legal servitudes, necessary for the use and benefit of the mining works and installations [a conflict arises] an appraiser will be asked to estimate the amount, within a term of thirty (30) days. Once the appraisement has been given, the Mayor will indicate the amount of such guarantee during the following five (5) days. The decision can be appealed before the Governor with no suspension effect and will be granted if the interested party provisionally constitutes such guarantee, in the amount fixed by the Mayor. When the amount of the guarantee is in force, it can be checked by a civil court judge with jurisdiction over the area of the corresponding lands (...)]

Administrative High Court as a sole instance in all other matters.[56] This includes conflicts regarding Indian/Afro-Colombian mining rights and areas.

According to article 20 of Law 1564 de 2012—the *Código de Procedimiento Civil* [Civil Procedure Code] the first instance is the "*Juece civile del circuito en primera instancia*" [Circuit Court judges in first instance] and according to article 30 of the Civil Procedure Code the court of appeal is: "*La Corte Suprema de Justicia*" [The Supreme Court of Justice].

Mining conflicts that touch upon Constitutional rights fall under the jurisdiction of the Constitutional Court of Colombia.[57]

There is also a traditional justice systems for Indian/Afro-Colombians. This justice system does not apply to mining licenses or land access.[58]

With the decree 1818 of 1998, el *Estatuto de los mecanismos alternativos de solución de conflictos* [The statute on alternative dispute resolution mechanisms], alternative dispute resolution mechanisms are available within the Colombian justice system. Their use is not obligatory or specifically encouraged for mining license or land access disputes.

Legal stability contracts that were established in 2005 to foster foreign investments furthermore open the door to arbitration rather than the jurisdiction of the courts as described supra.[59]

In the mining industry, those rules relate to tax law and mining concessions terms. According to article 5 of the Legal Stability Law 2005, the investor will have to pay 1 % of the amount invested per annum as a consideration for entering into a legal stability contract. While disputes arising out of the legal stability clause fall

---

[56] According to article 295 of the Mining Law 2001 all other mining related matters [which are not land access matters]: "(. . .) *conocera el Consejo de Estado en unica instancia.*" [(. . .) falls under the jurisdiction of the Administrative High Court as a sole instance].

[57] Article 241 of the Constitution of Colombia states: "*A la Corte Constitucional se le confía la guarda de la integridad y supremacía de la Constitución, en los estrictos y precisos términos de este artículo.* (. . .)"

[The Constitutional Court is entrusted with safeguarding the integrity and supremacy of the Constitution, (. . .)].

[58] Zuleta and Araque (2013).

[59] According to article 1 of law 963 of 2005 (Legal Stability Law 2005) Colombia decided to: "*Se establecen los contratos de estabilidad jurídica con la finalidad de promover inversiones nuevas y de ampliar las existentes en el territorio nacional.*"

[Establish legal stability contracts with the aim of promoting new investment and expanding existing investments in the country.]

Under article 2 of the Legal Stability Law 2005: "(. . .), *el Estado garantiza a los inversionistas que los suscriban, que si durante su vigencia se modifica en forma adversa a estos alguna de las normas que haya sido identificada en los contratos como determinante de la inversión, los inversionistas tendrán derecho a que se les continúen aplicando dichas normas por el término de duración del contrato respectivo.*"

[(. . .), the State guarantees to the investors that if throughout the duration of the contract any of the rules identified in the contract as a determinant of the investment are modified, the investors are entitled to be treated under the law that it had entered in at that time of the conclusion of the contract.]

under the jurisdiction of the Colombian judiciary, article 7 of the Legal Stability Law 2005 opens the possibility to include a clause in legal stability contract to refer disputes to an arbitration tribunal, which will be subject to Colombian arbitration law.[60]

10.4.3.1.2 Past Legal Developments and Future Political Trends

Until 2012, 66 legal stability contracts were concluded, 10 of which were directly related to mining investments.[61] The Legal Stability Law 2005 has been challenged to be unconstitutional several times:

One legal argument was that the Legal Stability Law 2005 violates the principle of equality inherited in article 13 of the Constitution of Columbia.

The Constitutional Court of Colombia dismissed the claim by stating: "(…) *en cuanto sus* [*legal stability contracts*] *fines y medidas son legítimos, como también estas son adecuadas al propósito previsto por el legislador, representado por la conveniencia de atraer capitales para destinarlos a actividades consideradas estratégicas dentro del sistema económico colombiano.*"[62]

[Legal stability contracts are legitimate, as they are appropriate measures to the purpose intended by the legislature, the desire to attract capital to be allocated to activities considered strategic in economic terms within Colombia.]

Thus it is within the discretion of the parliament to focus an economic stimulus on a particular type of investments, in this case, foreign investment.[63]

Another challenge was on the basis that legal stability contracts would unconstitutionally restrict the power of Parliament to change its laws.[64] The Constitutional Court of Colombia dismissed the claim by arguing: "(…) *el artículo legal demandado debe ser entendido en el sentido de que mediante los contratos de estabilidad jurídica no se les garantiza a los inversionistas la inmodificabilidad de la ley, sino que se les asegura la permanencia,* (…), *las mismas condiciones legales existentes al momento de la celebración de aquél, de tal manera que en caso de modificación de dicha normatividad, y el surgimiento de alguna controversia sobre este aspecto, se prevé la posibilidad de acudir a mecanismos resarcitorios* (…)"

[(…) the legal article must be understood in the sense that through legal stability contracts investors are not guaranteed an unchangeable law, but ensures (…) the same legal conditions existing at the time of the conclusion of the contract, so that in case of modification of the regulations, and the emergence of some controversy

[60] Pereira (2013).

[61] Ministerio de Commercio (2014).

[62] Corte Constitucional de Colombia (2006), para 5.9.

[63] Silva (2012), p. 11.

[64] Silva (2012), p. 11.

on this point, it allows for the possibility of a compensatory mechanisms [e.g. in the case of a breach of a legal stability contract](. . .)].[65]

10.4.3.2 Specific Foreign Investor: Host State Conflict Resolution Mechanisms

10.4.3.2.1 Current Situation

Colombia has concluded bilateral investment treaties with several countries. The bilateral investment treaties with the United States and the European Union are still being negotiated. The bilateral investment treaties in place include either an ICSID or a UNICTRAL arbitration clause.

10.4.3.2.2 Past Legal Developments and Future Political Trends

Colombia signed the ICSID convention on May 18th, 1993.

Based upon Law 266 of 1996 and with the deposition of the ratification on July 15th, 1997 the ICSID convention entered into force for Colombia on August 14, 1997.[66] Law 315 of 1996 furthermore accepted international arbitration, such as the procedure before ICSID as a valid means of conflict resolution for investor-state disputes in Colombia.[67] So far no ICSID cases have been brought against Colombia.[68]

References

Buckley RP (1993) Some jurisdictional difficulties with Australia's ratification of the ICSID convention. Asia Pac Law Rev 2:92

Clapham J (2013) Australian companies' use of BITs to protect foreign investments on the increase. Available online at: http://www.mallesons.com/publications/marketAlerts/2013/Pages/Australian-Companies-use-of-Bilateral-Investment-Treaties-to-protect-foreign-investments-on-the-increase.aspx. Last checked on 15 February 2014

Collins D (2010) Review of 2010 ICSID Decisions, ICSID Case No. ARB(AF)/07/1. Manch J Int Econ Law 7(3):60–66

Commonwealth Law Bulletin (2014) International developments. Commonw Law Bull 1991 (17):1001

Corte Constitucional (2006) Demanda de inconstitucionalidad contra la ley 963 de 2005, - Por cual se instaura una ley de establidad jurídica para los inversionistas en Colombia, Judgment of

---

[65] Corte Constitucional de Colombia (2006).

[66] ICSID (2013).

[67] ICSID (2013).

[68] Law Business Research Ltd (2014).

29 March 2006. Reference: C-242/2006. Available online at: http://www.corteconstitucional.gov.co/relatoria/2006/C-242-06.htm. Last checked on 15 February 2014

Department of Health and Ageing (2014) Pharmaceutical Benefits Scheme (PBS) - Introduction. Edited by Government of Australia. Available online at: http://www.pbs.gov.au/info/healthpro/explanatory-notes/section1/intro. Last checked on 15 February 2014

Department of Trade and Industry South Africa (2012) SA's Minister of Trade and Industry, arrived in Geneva on an official visit. Available online at: http://www.thedti.gov.za/editmedia.jsp?id=2504. Last checked on 15 February 2014

Department of Trade and Industry South Africa (2013) Update on the Review of Bilateral Investment Treaties in South Africa. Available online at: http://www.thedti.gov.za/parliament/bit%27s_in_sa.pdf. Last checked on 15 February 2014

Dolzer R, Schreuer C (2008) Principles of international investment law. Oxford University Press, Oxford

Federal Court of Australia (2014) The Courts Jurisdiction. Available online at: http://www.fedcourt.gov.au/about/jurisdiction. Last checked on 15 February 2014

Government of Australia (2011) Gillard Government Trade Policy Statement: Trading our way to more jobs and prosperity. Available online at: http://www.dfat.gov.au/publications/trade/trading-our-way-to-more-jobs-and-prosperity.pdf, updated on 4/12/2011. Last checked on 15 February 2014

Government of Australia - Attorney-General's Department (2014) Investor-state arbitration - tobacco plain packaging. Available online at: http://www.ag.gov.au/Internationalrelations/InternationalLaw/Pages/Tobaccoplainpackaging.aspx. Last checked on 15 February 2014

Government of Queensland (2014) The Land Court of Queensland, Australia. Available online at: http://www.landcourt.qld.gov.au/. Last checked on 15 February 2014

Green A (2012) South Africa: BITs in pieces. Beyondbrics, 10/19/2012. Available online at: http://blogs.ft.com/beyond-brics/2012/10/19/south-africa-bits-in-pieces/#. Last checked on 15 February 2014

High Court of Australia (2014) Operation of the High Court. Available online at: http://www.hcourt.gov.au/about/operation. Last checked on 15 February 2014

Howard D, McWhinney G (2014) Queensland Land Court: key forum for mining and petroleum. Available online at: http://www.lexology.com/library/detail.aspx?g=20db57d6-9413-4478-871b-dc76a54ce43a. Last checked on 15 February 2014

ICSID (2010) Piero Foresti, Laura de Carli and others v. Republic of South Africa, award of 04 August 2010. Reference: ARB(AF)/07/1. Available online at: https://icsid.worldbank.org/ICSID/FrontServlet?requestType=CasesRH&actionVal=showDoc&docId=DC1651_En&caseId=C90. Last checked on 15 February 2014

ICSID (2013) International Centre for Settlement of Investment Disputes. Available online at: https://icsid.worldbank.org/ICSID/FrontServlet?requestType=ICSIDDocRH&actionVal=ShowDocument&language=English, updated on 8/31/2013. Last checked on 15 February 2014

JDSupra (2014) Australia's New Bilateral Investment Treaty Stance: An Open Amicus Curiae Submission|JD Supra. Available online at: http://www.jdsupra.com/legalnews/australias-new-bilateral-investment-tre-99291/. Last checked on 15 February 2014

Joubert J (2014) Embedding mediation in South African Justice. Mediate.com. Available online at: http://www.mediate.com/articles/Joubertj1.cfm. Checked on 9/18/2013

King F, Deputy President Land and Resource Tribunal (2011) Reforming Queensland's Tribunals. Available online at: http://www.landcourt.qld.gov.au/documents/articles/Reforming%20Queenslands%20Tribunals.pdf, updated on 12/12/2011. Last checked on 15 February 2014

Kurtz J (2012) Australias' Rejection of Investor-State Arbitration. Causation, Omission and Implication. ICSID Rev Foreign Invest Law J

La Croix SJ (1992) Property rights and institutional change during Australia's gold rush. Explor Econ Hist 29(2):204–227. doi:10.1016/0014-4983(92)90011-K

Langalanga A (2014) South African Courts and the Expropriation Conundrum: Caveat Foreign Investor. African International Legal Awareness. Available online at: http://blogaila.com/2013/05/31/south-african-courts-and-the-expropriation-conundrum-caveat-foreign-investor-by-azwimphelele-langalanga/. Last checked on 15 February 2014

Law Business Research Ltd (2014) http://www.lbresearch.com: Colombia - Mining - Reference - Latin Lawyer. Available online at: http://www.cardenasycardenas.com/archivos/52.M2013%20-%20Colombia%20%282%29.pdf. Last checked on 15 February 2014

Marais J (2012) South Africa, European Union lock horns. Business Day, 9/23/2012. Available online at: http://www.bdlive.co.za/businesstimes/2012/09/23/south-africa-european-union-lock-horns. Last checked on 15 February 2014

Ministerio de Commercio (2014) Contratos de Estabilidad Jurídica-Firmados. Available online at: https://www.mincomercio.gov.co/minindustria/publicaciones.php?id=17145. Last checked on 15 February 2014

Paleker M (2011) Civil procedure in Africa: the past, the present and the future. In: Leipold D, Stürner R (eds) Jahrbuch des Internationalen Zivilprozessrechts. Carl Heymanns Verlag (16), pp 343–368

Pereira A (2013) Legal Stability Contracts in Colombia: an appropriate incentive for investments? Richmond J Glob Law Bus 12(2):237–276. Last checked on 15 February 2014

Peterson LE (2006) South Africa's bilateral investment treaties. Implications for development and human rights. Berlin u. a: Friedrich-Ebert-Stiftung (Dialogue on globalization Occasional papers, 26)

Queensland Government (2014) Creation of a state. Available online at: https://www.qld.gov.au/about/about-queensland/history/creation-of-state/. Last checked on 15 February 2014

Silva MP (2012) Legal Stability in Colombia, an invitation to invest. In: Dundee, LL.M. papers. Last checked on 15 February 2014

Sornarajah M (2010) The international law on foreign investment, 3rd edn. Cambridge University Press, Cambridge

South African Government News Agency (2014) Controversial Traditional Courts Bill withdrawn. Available online at: http://www.sanews.gov.za/south-africa/controversial-traditional-courts-bill-withdrawn-0. Last checked on 15 February 2014

Tayob RK (2009) South African Judge offers view as to advantages of South Africa acceding to ICSID (Or did the previous administration "sign" away BEE?). Available online at: http://lists.fahamu.org/pipermail/debate-list/2008-September/016843.html, updated on 6/29/2009. Last checked on 15 February 2014

Trakman LE (2012a) Choosing domestic courts over investor-state arbitration: Australia's repudiation of the status quo. Univ N S W Law J 35(3):979–1012. Last checked on 15 February 2014

Trakman LE (2012b) Investor state arbitration or local courts: will Australia set a new trend? J World Trade 46(1):83–120

UNCTAD (2012) BIT South Africa - Zimbawbe. Available online at: http://unctad.org/sections/dite/iia/docs/bits/SA_Zimbabwe.pdf, updated on 3/16/2012. Last checked on 15 February 2014

Woolfrey S (2014) South Africa's new investment policy framework and protection for SA firms investing abroad. Tralac. Available online at: http://www.tralac.org/2013/03/06/south-africas-new-investment-policy-framework-and-protection-for-sa-firms-investing-abroad/. Last checked on 15 February 2014

Zuleta E, Araque W (2013) Jurisdiction Indigenous Colombia. Available online at: http://latinlawyer.com/reference/topics/60/jurisdictions/8/colombia/, updated on 9/18/2013. Last checked on 15 February 2014

Chapter 11
Applying for the Social License to Operate by Corporate Social Responsibility Policies and Actions

11.1 Introduction and Disambiguation

Foreign investments in mining projects used to be an issue between international mining companies and the national, at most local governments.

It has now been recognized that: "*Today, there is the need to gain and maintain the support of the people that live and work in the area of impact and influence of any given project – to have the Social License to Operate. There is ample evidence that a failure to gain and maintain this Social License can lead to conflict, delays or cost for the proponents of a project.*"[1]

The Social License to Operate ("***SLO***") has been defined as: "(...) *a set of concepts, values, tools and practices that represent a way of viewing reality for industry and stakeholders. Its purpose is to create a forum for negotiation whereby the parties involved are heard, understood and respected. SLO is a means to earn accountability, credibility, flexibility and capacity for both stakeholders and industry.*"[2]

But where and how should one apply for the SLO? Pierre Lassonde, the President of Newmont Mining Corporation has been quoted saying: "*You don't get your social license by going to a government ministry and making an application or simply paying a fee... It requires far more than money to truly become part of the communities in which you operate.*"[3]

The Social License to Operate is not a "*legal*" license in the narrow sense of for example a mining licenses (see supra in Chap. 5), but it helps to frame ones thinking in legal terms to better understand the concept of the Social License to Operate, therefore looking for the parties, the offer and the acceptance.[4] As consideration is a

[1] Thomson (2012).

[2] Nelsen (2006), p. 161.

[3] Thomson (2012).

[4] Fulcher (2012).

R.W. Roeder, *Foreign Mining Investment Law*, DOI 10.1007/978-3-319-31217-0_11

concept only necessary in the contract law of some jurisdictions, but alien to others, it will be left out at this point.

The parties of the SLO "*agreement*" are the foreign investor on one side and local institution and the local/Indigenous Australians/Tribal Authorities and Indian-/Afro-Colombian population and NGOs on the other side.

The offer of the foreign investor is to go "*beyond compliance*" and to adhere to the socio-economic and environmental requests of local institutions, the Indigenous Australians/Tribal Authorities and Indian-/Afro-Colombian population and NGOs on the other side. The acceptance refers to the goodwill of the institution and (Indigenous) population of the host state necessary for the successful realization of a mining project.

This work will focus on the offer of the foreign investor to go "*beyond compliance*" by means of Corporate Social Responsibility ("**CSR**") policies and actions.

There are several definitions for CSR used in the scholarly literature.[5] For the purpose of this work the definition of CSR as used by the European Commission in their Green Paper on: "*Promoting a European Framework for CSR*" shall be used. It states:

> Being socially responsible means not only fulfilling legal expectations, but also going beyond compliance and investing more [than required by law] into human capital, the environment and the relations with stakeholders.[6]

Using a non-Australian/South African/Colombian definition of CSR allows for a more objective comparison.

What CSR means in theory and practice might also differ from region to region.[7] While in developed countries the focus of CSR might be in human resource development and environmental issues, in developing countries the focus of CSR might very well shift to satisfaction of the basic needs of the local community such as food, housing and healthcare.

11.2 Relevance

Considering the high capital investments and the long duration of mining projects it is crucial for a foreign investor to develop his project without interruption and delays and to acquire and maintain his SLO.[8]

---

[5] The World Bank defines CSR as: "*Corporate social responsibility is the commitment of business to contribute to sustainable economic development—working with employees, their families, the local community and society at large to improve the quality of life, in ways that are both good for business and good for development.*", see: Ward 2014, p. 3.

[6] Commission of the European Communities (2001), p. 6.

[7] Ramlall (2012), p. 275.

[8] Nelsen (2006), p. 161.

If the concerns of local communities, Indigenous groups and non-governmental organizations are not adequately addressed and the foreign investor is not "*granted*" the SLO or loses it in the process, the resulting opposition to the project may delay, interrupt or even fail a mining project.

Acquiring and maintaining the SLO by means of going beyond compliance and establishing widely accepted CSR policies is a substantial means to significantly reduce risks to the success of a mining project.

11.3 Observation Horizon

This question will analyze how mining companies aim to "*apply*" for the SLO with their CSR policies and initiatives.

This work will compare CSR policies and initiatives of Rio Tinto in Australia, and AngloGold Ashanti South Africa and AngloGold Ashanti Colombia. This choice allows for an inter-company comparison as well as an intra-company comparison.

The focus will be on CSR policies regarding the employment and training of the local/Indigenous Australians/Tribal Authorities and Indian-/Afro-Colombian staff. While today CSR policies may encompass further topics, such as environmental and cultural concerns, the question of local employment has been and is a crucial factor for acquiring a Social License to Operate.[9]

The work does not attempt to judge whether or not the CSR policies and the actions of the analyzed mining companies match, and/or whether the CSR policies of the analyzed mining companies are appropriate CSR policies in the given contexts. CSR performance rankings for the mining industry have been established elsewhere.[10]

The work will assess the role that the SLO and the establishment of CSR policies by mining companies plays within the legal framework for foreign investments in mining projects.

---

[9] Nelsen (2006), p. 161.

[10] Diniz (2013).

11.4 Countries

11.4.1 Australia

11.4.1.1 Current Situation

The following paragraphs will discuss examples of how mining companies in Australia, specifically Rio Tinto, apply for their Social License to Operate by addressing some of the issues prevalent of the local population by their Corporate Social responsibility policies and actions. It will then be discussed how this shapes the legal framework for foreign investments in Australian mining projects.

By establishing and applying CSR policies the foreign investor offers to go "*beyond compliance*" and to adhere to the socio-economic and environmental requests of local institutions, local population and environmentalists. It constitutes one of the ways to apply for a Social License to Operate. The acceptance then refers to the goodwill of the institution and local population of the host state necessary to allow a successful mining project to be realized.

The outlined example concentrates on the CSR policies and actions of Rio Tinto Australia. Coordinated industry efforts such as the Australian Employment Covenant initiatives regarding the employment of local and Indigenous Australian personnel are described elsewhere.[11]

Rio Tinto's CSR statement reads as follows: "*Our approach to sustainable development: We believe that our business can make an important contribution to the ongoing, global transition to sustainable development. Our diverse global operations give us the opportunity to bring positive, long-term benefits to the communities, regions and countries where we work.*

Our strategy of investing in large, long-term mines and businesses means that we operate on extended time horizons, representing considerable investments in fixed capital. These long-term commitments provide opportunities for us to plan, implement and deliver sustainable contributions to social wellbeing, environmental stewardship and economic prosperity.

Delivering social and environmental benefits: The nature of our business means we forge close relationships with the environment - and with local communities - wherever we operate. By promoting the employment of local people, and

---

[11] An initiative masterminded by Andrew Forrest is "*The Australian Employment Covenant ("AEC")*". *Industry-led, it is in a way a national CSR policy and at least a coordinated CSR effort for several Australian mining companies. It aims to unite Australians to work together to "break the vicious cycle of unemployment and poverty amongst Indigenous Australians*". The initiative, which started in 2008, created the largest team-up of various employers in the history of the Commonwealth of Australia and by June 30th, 2011 over 290 employers committed to creating over 55,000 job opportunities for Indigenous Australians. By the end of 2012, this had grown to over 330 employers and over 60,000 job commitments. Even more importantly, at that time already 12,000 jobs had actually been filled with Indigenous Australians. Initiatives such as "*Generation One*" now urge the employers to act upon their commitment in full.

developing practical programs for environmental management, we aim to make a lasting contribution to the (often remote) areas of our operations. We also aim to contribute to the development of new approaches to solving the world's environmental and human development challenges, such as climate change and poverty."

Rio Tinto specifically recognizes indigenous employment as crucial, both for maintaining the Social License to Operate and in order to maintain a stable "*talent-pool*".[12]

Within the engagement in the sector Rio Tinto aims to not only focus on employment as such, but also on "*employability*" [for jobs outside the mining industry] and through this hopes for an indirect benefit for the community.[13]

The first response after the Mabo decision was reserved. A press statement written by Assistant Director Geoffrey Ewing of the Australian Mining Industry Council ("***AMIC***"), where CRA Limited (Rio Tinto's predecessor) was a significant member, stated in 1993:

> The High Court decision in the Mabo case has undermined Australia's ordered system of commerce and unless the system can adapt to accommodate Mabo then the nation will face serious economic and perhaps social difficulties.[14]

The approach of Rio Tinto and the industry changed with the appearance of new actors, such as CRA Vice President External Affairs, George Littlewood. He worked towards change and the new policies were then voiced by then CEO Leon Davis. Leon Davis decided to move forward the agenda and stated in 1995 that: "... *the next decade will see a series of CRA operations developed in active partnership with Aboriginal people.*"[15]

The same year saw the idea: "... *to establish innovative ways of sharing with and/or compensating Indigenous people*" which opened channels of thought for CSR policies that included Indigenous Australian employment.[16]

Rio Tinto then developed its first Aboriginal and Torres Strait Islander Policy in 1996 and directly addressed the issue of Aboriginal Australian employment: "*Economic independence through direct employment, business development and training are among advantages that Rio Tinto will offer.*"[17]

By the end of 2012, Rio Tinto had negotiated more than 100 such exploration access agreements.[18]

---

[12] Rio Tinto (2014b); "*We're committed to providing employment and career development opportunities to local communities. This mutually beneficial arrangement not only contributes to local economic growth, it also provides a stable talent-pool for our operations. In 2012, around seven per cent of our Australian employees were Indigenous Australians.*"

[13] Rio Tinto (2014a), Bruce Harvey, p. 3.

[14] Bauman and Glick (2012), p. 4.

[15] Bauman and Glick (2012), p. 6.

[16] Bauman and Glick (2012), p. 6.

[17] Bauman and Glick (2012), p. 7.

[18] Bauman and Glick (2012), p. 7.

Rio Tinto's explanation of its motivation for CSR has slightly changed over the past years. In 2008 Rio Tinto stated that it was foremost active in the area of CSR to gain better access to *to land, people and capital.*[19] In 2013 Rio Tinto stated that the CSR activities would help them to better manage their risks, mitigate *environmental impacts and interact with the local communities.*[20]

A discussion paper of Rio Tinto outlines the reasons of this change in more detail. Among the new reasons for its CSR engagement it lists "*avoidance of negative public sanction and securing expedited government permitting*" and acquiring the "*social license to operate*".[21]

While this social license to operate is not a legal permit (yet) it refers to the general goodwill of the people towards the operation of Rio Tinto in a specific area. A further reason mentioned is the belief of Rio Tinto that "*high productivity workforces are increasingly motivated by accomplishing societal purposes...*". By performing in a way that people who work for Rio Tinto can be proud of it in front of the their community members, Rio Tinto hopes to motivate its workforce.

Rio Tinto furthermore names "*heightened stakeholder and community expectations*" as a reason for its engagement.[22]

Within the research undertaken only one direct reference to "*moral*" reasons could be found—also within the Rio Tinto discussion paper. It states: "*Notwithstanding the need for a clear business case [for resources to be used in CSR programs], Rio Tinto should not be oblivious to moral concerns. [Actions should be undertaken...] simply because it is the right thing to do.*"[23] For Rio Tinto the Mabo Case has led to change in the institution and has been called: "*a catalyst that triggered constructive conflict*".[24]

11.4.1.2 Past Legal Developments and Future Political Trends

The development of CSR policies in Australia has been categorized into three distinct phases:

---

[19] Coronado and Fallon (2010), p. 671; "(...) *by earning a good reputation for our care of the environment and contribution to social improvement and the economic conditions of local [Indigenous] communities . . . we gain improved access to land, people and capital, the three critical resources on which our business success is built.*"

[20] Rio Tinto (2014c); "*Our approach enables us to manage risks effectively, reduce environmental impacts and engage with our host communities. It can also decrease operating costs, provide additional business opportunities and attract high-caliber employees. Ultimately, it allows us to deliver better returns for our shareholders.*"

[21] Rio Tinto (2014a), Bruce Harvey, p. 2.

[22] Rio Tinto (2014a), Bruce Harvey, p. 2.

[23] Rio Tinto (2014a), Bruce Harvey, p. 2.

[24] Bauman and Glick (2012), p. 16.

Throughout the 1960s and 1970s the government specifically demanded that companies address certain issues in their CSR policy. This phase was named "*command-and-control*" phase.[25]

The second phase focused on self-regulation and took place in the 1980s and 1990s. The initiative shifted towards the companies themselves.[26]

A further shift then became visible from 2000 until today and has been labeled: "*co-regulation*". This time, CSR policies were said to be neither mandated directly by government, nor decided upon unilaterally by the companies, but instead attempted to include the various stakeholders not only as targets, but also as participants in the development of the CSR policies.[27]

Considering the developments in the employment of Indigenous Australians outlined supra it is unlikely to see any major changes in the CSR policies of foreign investors in Australia in the near future. Whilst Rio Tinto's policies are likely to be amongst the furthest developed ones, other mining companies might catch up, but are unlikely to go any further at this point.

11.4.2 South Africa

11.4.2.1 Current Situation

The following paragraphs will discuss examples of how mining companies in South Africa, specifically AngloGold Ashanti, apply for their Social License to Operate by addressing some of the issues prevalent to the local population by their Corporate Social responsibility policies and actions—and how this shapes the legal framework for foreign investments in South African mining projects.

The process of acquiring the Social License to Operate may—in a non-technical way—be framed in legal terms to better grasp the issue:

By establishing and applying CSR policies the foreign investor offers to go "*beyond compliance*" and to adhere to the socio-economic and environmental requests of local institutions, local population and environmentalists. It constitutes one of the ways to apply for a Social License to Operate. The acceptance then refers to the goodwill of the institution and local population of the host state necessary to allow a successful mining project to be realized.

The examples outlined infra focus on CSR policies regarding the employment of local and HDSA and more specifically concentrate on the CSR policies and actions of AngloGold Ashanti.

On a global level, AngloGold Ashanti's CSR policies are guided by its Code of Business Principles and Ethics and its Community and Environment Management

---

25 Coronado and Fallon (2010), p. 669.

26 Coronado and Fallon (2010), p. 669.

27 Coronado and Fallon (2010), p. 670.

Standards. The Code of Business Principles and Ethics is a rather broad guidance document regarding good corporate governance and:

> (...) is intended as a source of direction and guidance for our actions and decisions internally and in our interactions with stakeholders and the public.[28]

The "*Community and Environment Management Standards*" are substantive global guidelines for specific mining projects on how to deal with issues arising from AngloGold Ashanti's stakeholder engagement.[29]

According to AngloGold Ashanti: "*Community and Environment Management Standards* (...) *have been designed to provide clarity to commitments made in the community and environment policy as well as the company's values* (...)."[30]

Community and Environment Management Standards encompass many key issues of the legal framework for foreign investment in mining projects, such as land access, local employment, local procurement and even dispute resolution mechanisms.[31]

In its section on socio-economic contribution, the Community and Environment Management Standards refer to the employment of local/indigenous population:

> It is AngloGold Ashanti's value intention that the communities and societies in which the Company operates will be better off for it having been there. This is achieved through, among other things, the Company's socio-economic contribution in the host country, including economic value generation and distribution. (...).
>
> This approach to sustainability calls for integration of community development and economic considerations into core business decision-making.
>
> AngloGold Ashanti's value -add is implemented through, (...), local employment, local procurement, (...).[32]

The global management standards include a reference to take into account the specifics of the community of each mining site managed by AngloGold Ashanti.[33]

---

[28] AngloGold Ashanti (2013b).

[29] AngloGold Ashanti (2013c).

[30] AngloGold Ashanti (2013c).

[31] AngloGold Ashanti (2013c).

[32] AngloGold Ashanti (2013c), p. 62; Under local employment, AngloGold Ashanti states: "*Local employees refers to individuals either born or who have the legal right to reside indefinitely,* (...) *aspects of expenditure associated with local employment are* (...): *Wages and benefits paid to local employees and contractors* [*and*] *total payroll, which means employees' salaries, including amounts paid to government institutions* (*employee taxes, levies, and unemployment funds*) *on behalf of employees. Total benefits, which include regular contributions* (*e.g. to pensions, insurance, Company vehicles, and private health*), *as well as other employee support such as housing, interest free loans, public transport assistance, educational grants, and redundancy payments.*"; Under local procurement, AngloGold Ashanti aims to purchase from: "(...) *providers of materials, products, goods and services that are based in the same geographic market as the site* (*i.e. excluding transnational payments*)."

[33] AngloGold Ashanti (2013c), p. 68; As for the objective of its global management standards, AngloGold Ashanti states that its: "*sites are* [*to be*] *managed in line with the Company's vision, mission and values, and to meet the Company's Environment and Community Policy commitment to undertake initiatives that contribute to sustainable futures in partnership with the societies in*

On a local level in South Africa, AngloGold Ashanti states (regarding local employment and local procurement) that it is determined to meet the targets set in its Social and Labour Plans ("***SLPs***").[34]

Regarding the employment of HDSA at AngloGold Ashanti in South Africa, Ashanti's Sustainability Report 2012 states that:

> In South Africa the Mining Charter specifies that 40% of management should be made up of historically disadvantaged South Africans (HDSAs). As at 31 December 2012, HDSAs made up 32% of senior management and 40% of top management for our South African management team.[35]

AngloGold Ashanti admits that the Broad-Based Economic Empowerment legislation and the deriving mining charter was a reason for some changes in their policies: ". . .*The second is a continuation of the trend where* [*Fund*] *initiatives are generally only considered if they are based in the regions where AngloGold Ashanti has operations* [. . .] *AngloGold Ashanti is following the requirement of the Broad-Based Socio-Economic Empowerment Charter that mining companies should concentrate on development in their host communities and in the major-labour sending areas.*"[36]

A specific challenge for the South African mining industry in general is the substantial number of migrant workers. Some claim that there are about 200,000 migrant workers involved in South African mining projects, mostly from the Eastern Cape or countries such as Mozambique or Lesoto.[37] Considering their diversity and number, CSR agreements have to be renegotiated again and again. The issue of migrant workers is not yet specifically addressed in the Community and Environment Management Standards.

---

which we operate." This broad aim is then narrowed down to require: "*Each site, regional and country office, as appropriate,* [*to*] *have a strategy to address its social and economic contribution in a manner appropriate to its size and stage of development, to the nature and magnitude of its impacts, to the environmental and social context, legacy issues, scope of engagement and, availability of funds and other resources*". This strategy is to be developed with the help of regularly updated studies and is at least to include: "*Local procurement objectives, targets and spend;* (. . .) [*and*] *Local employment strategy and associated targets.*"

[34] AngloGold Ashanti (2012b); "(. . .) *continues to meet the targets set in its Social and Labour Plans (SLPs). The region has developed a framework to address the socio-economic focus areas within and outside of the business over a three-year period. This involves partnerships with government as well as with social and industry stakeholders to address economic gaps created as the operations mature and production declines.*"

[35] AngloGold Ashanti (2012a).

[36] AngloGold Ashanti (2014).

[37] Crush and Williams (2006).

11.4.2.2 Past Legal Developments and Future Political Trends

CSR was not a predominant focus either for mining companies or for the South African government before the end of the Apartheid.[38] While mining companies were confronted with a higher level of scrutiny regarding their ecological footprint from the 1980s onward,[39] their focus only started to shift towards their social footprint after the end of the Apartheid area and with the introduction of the Constitution of South Africa in 1996 and the Mineral and Petroleum Resources Development Act 28 in 2002.[40]

It has to be noted that in South Africa, companies now prefer to use terms such as corporate social investment and corporate citizenship rather than CSR.[41] One explanation for the use of such specific terminology could be that neither corporate social investment nor corporate citizenship links firmly to past ethical or moral responsibilities, i.e. deficiencies that might have been accumulated in the time of Apartheid.[42]

Examples of CSR projects can now frequently be found. A documented example of a CSR project is the HIV awareness project "*Lesedi*". The government of the South African province "*Free State*", the mining company Harmony Gold, the local community and workers participated in this project, which led to the reduction of HIV not only within the mining workforce but also in the local community.[43,44]

CSR policies of mining companies have been challenged on the basis that a director must only focus on what is best for the company. Before 1994, the common law position of the South African courts was very restrictive on any director's CSR action taken. It was argued that such action does not specifically take into account the interests of the company, but looks for a broader, social responsible behaviour that does not lie within the duties of the director.[45]

In "*Amalgamated Society of Wood Workers of South Africa v. Die 1963 Ambagsaalverenigung*"[46] the court held that:

> … the power of a corporate body to donate a major asset cannot be lightly inferred … donation should be limited to such donations as are reasonable incidental to the carrying on of the activities of the donor or which are for the benefit of the donor (at 594).

[38] Kloppers and du Plessis (2008), p. 91.

[39] Kloppers and du Plessis (2008), p. 92.

[40] Kloppers and du Plessis (2008), p. 91.

[41] Fig (2005), p. 599.

[42] Fig (2005), p. 601.

[43] UNAIDS (2013).

[44] Kloppers and du Plessis (2008), p. 115.

[45] Ramlall (2012), p. 272.

[46] Ramlall (2012), p. 273.

Post-Apartheid, most business entities in South Africa now avoid legal challenges to their CSR actions by including provisions in their memoranda of association that allow for the making of donations or other CSR activities.[47]

While these provisions avoid litigation regarding the director's breach of responsibilities towards the company, it could now also be argued that the aim of a company has changed. Especially in the setting of South Africa, it can certainly be argued that environmental and social concern have been added to the responsibilities of a company.[48]

By arguing on this basis, the director in the future might not have breached his or her duties by addressing environmental and social challenges, but rather the opposite: when those issues are not addressed, the director may be in breach of director's duties.

This is now supported by legislative measures. The Companies Act 2008, reaffirmed by the Companies Amendment Act 2011 and the Companies Regulations 2008, and again reaffirmed by the Companies Regulations 2011 which came into force May 1st, 2011, require a public or state owned company to establish a social and ethics committee as part of its governance arrangements.[49,50] The function of such a committee inter alia is to monitor a company's approach towards good governance and CSR.[51]

Considering that many goals of the Black Economic Empowerment have not been reached in the mining business in South Africa it is likely that further changes in CSR policies are to come, which will most likely improve the situation of HDSA to the detriment of the flexibility of foreign investors regarding the choice of hiring.

The Mining Charter of October 11th, 2002 included voluntary goals that were subsequently addressed in CSR policies. The Amended Mining Charter of 2010 forces its addressees into compliance by stipulating punitive measures for non-compliance—whether they address the respective issue in their CSR policies or not. The latest changes in the new mining charter therefore have moved the actions for the employment of HDSA away from a voluntary CSR perspective to a mandatory compliance mechanism (see infra).

---

[47] Ramlall (2012), p. 281.

[48] Ramlall (2012), p. 281.

[49] Ramlall (2012), p. 281.

[50] BDO (2013).

[51] Ramlall (2012), p. 281.

11.4.3 Colombia

11.4.3.1 Current Situation

The following paragraphs will discuss examples of how mining companies in Colombia, specifically AngloGold Ashanti, apply for their Social License to Operate by addressing some of the issues prevalent to the local population by their Corporate Social responsibility policies and actions—and how this shapes the legal framework for foreign investments in Colombian mining projects.

As discussed supra the Social License to Operate may be framed legal terms to better grasp the issue.

By establishing and applying CSR policies the foreign investor offers to go "*beyond compliance*" and to adhere to the socio-economic and environmental requests of local institutions, local population and environmentalists. This is one of the ways to apply for a Social License to Operate.

The acceptance then refers to the goodwill of the institution and local population of the host state necessary to allow a successful mining project to be realized.

The outlined examples focus CSR policies regarding the employment of local and Indian/Afro-Colombian personnel and as examples, on the CSR policies and actions of AngloGold Ashanti Colombia.

On a global level, AngloGold Ashanti's CSR policies are guided by its Code of Business Principles and Ethics and its Community and Environment Management Standards. The Code of Business Principles and Ethics is a rather broad guidance document regarding good corporate governance and is:

> (...) is intended as a source of direction and guidance for our actions and decisions internally and in our interactions with stakeholders and the public.[52]

The "*Community and Environment Management Standards*" are substantive global guidelines for specific mining projects on how to deal with issues arising from AngloGold Ashanti's stakeholder engagement.[53]

According to AngloGold Ashanti: "*Community and Environment Management Standards* (...) *have been designed to provide clarity to commitments made in the community and environment policy as well as the company's values* (...)."[54]

Those Community and Environment Management Standards encompass many key issues of the legal framework for foreign investments in mining projects, such as land access, local employment, local procurement and even dispute resolution mechanisms.[55]

---

[52] AngloGold Ashanti (2013b).

[53] AngloGold Ashanti (2013c).

[54] AngloGold Ashanti (2013c).

[55] AngloGold Ashanti (2013c).

In its section on socio-economic contribution, the Community and Environment Management Standards refers to the employment of local/indigenous population and states that it is AngloGold Ashanti's value intention to make sure that the local communities are better off with it operating in the area than without, inter alia by actively undertaking local employment and local procurement.[56]

The global management standards include a reference to take into account the specifics of the community of each mining site managed by AngloGold Ashanti.[57]

This strategy is to be developed with the help of regularly updated studies and shall at least include: "*Local procurement objectives, targets and spend*; (...) [*and*] *Local employment strategy and associated targets.*"[58]

On a site and country level in Colombia, the broad management guidelines are then reflected in specific "*Politicas de Relacionamiento*" [Relationship Policies]. Regarding local employment and local procurement it states to prioritize for

[56] AngloGold Ashanti (2013c), p. 62; "*It is AngloGold Ashanti's value intention that the communities and societies in which the Company operates will be better off for it having been there. This is achieved through, among other things, the Company's socio-economic contribution in the host country, including economic value generation and distribution.* (...) *This approach to sustainability calls for integration of community development and economic considerations into core business decision-making. AngloGold Ashanti's value-add is implemented through,* (...), *local employment, local procurement,* (...)."; Under local employment, AngloGold Ashanti refers to: "(...) *individuals either born or who have the legal right to reside indefinitely*," and states that: "(...) *aspects of expenditure associated with local employment are* (...): *Wages and benefits paid to local employees and contractors. Total payroll, which means employees' salaries, including amounts paid to government institutions (employee taxes, levies, and unemployment funds) on behalf of employees. Total benefits, which include regular contributions (e.g. to pensions, insurance, Company vehicles, and private health), as well as other employee support such as housing, interest free loans, public transport assistance, educational grants, and redundancy payments.*" Under local procurement AngloGold Ashanti refers to and fosters: "(...) *providers of materials, products, goods and services that are based in the same geographic market as the site (i.e. excluding transnational payments).*"

[57] AngloGold Ashanti (2013c), p. 68; As the objective of its global management standards AngloGold Ashanti states that: "*sites are* [*to be*] *managed in line with the Company's vision, mission and values, and to meet the Company's Environment and Community Policy commitment to "undertake initiatives that contribute to sustainable futures in partnership with the societies in which we operate.*" This broad aim is then narrowed down so that: "*Each site, regional and country office, as appropriate, must have a strategy to address its social and economic contribution in a manner appropriate to its size and stage of development, to the nature and magnitude of its impacts, to the environmental and social context, legacy issues, scope of engagement and, availability of funds and other resources*".

[58] AngloGold Ashanti (2013c), p. 69.

employment, contracting and purchasing, the people in the communities where the mining activities are carried out[59] while maintaining competitive tender processes.[60]

---

[59] AngloGold Ashanti (2011); it states: "*La generación de riqueza e inclusión que AngloGold Ashanti Colombia de forma voluntaria hace en las comunidades, parte del inventario de la capacidad instalada con el fin de encontrar oportunidades en contratación de empresas, compras locales y empleo. Es por esto que AngloGold Ashanti Colombia ha decidido priorizar a las comunidades, los municipios y región donde se realizan sus operaciones de exploración y producción para el empleo, la contratación y las compras, priorizando al proveedor en los casos que se presenten igualdad de condiciones.*"

[The wealth generation and inclusion that AngloGold Ashanti Colombia voluntarily does in local communities originates from the available local capacity, for finding opportunities to hiring companies, local purchases and employment. It is due to this that AngloGold Ashanti Colombia has decided to prioritize for employment, contracting and purchasing, the communities, municipalities and region where their exploration and production operations are carried out, giving priority to the supplier in equality of conditions.]

"[*Eso*] *nos exige un acompañamiento permanente a los contratistas con el fin de hacer realidad con ellos la Política de Responsabilidad Social Corporativa y en particular la inclusión del Componente Local a través de la generación de oportunidades laborales y del excelente desempeño de las relaciones entre los contratistas con sus empleados, a través de procesos de búsqueda, selección, enganche, desarrollo y desvinculación transparentes, coherentes, justos y amables cumpliendo con la ley, honrando los principios y haciendo realidad la Política de Responsabilidad Social Corporativa de AngloGold Ashanti Colombia.*"

[[This] demands a permanent support of the contractors in order fulfil with them the CSR policies and particularly the "Local Component" inclusion through the generation of labour opportunities and the excellent performance of the contractor-employee relations through transparent, coherent, just, amiable and law complying processes of search, selection, connection, development and detachment, honouring the values of and fulfilling AngloGold Ashanti Colombia's CSR Policies.

> Es responsabilidad de AGAC y del contratista dar preferencia en la participación de empleo al personal de la región donde se realizan los trabajos, en igualdad de preparación, calidad de trabajo y capacidades, de acuerdo con los perfiles de cargos elaborados por el contratista. Toda vinculación de personal de las comunidades y de la región deberá hacerla AGA y el contratista bajo los parámetros establecidos por la Compañía.
>
> En la oferta se deberán entregar los perfiles de todos los cargos tanto calificados como no calificados que vayan a ser ocupados en la ejecución del contrato.

[AngloGold Ashanti Colombia and the contractors are then responsible for giving preference to employment to the personnel of the region where the operations are carried out, in equality of preparation, quality of work and capacities, in agreement with the position profiles prepared by the contractor.

All entailment of personnel of the communities and of the region will have to be carried out by AngloGold Ashanti Colombia and the contractors under the parameters established by the Company. All profiles covered under (...) the agreement should be delivered to offer positions to both, qualified and not qualified personnel.]

[60] AngloGold Ashanti (2011), p. 11; "*Una vez finalizados los contratos individuales de trabajo, el contratista evaluará a cada trabajador. También se deberán aplicar a todos los trabajadores vinculados al contrato la encuesta de satisfacción laboral. Dichas evaluaciones y encuestas deberán ser entregadas y discutidas con el gerente del contrato. Por otra parte, la adquisición local de bienes y servicios facilitan la aceptación del contratista en el área y por ende su eficiencia*

A specific challenge for AngloGold Ashanti, as well as Colombian mining industry in general, are artisanal mining activities (see supra). In its section on Artisanal and Small Scale Mining (Legal and Illegal) the Community and Environment Management Standards inter alia refer to the employment of artisanal miners as a way to respond to the challenge.[61]

It states: "*It is AngloGold Ashanti's view that the challenges of Artisanal and Small Scale Mining* ("***ASM***") *can best be addressed by adopting a multi stakeholder approach, with governments taking a lead role in addressing the issue along with artisanal miners, large-scale miners, NGOs and development agencies. In keeping with AngloGold Ashanti's values, the Company fully supports well-coordinated strategies to regulate and manage ASM where it exists.*"

AngloGold Ashanti states that: "*The objective of this management standard is to ensure that where ASM is present in our tenement or lease areas, site specific strategies are developed and implemented. These strategies will aim to enable co-existence, reduce the negative safety, security, environmental, social and health impact of ASM and promote the development of orderly, viable ASM sectors in collaboration with host communities and governments.*"[62] These strategies are to be developed with government and interested and affected parties.

The global requirements however do not address hiring of the artisanal miners, but rather addresses security measures to avoid illegal mining activities.

On a site and country level in Colombia, the broad management guidelines are then reflected in a specific paper on artisanal mining: "*Hacemos grande la pequena mineria*" [Let's make small mining big/great] which has a very different tone from the security focused global Community and Environment Management Standards.

It first acknowledges that artisanal mining has had a long history in Colombia and at the site of the new AngloGold Ashanti project.[63] It then outlines the approach of AngloGold Ashanti Colombia at its site at Gramalote en San Roque, Antioquia as

---

y rendimiento en la ejecución de los trabajos contratados, por tanto será preferible su obtención local, sin detrimento de la calidad y competitividad en precios."

[Once the individual work contract is completed, the contractor will evaluate every worker. In addition, all workers entailed to the agreement should fill out the labour satisfaction survey. The above mentioned evaluations and surveys will have to be delivered to and discussed with the manager of the contract.

Besides, the local acquisition of goods and services ease the acceptance of the contractor in the area and thus its efficiency and performance in the execution of the contracted works, therefore the local procurement will be preferable, without detriment to quality or to competitiveness in prices.]

[61] AngloGold Ashanti (2013c), p. 89; [ASM] refers to artisanal and small-scale mining as including: "(…) *any mining and or processing activities undertaken by individuals who may have formed a collective or cooperative to undertake these activities. The scale of activity can range from one individual to large collectives of hundreds or even thousands of individuals working an area with the common denominator being a low level of mechanization. Activity is often well coordinated, although it may seem informal, and is sometimes regulated by local legislation, though often the activities are unregulated.*"

[62] AngloGold Ashanti (2013c), p. 68.

[63] AngloGold Ashanti (2013a).

a 13 month negotiation process. At the end of the negotiation process, 69 of the artisanal miners became part of the workforce of AngloGold Ashanti Colombia and another 84 became suppliers to the mining project. AngloGold Ashanti Colombia claims to have provided training and professional development support for all of them. AngloGold Ashanti Colombia summarizes its local approach in Colombia stating:

> Nos comprometemos con los mineros artesanales: Los invitamos a ser parte de la industria y a mejorar su calidad de vida y el futuro de sus familias. [We are committed to the artisanal miners: We invite them to be part of the industry and improve their quality of life and the future of their families.]

11.4.3.2 Past Legal Developments and Future Political Trends

The notion of CSR has a history and dates back to the beginning of the twentieth century. It was partly based on the catholic background of Colombian businesspersons at the time.[64]

In the last decades much of the development of CSR policies and initiatives derives from the engagement of foreign investors, especially from Spain, and has been described in detail elsewhere.[65]

Besides the approach of AngloGold Ashanti outlined supra, another key example of CSR policies and projects in Colombia is the one of the mining project *Cerrejón*.

The mining project *Carbones del Cerrejón* is one of the largest open air carbon mine in the world situated at the Department La Guajira. After some merger activities the project Cerrejón is independently operated, but belongs in three equal parts to subsidiaries of BHP Billiton, Anglo American, and Glencore Xstrata.[66]

This project, well documented elsewhere,[67] was a major milestone in the development of social responsibility policies and initiatives in Colombia. It included a development plan for the Indian community in the proximity of the mining project, the "*Plan de Ayuda Integral a las Comunidades Indígenas-PAICI*" [The Plan of Integral Help to the Indigenous Communities of the companies Carbocol-Intercor] that dates back to 1982.[68]

---

[64] Gutierrez and Lobo (2007), p. 40.

[65] Pulido and Ramiro (2014), p. 106.

[66] Cerrejón (2014).

[67] Szegedy-Maszák (2008), p. 295.

[68] Szegedy-Maszák (2008), p. 305; Further analysis on CSR initiatives in Colombia can be found at: Lindgreen et al. (2010), p. 229; and specifically for the case of the energy industry: Heincke (2006).

References

AngloGold Ashanti (2011) Politica_de_relacionamiento. Available online at: http://www.anglogoldashanti.com.co/Sostenibilidad/Politicas/Politica_de_relacionamiento.pdf, updated on 7/13/2011. Last checked on 9/28/2013

AngloGold Ashanti (2012a) AngloGold Ashanti sustainability report 2012. Available online at: http://www.aga-reports.com/12/os/performance/attracting-developing-retaining-people. Last checked on 15 February 2014

AngloGold Ashanti (2012b) South Africa 2012 in summary - Integrated report 2012. Available online at: http://www.aga-reports.com/12/ir/operating-reviews/south-africa. Last checked on 15 February 2014

AngloGold Ashanti (2013a) Formalización Mineros SMGE. Available online at: http://www.anglogoldashanti.com.co/saladeprensa/Presentaciones/Formalizaci%C3%B3n%20Mineros%20SMGE.pdf, updated on 2/22/2013. Last checked on 15 February 2014

AngloGold Ashanti (2013b) Code of business principles and ethics. Available online at: http://www.anglogoldashanti.com/NR/rdonlyres/A8D58370-3B9E-4064-AE1F-A97A3ECB5B92/0/COE_A4ENGLISH.pdf, updated on 9/20/2013. Last checked on 15 February 2014

AngloGold Ashanti (2013c) Community and environment management standards. Available online at: http://www.anglogoldashanti.com/NR/rdonlyres/91825948-F0BF-40CA-AA0E-D43024F2DD26/0/CommunityandEnvironmentManagementStandards.pdf, updated on 9/20/2013. Last checked on 15 February 2014

AngloGold Ashanti (2014) The AngloGold Ashanti Fund and Trust empowering people. Available online at: http://www.anglogold.com/subwebs/informationforinvestors/reporttosociety06/AGA-fund.htm. Last checked on 15 February 2014

Bauman T, Glick L (eds) (2012) The limits of change. Mabo and native title 20 years on. Canberra, A.C.T: AIATSIS

BDO (2013) The New Companies Act 2008 - what you need to know. Edited by BDO. Available online at: http://www.bdo.co.za/displaycontent.asp?contentpageid=505, updated on 12/31/2013

Cerrejón (2014) Our Company. Available online at: http://www.cerrejon.com/site/english/our-company.aspx. Last checked on 29 September 2013

Commission of the European Communities (2001) Green paper on: "Promoting a European framework for corporate social responsibility". Brussels. Available online at: http://eur-lex.europa.eu/LexUriServ/site/en/com/2001/com2001_0366en01.pdf. Last checked on 15 February 2014

Coronado G, Fallon W (2010) Giving with one hand. On the mining sector's treatment of Indigenous stakeholders in the name of CSR. Int J Sociol Soc Policy 30:666–682

Crush J, Williams V (2006) Migration in South Africa. Available online at: http://www.iom.int/jahia/webdav/site/myjahiasite/shared/shared/mainsite/policy_and_research/gcim/rs/RS7.pdf, updated on 11/10/2006. Last checked on 1/6/2014

Diniz V (2013) Corporate social responsibility: benefiting miners and communities. In Resource Investing News, 8/29/2013. Available online at: http://resourceinvestingnews.com/60425-corporate-social-responsibility-benefiting-miners-and-communities.html?utm_source=Resource+Investing+News&utm_campaign=f7c246ca8c-RSS_EMAIL_CAMPAIGN&utm_medium=email&utm_term=0_f83d87db0f-f7c246ca8c-248794225. Last checked on 15 February 2014

Fig D (2005) Manufacturing amnesia: corporate social responsibility in South Africa. Int Aff 81(3):599–617. doi:10.1111/j.1468-2346.2005.00471.x

Fulcher J (2012) The social license to operate: how do I get mine granted? Paper presented at the 2012 conference the Australian Petroleum Production and Exploration Association on 15 May 2012 in Adelaide, South Australia. Available online at: http://www.appeaconference.com.au/2012/images/Documents/APPEA%202012%20Final%20Program.pdf. Last checked on 15 February 2014

Gutierrez R, Lobo ID (2007) Corporate social engagement in Colombia. Soc Responsibility J 3 (1):40–51. doi:10.1108/17471117200700005

Heincke M (2006) Sustainable development, corporate social responsibility and oil. The case of BP in the complex political games of Colombia. Library and Archives Canada = Bibliothèque et Archives Canada (Canadian theses = Thèses canadiennes), Ottawa

Kloppers H, du Plessis W (2008) Corporate social responsibility, legislative reforms and mining in South Africa. J Energy Nat Resour Law 26:91–119

Lindgreen A, Córdoba J-R, Maon F, Mendoza JM (2010) Corporate social responsibility in Colombia: making sense of social strategies. J Bus Ethics 91(S2):229–242. doi:10.1007/s10551-010-0616-9

Nelsen JL (2006) Social license to operate. Int J Mining Reclam Environ 20(3):161–162. doi:10.1080/17480930600804182

Pulido A, Ramiro P (2014) La Responsabilidad Social Corporativa de las Multinacionales Espanoles en Colombia. Available online at: http://web.usbmed.edu.co/usbmed/elagora/htm/v10nro1/pdf/7.pdf. Last checked on 15 February 2014

Ramlall S (2012) Corporate social responsibility in post-Apartheid South Africa. Soc Responsibility J 8(2):270–288. doi:10.1108/17471111211234888

Rio Tinto (2014a) Rio Tinto communities and social performance - a discussion paper. Available online at: Provided by Bruce Harvey

Rio Tinto (2014b) Communities. Available online at: http://www.riotinto.com/ourcommitment/sthash.OE9bkXaO.dpuf. Last checked on 15 February 2014

Rio Tinto (2014c) Our approach. Available online at: http://www.riotinto.com/ourcommitment/our-approach-4802.aspx. Last checked on 15 February 2014

Szegedy-Maszák I (2008) Corporate social responsibility, the example of the mining project Cerrejón and its relation with the Indigenous group Wayüu in Colombia. In Vniversitas Bogota 117, pp 295–322. Available online at: http://www.scielo.org.co/pdf/vniv/n117/n117a12.pdf. Last checked on 15 February 2014

Thomson I (2012) The social license to operate. Available online at: http://socialicense.com/index.html, updated on 6/16/2012. Last checked on 15 February 2014

UNAIDS (2013) Employers' handbook on HIV/AIDS. Edited by UNAIDS. Available online at: http://www.unaids.org/en/media/unaids/contentassets/dataimport/publications/irc-pub02/jc767-employershandbook_en.pdf, updated on 12/31/2013. Last checked on 15 February 2014

Ward H (2014) Public sector roles in strengthening corporate social responsibility: taking stock. Available online at: http://pubs.iied.org/pdfs/16014IIED.pdf. Last checked on 15 February 2014

Chapter 12
Summary, Comparison and Analysis

This section will summarize the results from the analysed jurisdictions, compare the findings and analyse similarities, differences, and key developments and trends in the legal frameworks for foreign investments in mining projects in Australia, South Africa and Colombia (section 12.1–12.10). In Chapter 13 it will finally be described whether these specific legal challenges can sufficiently be analysed by the legal framework provided for by general foreign investment law.

12.1 Admission of Foreign Investment

The control of the admission of foreign investment provides a flexible tool for national governments. Depending on the necessity of attracting foreign technical expertise and capital for their national mining industry, governments choose to opt for a restrictive or an open approach towards foreign investment.

Australia has developed a specific and complex legal screening process dealing with the admission of foreign investment.

The "*national interest test*" gives the Treasurer a high level of discretion. The Treasurer is solely responsible for making decisions about the admission of foreign investment. He is guided by the Foreign Investment Review Board. Judicial review of his decisions is limited.

The competition law regime has overlapping power of control, but executes those powers in coordination with the foreign investment screening process.

The legal screening process has not changed substantially over the last decades, but the way "*national interest*" is interpreted by different governments differs.

Political and public controversies are frequent and show periodic community resentment to a high level of foreign investment. Nonetheless, very few foreign investment proposals have been turned down.

R.W. Roeder, *Foreign Mining Investment Law*, DOI 10.1007/978-3-319-31217-0_12

In the Apartheid period South Africa did not have a restrictive policy or a screening process in place, but foreign investment was scarce due to anti-Apartheid boycotts and the Apartheid legislation that discouraged investors.

Nevertheless in post-Apartheid South Africa, a specific legal screening process dealing with the admission of foreign investment into South Africa has not been established either.

The admission of foreign investment is only regulated via the administration of exchange controls. Regarding foreign investment, it is stated that non-residents may freely invest in South Africa. Political controversies rather touch upon how to better attract, than how to avoid foreign investment.

A certain amount of control and discretion can be executed via the South African competition law regime that includes goals such as the promotion of employment, social, economic welfare and the redistribution of ownership to historically disadvantaged persons.

Decisions under the competition law regime are open to judicial review by South African courts.

The Colombian regime regarding foreign investment was very protective before the 1990s. The former regime included a very detailed list of indicators that the decision makers had to take into account, e.g. the effect on Colombian employment and the inclusion of national investors. This approach has changed substantially towards a very liberal legal regime.

A specific legal screening process dealing with the admission of foreign investment into Colombia does not exist. The mining code specifically guarantees foreign investors the same rights as Colombian investors enjoy.

A certain amount of control and discretion can be executed via the Colombian competition law regime, but mining specific laws declare foreign investors to be equal to national investors, reducing the probability of the competition law regime to be used as an indirect foreign investment screening process.

Political controversies instead touch upon how to better attract rather than how to avoid foreign investment.

Australia is the only country of those examined in this work to have a specific screening process dealing with the admission of foreign investment; this includes the nebulous "*national interest*" as a basis of determination. This screening process provides the government of Australia a high level of power and discretion when deciding whether to admit foreign investment into the Australian mining sector or not.

During the Apartheid period, South Africa did not have a restrictive policy or a screening process in place, yet struggled to attract foreign investments due to the Apartheid regime. In post-Apartheid South Africa a specific legal screening process dealing with the admission of foreign investment into South Africa was not introduced, despite an increase in foreign investments.

In Colombia a screening process comparable to the one in Australia was in place before the 1990s. To attract more foreign investment Colombia decided to abolish it.

Australia also has the only official specific "*foreign investment policy*", whereas the foreign investment policies of South Africa and Colombia need to be ascertained from statements of politicians, legislative remarks and statements of investment agencies.

While the respective regulatory regimes differ substantially, ranging from the highly regulated approach of Australia to the nearly non-existent regulatory regimes in South Africa and Colombia, the difference for foreign investors is marginal. All three analysed countries welcome foreign investment. This holds true even for the Australia, which despite the rather careful Australian mindset with respect to foreign, especially Asian influence into the countries affairs, has in fact turned down very few investment proposals for international mining projects.

By formulating a more open or stricter policy and a more liberal or rigid screening process in regards to the admission of foreign investments in the mining sector countries position themselves according to their self-perceived or factual strength as a player on the global minerals market. The weaker their self-perceived or factual strength as a player on the global minerals market, the more open their policy and the more liberal their screening process in regards to the admission of foreign investments in the mining sector tends to be. The stronger their self-perceived or factual strength as a player on the global minerals market, the stricter their policy and the more rigid their screening process in regards to the admission of foreign investments in the mining sector tends to be.

As the Australian example, specifically in regards to the interpretation of "*national interest*" shows, such assessment is quickly modified in the light of current economic and political developments.

12.2 Corporate Structure

In all three analysed countries, a foreign investor will find broadly similar corporate structure requirements. Global corporate law developments and national adoption in Australia, South Africa and Colombia have led to a legal framework that provides a choice of a foreign investor between establishing various forms of national subsidiaries, incorporating a joint-venture with a local partner or to conclude contractual arrangements such as farm-in agreements and unincorporated joint-ventures.

To conduct business in Australia as a foreign investor is to establish an own Australian legal entity, e.g. in the form of a subsidiary, to form a joint-venture with a local partner in the form of a incorporated joint-venture or to register itself as a foreign legal entity and then conclude contractual arrangements such as a farm-in agreement or an unincorporated Joint-Venture. No foreign legal entity may conduct business without such registration.

There is no requirement to include state or local ownership when structuring the mining project and nationalization of the mining industry is not a regular topic of debate.

The most common corporate structure for mining projects in South Africa are joint ventures, South African subsidiaries, a branch office or farm-in agreements.

A company must register itself within 20 business days after it first begins to conduct business.

There is no requirement to include state ownership when structuring the mining project, but the Broad-Based Black Economic Empowerment legislation requires 26 % ownership by Historically Disadvantaged South Africans.

There is a requirement to apply for Ministerial consent when transferring certain types of shares of unlisted companies. That might be expanded to listed companies under the new MPRDA 2002 Amendment Bill 2011.

There is furthermore a continuous and highly emotional nationalization debate in South Africa that specifically aims at the mining industry.

The most common corporate structure for mining projects in Colombia are joint ventures, Colombian subsidiaries, a branch office or farm-in agreements.

A representative domiciled in Colombia suffices to present and transact proposals. For the execution of a mining project a joint venture, Colombian subsidiary or a branch office needs to be established and/or registered. The latest development was the establishment of the simplified share corporation, that reduced formalities and has proven highly attractive.

There is no requirement to allow state or local ownership when structuring the mining project. Nationalization of the mining industry was a topic of debate in the early 1990s, but ended with the privatization of the majority of the remaining state-owned companies.

In Australia and South Africa the corporate law is the key guidance for the foreign investor. South Africa additionally uses corporate law to control the ownership of mining tenements. Only the mining code of Colombia specifically addresses corporate structure requirements in more detail before referring to the Colombian Corporate Law.

Differences between the three countries are clearly visible regarding the requirement to register a foreign legal entity with the respective administration before conducting business. While South Africa allows for 20 business days of non-registered business activity, Australia requires registration before business is conducted. With its demand that a foreign investor is to register his business activities before even conducting any form of business, Australia has established tight control over foreign investors. To explain the registration requirement in Australia as a general adversity against foreign influence falls short of reality. Australia provides for a very efficient, transparent and fast administration which does make it possible to register planned business activities online and from abroad or via a local agent.

Colombia differentiates between presenting and transacting proposals on the one hand, and other business activity on the other. Colombia and South Africa cannot provide the same level of administrative efficiency—the more relaxed approach to foreigners conducting business in the country without registration might therefore originate from practical necessity.

In both Colombia and Australia, there are no requirements to include the state or locals in the ownership of a mining company. In South Africa there is a requirement to establish a minimum of 26 % ownership for Historically Disadvantaged South Africans. The enforcement of this policy has become more rigid in the course since the end of Apartheid.

For foreign investors, especially those entering the South African mining industry for the first time, the 26 % HDSA ownership requirement and its wide acceptance might be surprising. This requirement can be explained taking into account the unique political history of South Africa. The corporate law consent requirements for the transfer of shares can be explained in the light of the B-BBEE ownership goals. The Ministerial consent gives the South African government another tool to achieve its B-BBEE goals.

While not directly comparable, it should be noted though that both Australia (Indigenous Australians) and Colombia (Indians/Afro-Colombians) also have marginalized groups within their societies that demand for a greater stake in the national wealth. While the topic is addressed in various aspects in Australia and Colombia as well a requirement for ownership has not yet been established.

The nationalization debate is heated in South Africa, but nearly non-existent in Colombia and Australia. It can be argued that this difference comes from the fact that the marginalized group in South Africa, the HDSAs, are the majority in their country, whereas in Australia and Colombia the marginalized groups are only a relatively small portion of the overall population.

Countries introduce corporate structures to enable and order economic activities in their respective mining sectors.

By formulating a strict or less strict registration requirement and respective process in regards to economic activities in the mining sector, countries position themselves according to their self-perceived or factual strength as a player on the global minerals market while acknowledging their internal regulatory power.

Australia and South Africa can regulate and are regulating every kind of mining activity in their countries and are able to enforce corporate structure requirements on every foreign investor and citizen. In the case of South Africa this goes so far as to require a minimum of 26 % ownership for Historically Disadvantaged South Africans.

Colombia does only have limited control over parts of its country and therefore allows its citizens to conduct artisanal and small-scale mining without enforced corporate structure requirements. To make themselves more attractive for foreign investors they also facilitate such foreign investments by requiring only a very informal registration requirement.

12.3 Ownership of Minerals and Mineral Rights

Australia, South Africa and Colombia have all opted for the supremacy of state ownership over minerals and mineral rights. In all three cases private ownership of mineral rights was recognized in the past, but has been diminished in the case of Australia and Colombia or extinguished completely in the case of South Africa.

In Australia the ownership of minerals and mineral rights is—with very limited exceptions—vested with the "*Crown*". The Crown refers to the governing political entity, in the case of Queensland, Australia, the State of Queensland, Australia.

Deriving from its British history, gold and silver have long been considered royal minerals and the property of the Crown, whereas private ownership of e.g. coal was common. Over the course of several legislative measures, the ownership of minerals and mineral rights was transferred to the state, with only very few private mineral rights remaining. The next generation of rights regarding the use of the subsoil, the potential to use geothermal energy and greenhouse gas storage reservoirs, has already been declared the property of the state.

In South Africa, mineral resources are considered to be the common heritage of all the people of South Africa with the State acting as its custodian. The principle of custodianship is a topic of complex legal debate, but for a foreign investor it is comparable to a situation where there is only a state ownership of minerals and mineral rights.

Private mineral rights ownership was possible before 2002 and had a long history. But with the MPRDA 2002 all private mineral ownership rights ceased to exist after a transformation period. The transformation period did not allow the re-registration of private ownership of minerals, but could be used to acquire a license for the use of minerals under the new regime on the basis of private mineral ownership as stipulated under the old regime.

The change of the structure of mineral rights ownership in South Africa brought by the MPRDA 2002 has been claimed to constitute expropriation, but the Constitutional Court declared it to be a form of non-expropriatory transformation.

In Colombia, with very few exceptions, all minerals are exclusively owned by the State. While the Mining Law 2001 recognizes the possibility of private mineral rights ownership, it attempts to abolish it step-by-step by extinguishing unused private mineral rights and acquiring them for the state. No compensation is paid for private mineral rights that are extinguished and become state owned mineral rights. The situation has been legally stable for some time and signs of change are not visible as the new bill does not substantially alter the approach to mineral right ownership.

The supremacy of state ownership of minerals and mineral rights signifies that foreign investors will have to deal directly with the state when aiming to utilize the economic potential of natural resources of the respective country.

While Australia and Colombia have a long-standing history of supremacy of state ownership over minerals with only limited exceptions, South Africa has made the strongest shift towards the supremacy of state ownership over minerals and mineral right: from the 1991 mining law that attempted to effectively privatize mineral rights it transitioned to the MPRDA 2002 that established the custodianship over natural resources by the state of South Africa. This can be explained by reference to the history of Apartheid in South Africa and the structure of the ownership of private mineral rights that was constituted by white people. The MPRDA 2002 aimed not only to manage the natural resources of South Africa in the best way possible, but also to promote equitable access to the nation's mineral resources and specifically to expand opportunities for Historically Disadvantaged South Africans.

As the development in South Africa shows the question of who owns the minerals of a country and who has the right to profit from the mineral wealth lies at the heart of the power relationship between the various types of actors within a nation, e.g. the wealthy vs. the poor, but also reflects the power relationship between foreign actors, such as foreign investors and the national government. Whether or not the sovereignty over natural resources of a nations which is reflected in such ownership questions is permanent and impermeable or not is the subject of current academic debate.[1] The analysis of Australia, South Africa and Colombia points towards a gradually increased acknowledgement and realization of such sovereignty over natural resources by nation states.

12.4 Mining Licenses

Queensland, Australia, provides a distinct license for the exploration phase—the exploration permit—and the production phase—the mining lease. The cyclic character of the commodities industry and the possibility of delay between exploration and production is addressed by the availability of a retention license—the mineral development license.

Concerning the question of granting licenses on a first come first serve basis vs. a competitive application process Queensland, Australia, has decided to opt towards the latter, including qualitative criteria such as minimum spending requirements as well as a cash-bidding component in some tenders for high quality resources.

Considering the question of security of tenure the holder of the exploration permit is granted priority over all other persons when applying for the grant of a mineral development license or a mining lease.

State agreements are another way to enhance security of tenure and expedite the licensing process. Those agreements become law by enactment by parliament and can help to provide a secure legal framework for investors. Nevertheless they were frequent until the 1970s, but have not been used in Queensland, Australia, since. They are still commonly used in one of Australia's other large mining states, Western Australia.

[1] Bungenberg and Hobe (2015).

The compulsory acquisition of mining tenures when the administration takes the underlying land and designates it to another purpose provides uncertainty for investors, especially as the compensation mechanism does not take into account the economic value of the mining asset, but only pays for expenses accrued.

There are no specific provisions for Indigenous Australians regarding a specific right to directly participate in the exploration of natural resources themselves.

The Commonwealth of Australia and especially Queensland has seen several changes in the management of their natural resources in the past decades. The "*Modernizing Queensland Resource Acts Program*" and the federal elections on September 9th, 2013 that led to a change in government from labour to liberal indicate that further changes are to come.

South Africa provides distinct licenses for the exploration phase—the prospecting right—and the production phase—the mining right. The cyclic character of the commodities industry and the possibility of delay between exploration and production is addressed by the availability of a retention license—the retention permit.

Concerning the question of granting licenses on a first come first serve basis vs. a competitive application process South Africa has opted towards the former with the exception that when two applications are entered at the same time preference is to be given to applications from Historically Disadvantaged South Africans.

Considering the question of security of tenure, the holder of a prospecting right is entitled to apply for and be granted a mining right in respect of the mineral and prospecting area in question without discretionary power of the Minister to be exercised.

Security of tenure was touched upon by statements of high-ranking ANC officials who have threatened that mining companies misrepresenting their economic "*intentions*" could have their licenses revoked.

The latest amendments to the MPRDA 2002 introduced competitive elements in the process of granting a prospecting right or transforming a prospecting right into a mining right, touching on both the first come first serve basis and security of tenure. But those recent changes are already reconsidered in the light of allegedly increased possibilities of corruption and litigation and a new Amendment Bill is already in the parliamentary process.

Colombia does not distinguish between the exploration and the production phase, but provides one single and all-encompassing license—the "*mining concession*". The cyclic character of the commodities industry and the possibility of delay between exploration and production is addressed by the availability of prolonging the timeframe of the concession agreement rather than by a retention permit.

Regarding the question of granting licenses on a first come first serve basis vs. a competitive application process, under the Mining Law 2001 Colombia chose to decide applications on a first come first serve basis.

The Mining Law 2010 introduced a competitive element into the application process, but was declared unconstitutional. Law 1440 of 2011 then reintroduced the possibility of a tender process.

The Mining Law 2010 furthermore attempted to take the tension out of the topic of artisanal mining by halting criminal prosecution against artisanal miners who with their activities exceeded the limits set by article 152 of the Mining Law 2001. For foreign investors the status of local miners that are tolerated to mine on the premises of a valid mining license of the foreign investor will remain to be a challenge and requires careful negotiations.

Some mining areas are declared as specific Indian or Afro-Colombian mining zones where those groups will be given exclusivity, priority or support to conduct mining activities.

When governments grant a mining license, they exercise their sovereignty over the management of their natural resources. The mining license regimes allow host states to fine tune the legal framework for foreign investments in mining projects.

Queensland, Australia, and South Africa leave themselves two possibilities for intervention by granting a distinct license for each the exploration and the production phase. They assure "*priority*" in Queensland, Australia, or "*entitlement*" in South Africa to the holder of the exploration license to apply for and be granted a production license in respect of the area of the exploration license. Queensland, Australia, and South Africa undertake a second technical, legal and environmental screening process of the mining project before granting the production license for the mining project.

Colombia has opted for a mining concession that resembles a one stop shop and all-encompassing exploration and production license and therefore for a relatively higher level of security of tenure for investors.

All three countries include a form of retention license in their mining license management system, in the case of Columbia by prolonging the mining concession.

Queensland, Australia, South Africa and Colombia have developed their mining license management systems from a first come first served basis to include various forms of competitive application elements. Those elements include qualitative elements such as the best technical, environmental, socio-economic project plans as well as quantitative criteria, such as a cash component. This allows countries to optimize the economic, environmental and socio-economic results of foreign investment in mining projects. While in Queensland, Australia, and Colombia the introduction of those elements is generally accepted, the South African opposition heavily criticizes them as opening the gates for corruption.

Queensland, Australia, and South Africa only recognize mining to be legal under a mining license and consider all other forms of mining illegal. In Colombia the situation is more complex because artisanal and small-scale mining is a common occurrence. Colombia differentiates between legal mining under a mining license, legal artisanal and small-scale mining without a mining license and illegal mining without a mining license.

Throughout this work, it has been shown that the three countries have various approaches in dealing with their local/indigenous/marginalized populations. Only Colombia has chosen to have them participate directly in the mineral wealth of the nation by granting them priority in mining concessions or allowing them to undertake non-licensed small-scale mining to finance their livelihood.

South Africa has provisions to give priority to HDSAs when two applications compete. Queensland, Australia, has no specific provisions for the granting of mining licenses to Indigenous Australians.

While the question of ownership of Minerals and Mineral Rights determines the question of distribution of the mineral wealth between the state and private actors on a general level, the mining licenses regime determines which of the private actors may undertake mining activities. Furthermore, mining licences allow the government to establish conditions for the grant of such mining license, such as minimum spending requirements or similar. If the state decides to opt for a competitive process, the mining licences also provide a source of additional income for the state. Again and again the cyclic nature of the mining industry is reflected in the applicable law: The distinction between a specific exploration license and a production license as well as the creation of a retention license is the now seemingly common approach to tackle the cycle nature. The two/three-step approach is not only a result of the economic conditions—in the e.g. 25 year life-span of a mining project governments might change several times and might have different priorities in regards to the use of mineral resources of a nation. From the analysed it can be said that mining is a heavily regulated industry. The situation in Colombia in regards to artisanal and small-scale mining seems simply a result of the fact that the national government does not have control over certain areas and mining activities—and rather legalizes them then to create an enforcement gap that would show its weakness. This also explains why the Mining Law has to emphasize that the right to explore and exploit the mines of State's ownership can only be given by the State itself with the exceptions of artisanal and small-scale mining and by terms provided in the mining concession granted—a notion that seems self-evident to the regulators of Australia and South Africa. South Africa and Colombia also use mining licences to specifically support their HDSAs or local/indigenous population. The grant of mining licences therefore also is a tool for governments to foster the economic prosperity of certain parts of their population.

12.5 Land Access

The question of land access to prepare and conduct mining activities has to be asked in relation to the owner of the land, Indigenous Australians, HDSAs/Tribal Authorities, Indian-/Afro-Colombians and in relation to local government.

12.5.1 *The Relationship of the Foreign Investor with the Owner of the Land*

The foreign investor will have to negotiate with the land owner to be allowed on the land of the mining license. The land access framework of Queensland, Australia, provides a complex framework that outlines detailed steps in the development of the relationship between foreign investors and land owners that usually ends with a compensation agreement.

Land owners do not have a veto against the access to land by mining companies and such veto was not even mentioned in a recent review of the applicable Land Access framework, although it was being publicly discussed beforehand.

Compensation is to be paid to the land owner by the mining company. The value of such compensation is based upon the disturbance of the usual use of the land and is not related to the mineral wealth in the subsoil of the land.

If settlement in the form of a compensation agreement cannot be reached, a judicial decision can be sought and enforced. Awarded compensation also takes into account the time needed for negotiations by land owners.

Land access has been and increasingly is a heated topic of debate. Uncommonly, conservative farmers and young political activists unite in campaigns such as "*Lock the Gate*", mainly aiming to stop or slow down the coal seam gas industry.

While most provisions regarding coal seam gas are found in the Petroleum and Gas (Production and Safety) Act 2004, provisions can also be found in the MRA 1989. As there is one common land access framework, any changes in legislation will impact on foreign investment in mining projects as well.

Land access is not dealt with in a separate common land access framework, but—regarding mining projects—is regulated in the South African Mining Code.

Land owners do not have a veto against the access to their land by mining companies, nor have they held such a right in the past. Under the Apartheid Mining Law of 1991 the land owner did have to convince the Minister that he is likely to suffer loss or damage as a result of the mining project before he could force the investor into negotiations. Under the MPRDA 2002 the investor has to negotiate with the land owner to be allowed on the land of the mining license.

Compensation must be paid if the land owner has suffered or is likely to suffer loss or damage as a result of the mining project. If such an agreement cannot be reached, the mining license holder has to approach the Regional Manager for help. The Regional Manager in turn requests and aids the parties to reach a settlement. If this does not suffice, the question is decided by arbitration or by a court. If the Regional Manager determines that further negotiations affect the objects of MPRDA 2002 he may recommend to the Minister that the land be expropriated or to stop further activities by the mineral license holder altogether. Post-Apartheid land reforms require investors to carefully study who the actual owner of land is and take into account restitution claims.

Land access is not dealt with in a separate common land access framework, but—regarding mining projects—is regulated in the Colombian Mining Code. Land owners do not have a veto against access to land by mining companies but the foreign investor will have to negotiate with the land owner to be allowed on the land of the mining license. Compensation must be paid for the disturbance of the usual use of the land and is not related to the mineral wealth in the subsoil of the land.

If such an agreement is not achieved, the mining concession holder can have the question of access and compensation determined by a court process. The Mining Law specifically allows for expropriation of the land in question in order to move forward with the mining project as another option.

Land access is a crucial topic for mining projects and a much-discussed political topic. Notwithstanding how detailed the frameworks for land access are—all three countries demand of the mining license holder that they negotiate with the land owner before land access rights are granted and mining activities can be commenced.

Land access is regulated in the respective mining codes of Queensland, Australia, Colombia and South Africa. In South Africa, the Regional Manager aids the parties to determine the terms of land access. In Queensland, Australia, mediators support the negotiations. Expropriation as a means of solving the dispute is specifically recognized in the mining law of South Africa and Colombia, but not in Queensland, Australia.

None of the three jurisdictions provide land owners with a veto against access to land by the holder of a valid mining license. This can be understood to be an expression of the notion that mining is the "*best*" use of land. Whether or not the owner of the land will agree that mining activities on his land are indeed the "*best*" use will certainly always be influenced by the way the owner of the land participates in the revenues from the mining and the decision making process that led to it. Analysing the developments it seems that the owner of the land is more and more involved in both. The recently published detailed Land Access framework in Australia is an indicator of such development.

12.5.2 The Relationship of the Foreign Investor with Indigenous Australians, HDSAs/Tribal Authorities, Indian-/Afro-Colombians

In relation to Indigenous Australians, a specific legal framework that regulates the relationship between foreign investors and Indigenous Australians exists in the form of the Native Title Act 1994. In Australia, native title is recognized in the form of a process for the recognition of customary title of Indigenous Australians to the land.

Indigenous Australians do not generally possess a veto against access to their land, but the investor will have to enter into negotiations over a native title agreement before entering the land for mining purposes.

Such an agreement will include compensation for the disturbance of the usual use of the land, but does not to reflect the valuation of the mineral wealth in the subsoil of the land. Native title agreements may include provisions on further topics, e.g. indigenous employment in the mining workforce. If agreement cannot be reached, the National Native Title Tribunal supports the negotiation e.g. by mediation and—if necessary—by handing down arbitral decisions.

With the end of Apartheid and homeland policies in South Africa, specific rules on land access to areas with predominantly HDSAs eased to exist. *De iure* negotiations with tribal authorities do not differ from the land access regime described supra. De facto, the negotiation will have to address the various interests in the tribe, as some tribes do not have individual, but rather collective ownership structures.

Compensation must be paid if the tribal land owner has suffered or is likely to suffer loss or damage as a result of the mining project.

If such an agreement cannot be reached, the mining license holder has to approach the Regional Manager for help. The Regional Manager in turn requests and helps the parties to reach a settlement. If this does not suffice, the question is decided by arbitration or by court.

There are no specific provisions for land access for Colombian Indians/Afro-Colombians, but they can regulate access to their land for mining purposes via the protection of the specific Indian/Afro-Colombian mining zones.

The Colombian Mining Law provides for Indian/Afro-Colombian groups' precedence for the grant of mining concessions. This forces foreign investors into negotiations with the Indian/Afro-Colombian groups if they wish to exploit the natural resources of a declared Indian/Afro-Colombian zone. This amounts to a veto right of Indian/Afro-Colombian mining communities in their respective zones.

Regarding the relationship with Indigenous Australians, HDSAs/Tribal Authorities and Indian/Afro-Colombians, the regimes between Australia, South Africa and Colombia differ substantially.

In Australia a formal recognition of the customary title rights of Indigenous Australians exists in the form of Native Title. Land access to areas where a native title group has rights is underpinned by a specific legal framework that must be followed.

In South Africa with the end of Apartheid and the end of homeland policies, specific rules regulating land access to areas with predominantly HDSAs ceased to exist. De iure negotiations with tribal authorities do not differ from the land access regime described supra. De facto, the negotiation will have to address the various interests in the tribe as some tribes do not have individual, but rather collective ownership structures.

In Colombia, no specific framework for land access regarding Colombian Indians/Afro-Colombians is in place, but Colombian Indians/Afro-Colombians can indirectly influence access to their land via the Indian/Afro-Colombian mining zones regime explained supra.

If an area has been recognized as specific Indian-/Afro-Colombian mining zones, Indian-/Afro-Colombians have the power to veto mining activities in their respective Indian-/Afro-Colombian mining zone.

Indigenous Australians, HDSAs/Tribal Authorities, Indian-/Afro-Colombians were or are some of the weakest members of their respective nations. The preferential treatment of these groups by law is an attempt to level the playing field in relation to the economic power of some of the key actors in the global mining industry. The veto provided to the Indian-/Afro-Colombians is rather the exception than the rule, and is itself limited to specific Indian-/Afro-Colombian mining zones. For a foreign investor the relationship to Indigenous Australians, HDSAs/Tribal Authorities, Indian-/Afro-Colombians is crucial, as many of the mining activities are in remote areas and populated (only) by Indigenous Australians, HDSAs/Tribal Authorities, Indian-/Afro-Colombians. A mining license granted by the central authority as explained supra might be a start, but by no means sufficient to undertake mining activities. The increased global media attention to the treatment of Indigenous Australians, HDSAs/Tribal Authorities, Indian-/Afro-Colombians is likely to lead to further importance of these relationships.

12.5.3 The Relationship of the Foreign Investor with Local Governments

In Queensland, Australia, local governments generally have the authority to develop regional plans regarding the use of the land of municipalities. Therefore mining licenses granted under the MRA 1989 on the one side and regional plans decided upon by local municipalities and their planning authority under local planning laws may collide. In Queensland, Australia, it is regulated that mining licenses prevail over planning instruments.

In South Africa, mining licenses granted under the MPRDA 2002 on the one side and local municipalities and their planning authority under local planning laws on the other side may collide. The national mining license does not include the local planning authority, giving the municipality a form of a veto against mining activities in their area unless their conditions are met.

Recent court cases have reaffirmed this position, but also triggered discussions on streamlining the applications to allow for a "*one-stop-one-window*" approach, at least for foreign investors.

In Colombia, local governments generally have the authority to develop plans regarding the management of their local premises. Therefore mining concessions granted under the Mining Law 2001 on the one side and local municipalities and their planning authority under local planning laws may collide. In Colombia it is regulated that national mining concessions and planning decisions prevail, but there are demands to strengthen the power of the local governments.

In Australia, South Africa and Colombia alike, local governments generally have the authority over the management of their local affairs.

In Queensland, Australia, and Colombia it is regulated that national and state mining licenses/concessions decisions prevail over local authority planning decisions. In Colombia, there are demands to strengthen the power of the local governments. In South Africa national mining laws and local planning laws coexist, creating—at least for the time being—a situation where a foreign investor will have to deal with two regulatory bodies that have power over the question whether or not a mining project can be realized in a specific area.

Foreign investment in mining projects used to be an affair between international mining companies and national governments. A common trend is the empowerment of the local population and municipal bodies due to an increase in the bargaining power via land access provisions and public awareness.

Municipal bodies are still overruled by state or national decision making processes in Queensland, Australia, and Colombia, but not in South Africa. The power given to South African municipalities via the Land Use and Planning Act might set a precedent.

The fact that mining licenses overrule local building permits and other planning tools once again reflects the idea that mining is the "best" use of the land. As with major energy projects, such as nuclear power plants and other major infrastructure projects the benefit of the project often leaves the area, whereas the disturbance of the land will be closely related to the mining site. The latest decision in South Africa to empower local governance might develop into a trend, creating a situation where a foreign investor will have to deal not only with the national government, but also with the local authorities.

Taking into account the development of the relationship of a foreign investor with the owner of the land, Indigenous Australians, HDSAs/Tribal Authorities, Indian-/Afro-Colombians and local governments a trend of empowerment of further stakeholders and affected individuals and communities can be seen—hinting towards an even more complex legal structure to deal with for foreign investors in order to successfully realize their mining projects.

12.6 Performance Requirements

In this work performance requirements refer to and focus on whether or not and to what extent a foreign investor is required to hire local/indigenous/Indian/HDSA employees. Whilst not de jure, this de facto includes the closely related visa regime and preferential procurement policies as well as local processing requirements.

There is no specific legislation in place that obliges mining companies to hire or train local/indigenous Australians as a local performance requirement.

It has become best practise to hire Indigenous Australians in areas that include a population of Indigenous Australians as not doing so could anger the local/

indigenous population and potentially disturb the smooth progression of the project. Thus, a de facto performance requirement was established.

Australia is reviewing its visa regime for skilled overseas workers and is discussing a limitation of the numbers. A limitation of the available visa numbers may lead to a de facto requirement to hire local employees when trying to realize mining projects.

Australia introduced legislation regarding preferential procurement for Indigenous Australian businesses. It is however not an active obligation to preferentially procure, but only a passive alteration of the laws to allow for preferential procurement against competition law barriers.

A recent development, but possibly a singular event regarding performance requirements was the obligation to build production sites close to a mining project in order to be awarded the mining license, e.g. in form of a development requirement stipulated in the conditions of the mining license.

Two decades after the end of the Apartheid regime South Africa has yet to cope with the inequality established under the Apartheid regime. Broad-Based Black Economic Empowerment, the policy addressing the inequality aims to increase effective and broad-based participation of black people in the South African economy.

The Constitution of South Africa, the South African Mining Law, the Mining Charter and several further laws set up specific rules on the employment and training of Historically Disadvantaged South Africans. A quota of 40 % of HDSA employees not only in the low income type of positions, but also in the management is to be achieved by 2014, clearly restricting the choice of a foreign investor whether to hire local personnel or not.

The South African visa regime is not specifically discussed as a bottleneck, but migrant workers are a topic of political debate.

An active preferential procurement policy favours companies with a high B-BBEE rating in public tenders. This procurement framework also has effects on private tenders, as companies can gain points towards their B-BBEE rating by procuring from companies with a high B-BBEE ranking themselves.

Building production facilities close to the mining project is favoured by the South African government, but no specific requirements could be found in mining licenses awarded or tendered.

Prior mining laws used to set a strict performance requirement regarding the hiring of local workers, requiring not less than ninety percent (90 %) of Colombian workers as staff and not less than eighty percent (80 %) of Colombian workers as qualified personnel and management, with some discretion by the Ministry of Mining. Furthermore, it demanded close to equal pay compared to foreign personnel. Those laws have been abolished.

The Mining Law still gives some discretion over quotas for hiring local personnel to the Ministry of Mining and Energy. No evidence could be found that the ministry actually exercised its discretion since article 74 and 75 of the Labour Code of Colombia had been abolished.

The Colombian visa regime is not being specifically discussed as a bottleneck.

Neither an active nor a passive preferential procurement policy is in place in Colombia.

No specific requirements regarding the building of production facilities close to mining project could be found in mining licenses awarded or tendered.

Australia has not established legal obligations to hire Indigenous Australians for mining projects. Colombia abolished strict performance requirements, but left itself some discretion that it currently does not exercise. South Africa has strict performance requirements in place.

As explained in the Constitution of South Africa, its history led South Africa to take a pro-active and openly advertised choice to eliminate the inequalities established through the Apartheid regime via a preferential treatment of HDSAs, especially in the crucial mining industry.

In South Africa, an active preferential procurement policy favours companies with a high B-BBEE rating in public tenders and indirectly also in private tenders.

Australia does not take such a pro-active approach towards favouring its indigenous population, but it has eliminated competition law barriers for preferential procurement. Colombia does not specifically address the issue.

Active preferential procurement is a strong political influence on the open (job) market. Only South Africa has made the conscious choice to prioritize the issue of HDSA employment to such an extent.

Australia has in one case specifically demanded that minerals are to be processed within Australia in order to be awarded a mining license. This is a substantial demand, as it changes the way a foreign investor can structure the financing of a mining project. A production site in a high-income and high-cost country such as Australia is a competitive disadvantage. No such demands have been found in South Africa or Colombia.

Performance requirements provide the government with further tools to influence foreign mining investments, directly impacting on the decision making freedom of foreign investors. The concrete rules are the outcome of the reconciliation of the interest of the foreign investor to freely pick his employees to get the best quality workers for the lowest salary on the one side and the interest of the government of the host state to have its constituencies profit to the highest extend possible from mining activities in its country.

While visa restrictions, general local hire, local procurement and local processing requirements limit the access of foreign workers, performance requirements can also be used to establish preferential treatment of one group of local workers over another. In South Africa, this choice was made in favour of HDSA. Considering the specific situation and history of South Africa outlined supra, this cannot be seen as a general trend. Whilst visa restrictions and local hire/procurement are a rather common occurrence, the requirement of local processing could vastly change the global mining industry that usually uses logistics to minimize processing costs. So far, no new legal development could be seen yet—the requirement was rather made under political pressure and is only reflected in a single mining license application process, rather than fixed in competitive mining license grant processes.

12.7 Distribution of Profits

Whether to invest in a mining project or not can sometimes be a matter of political choice, nearly always the key question is whether the investment will generate profits. The question of how such profits are distributed between foreign investors on the one side and host states and local communities on the other side is predominantly determined by the tax and royalty structures.

A constant development are the cuts in Australia's corporate income tax rate, from a 49 % in the mid-80s to 30 % ever since 2001. A further cut from 30 % to 29 % is currently being discussed.

The resource boom in Australia and elsewhere let to the Australian national government's attempt to profit from the resource boom in form of a specific windfall tax aimed at mining revenues. The Resource Super Profits Tax was planned to expand to all minerals. A strong lobby engagement of the mining industry paid off, leading to the Mineral Resources Rent Tax being applicable to coal and iron ore. The Mineral Resources Rent Tax furthermore includes several tax breaks. The liberal national coalition party government, in power since September 2013 had decided to abolish the MRRT when elected, but does not as yet hold the necessary majority in the Senate (the Upper House of the Commonwealth parliament) to do so.

The state government in Queensland, Australia, charges royalties on produced minerals. If the minerals are privately owned the state collects the royalties on behalf of the private mineral holder and passes the royalties on after taxation.

The royalty rate frequently changes when commodity prices change. The legislation facilitates this frequent change by determining the royalty rates in a schedule of the Mineral Resource Regulations rather than in the Mineral Resource Act 1989. There is no formula in place that would determine the exact relationship between commodity price development and royalty development, leaving a wide discretion for the Queensland government and economic uncertainty for foreign investors.

The Fiscal Repair Amendment Act included exploration permits in the scope of the stamp duty. Farm-in agreements are still excluded, but there is a trend to include more and more types of transactions in the stamp duty regime.

The latest development important from a foreign investor's point of view in South Africa was that from April 1st, 2012 branches of foreign companies which are effectively managed from the outset are also taxed at 28 %. Prior to April 2012 those companies were taxed at a higher rate of 33 %.

A windfall tax has not been levied. The idea is discussed and a form of "*resource rental tax*" is supported by the ANC. It was suggested to introduce a windfall tax of 50 % that would apply to profits made after investors have made a "*reasonable return*", without specifying further what "*reasonable*" means.

Before the MPRDA 2002 South Africa did not collect royalties for the state. The Mining Law 1991 was generally viewed as providing for private mineral rights. This in turn prohibited the state from collecting royalties for its own use, as the royalties would be *ius usus* fructus of the private owner, they would belong to him as the yield of the private mineral right.

With the MPRDA 2002 the former regime changed. As the custodian of South Africa's mineral resources, South Africa is entitled and through the Mineral and Petroleum Resource Royalties Act 2008 obliged to secure that any person who wins or recovers a mineral resource from within the Republic of South Africa pays royalties.

The MRPD Amendment Bill 2011 also raises the possibility of empowering the South African Minister for Natural Resources to influence the pricing of natural resources sold from South African mining projects and to impose export permits on minerals. A windfall tax is not being levied.

The national government in Colombia collects royalties as the state is the owner of the subsoil and of the natural, non-renewable resources. In the few cases where the government is not owner of the minerals, the state does not collect royalties.

A specific feature of the Colombian mining tax system is the surface fee. The surface fee is levied on the total area of the mining license during its tenure. It is to be paid by the mining concession holder without taking into consideration as to who has the property or possesses the lands of the contract.

Considering the different types of taxes and the various incentive schemes as well as possible tax breaks or different applications of tax codes the following Table 12.1 is meant for a broad overview.

For mining projects, it is crucial to analyse the combination and interaction of the general corporate tax with mining specific taxes and royalties. Comparing Australia, South Africa and Colombia, the corporate income tax varies within a small range.

In Australia, the corporate tax rate has been continuously reduced from 49 % to 30 % today and will possibly be further reduced. At the same time, mining specific taxes and royalty schemes have been increased or even introduced as in the case of the MRRT windfall tax.

Table 12.1 Overview over taxes relevant for the mining industry

Type of tax	Australia	South Africa	Colombia
(Corporate) income tax	30 %	28 %	33 %
Windfall-tax	MRRT 30 %	No windfall tax	No windfall tax
Royalties	Depending on the value of the mineral and mineral type, e.g.: Coal: 7–15 %	Depending on production chain: refined: 5 % unrefined: 7 %	Depending on amount of the mineral & mineral type e.g.: Coal: 5–10 % Iron Ore: 5 %
Mining specific surface fee	No mining specific surface fee	No mining specific surface fee	Depending on area and current minimum wage
Stamp/transfer duty	Depending on value of transaction: 1.5–5.75 %	Depending on value of transaction: 3–8 %	1.5 %

Source: Own compilation

In South Africa, the latest changes in corporate income tax levelled the playing ground for foreign investors seeking to undertake mining activities with their original legal entity with those foreign and national investors who are willing to set up an own South African corporate entity. A windfall tax, potentially about twice as extensive as the Australian MRRT, is being discussed in South Africa but has not been levied so far.

The importance of the discussion of mineral ownership finds its echo in the discussion on royalties. While Queensland, Australia, and Colombia were able to levy royalties for decades, South Africa had to change its mineral resource ownership framework in order to be able to levy royalties for the state. It is important to note not only the difference in royalty rates, but also the difference in the basis of their calculation. South Africa distinguishes between refined and unrefined minerals, establishing an incentive—or one might even say indirect performance requirement—to process minerals within the country. The Colombian calculations scheme—a percentage of the value of the tonnage in combination with a reference price set by the Energy Mining Planning Unity—leaves a high level of discretion with the government of Colombia and in turn a high level of uncertainty for a foreign investor.

The discussion over the empowerment of the South African Minister for Natural Resources to influence the prices of natural resources and to impose export permits on minerals is unique when compared to Queensland, Australia, and Colombia.

This discussion on such export permits has to be seen in the light of the current energy crisis in South Africa. With the regulation of pricing and the imposition of export permits on coal, South Africa aims to provide its state owned energy provider Eskom with cheap coal for its energy production. Price fixing for the benefit of a state-owned energy company means the state takes a bigger part of the profits away from the investor to use for national purposes.

A specific feature of the Colombian mining tax system is the surface fee. Unlike corporate tax or royalties, surface fees are levied on the basis of the area of the concessions only.

Comparing Australia, South Africa and Colombia, the corporate income tax varies within a small range. This can be explained by a globalized market for general foreign investment and capital.

Furthermore, the governments acknowledge the dangers of the resource curse and that mining taxation requires a specifically tailored tax system. A low corporate tax rate will benefit the overall economy by allowing other industries to produce goods at prices that are more competitive. This can offset at least a part of possible high exchange rates of the national currency through mining revenue in foreign currency.

Increased mining specific taxes allow for a high revenue for the government and a flexible instrument that allows adaptation to fluctuating commodity prices, without affecting the tax system as a whole. Unlike taxes on nearly all other industries mining companies may not shift their production site to avoid taxation. Mining production is simply taxed at the site where the minerals are located before they are produced.

The discussion on the extensive windfall tax in South Africa has to be understood against the background of the nationalization debate in South Africa outlined supra. South Africa has yet to decide how to capture a higher profit yield from its mineral wealth without losing investors' trust. The reason why a windfall tax has not yet been introduced might be the same as in Colombia: unlike Australia—where the MRRT was finally introduced—neither South Africa nor Colombia can afford to lose foreign investments.

12.8 Repatriation of Foreign Investments

Australia, South Africa and Colombia have a foreign exchange control system in place that has the potential to regulate the repatriation of foreign investments. Further options include the requirement to for export permits and price controls.

Australia's foreign exchange control regime gives the Governor General the power to enact regulations at his discretion to protect Australia's national interest.

Regarding the repatriation of foreign investment, both the local sale or redemption proceeds of non-resident owned assets in Australia and any income earned from the foreign investment in Australia may be freely transferred abroad.

Besides export permits and controls regarding the export of uranium, price controls, export permits and the requirement for the transfer of the controlling interests (outside the competition law regime) do not exist in Australia.

South Africa has a foreign exchange control regime in place that is administered by the South African Reserve Bank on behalf of the Minister of Finance.

Regarding the repatriation of foreign investment, both the local sale or redemption proceeds of non-resident owned assets in South Africa and any income earned from the foreign investment in South Africa may be freely transferred abroad.

The discussed empowerment of the South African Minister for Natural Resources to influence the pricing of natural resources sold from South African mining projects and to impose export permits on minerals would restrict the free repatriation of foreign investment and related profits.

The restrictions on the transfer of the controlling interests of a (un-)listed company that holds a mining right by requiring the consent of the Minister of Mineral Resources also impacts on the free repatriation of foreign investment. The current requirement for transfer of unlisted companies might be expanded by an Amendment Bill. Considering the corporate structures of many mining projects this provision could lead to a situation in which a multinational company would need the consent of the South African Minister for Natural Resources to trade shares, restricting the way a foreign investor can disinvest.

Colombia had a strict foreign exchange control regime in place that did not allow for the free repatriation of assets and profits. The regime was liberalized in line with the regime regarding the admission of foreign investment outlined supra. Now each foreign investment must be registered with the Central Bank of Colombia to allow repatriation of capital and profits.

When the foreign investment is registered, the repatriation of capital and profits (also in the form of dividends) is permitted without restriction.

Mining companies in Colombia have to exchange into Colombian pesos all funds necessary to pay for mining activities in Colombia.

Price controls, export permits and the requirement for the transfer of the controlling interests (outside the competition law regime) do not exist. The latest development is a registration of minerals on a single trader desk.

Australia, South Africa and Colombia have a foreign exchange control system in place that has the potential to regulate the repatriation of foreign investments.

While Australia remains committed to the free repatriation of foreign investment and Colombia is moving towards abolishing foreign exchange controls completely, developments in South Africa point the other way: Discussions on price controls, export permit requirements and transfers of controlling interests add to the picture of resource nationalism tendencies in South Africa seen throughout this research.

Only the Colombian foreign exchange control system remains active, but its impact has been substantially reduced. The obligation to exchange into Colombian pesos all funds necessary to pay for mining activities aims to stimulate Colombian currency reserves, but is a marginal measure compared to possible repatriation restrictions. The registration of minerals on a single trader desk aims to fight illicit mining activities rather than to restrict repatriation of profits via the sale of minerals abroad.

The question of repatriation of foreign investments and export controls directly touches upon the field of tension between the interest of a state to attract foreign investment and its interest to maintain control and protect its sovereignty. Little or non-export controls attract foreign investments, but take away a powerful tool of governments to react to currency fluctuations. The analyzed countries have reacted by each establishing a system that would quickly allow them to introduce blockades to the repatriation of foreign investments and export stops. The single trader desk registration requirement could also be seen in this light. At this point of time the states do not make use make use of these mechanisms.

12.9 Conflict Resolution

Considering the wealth of stakeholders and actors in international mining investments and the impact on economic, political, cultural and environmental issues the possibility of conflict is manifold. The analysis in this work structures the types of conflicts in conflicts, that utilize national conflict resolution mechanisms, and conflicts, that utilize international conflict resolution mechanisms.

On a state level in Australia, mining licenses and land access fall under the jurisdiction of the specialized Land Court with the Land Appeal Court as the second instance.

Native title issues fall under the jurisdiction of the Federal Court, with the specialized National Native Title Tribunal acting in some cases.

Mining conflicts that touch upon Constitutional rights fall under the jurisdiction of the High Court of Australia.

A traditional judiciary system is in place in Australia, but does not have the jurisdiction over mining licenses and land access issues except on (limited) appeal.

Both the Land Court system and the Federal Court system heavily focus on Alternative Dispute Resolution mechanisms to aid the parties to come to a non-litigations solution of disputes.

On an international level, Australia signed the ICSID convention in 1975 but only enacted it in 1991. This was welcomed as a step towards security of investments for foreign investors.

In Australia, investor-state arbitration agreements referring to ICSID are used by foreign investors into Australia and by Australian companies investing abroad.

International arbitration is available for foreign investors in the case of disputes covered by the relevant bilateral investment treaty.

In April 2011 the Australian government announced that it will no longer include in its investment treaties clauses that refer disputes between foreign investors and the Commonwealth of Australia or states to an international arbitration body.

Legal stability contracts or similar offers to maintain the legal framework of the time of the investment are not available to foreign investors.

On a national level, the South African Parliament did not exercise its power to establish a specialized court for mining license and land access matters.

In South Africa, mining licenses and land access issues including both tribal land owners and any other land owners will be heard before a Magistrates Court or a High Court in the first instance, depending of the value of compensation in question.

Before judicial review, an administrative review in the form of an appeal to the Director-General of the relevant department or the Minister is obligatory.

The Supreme Court of Appeal is the highest court of appeal except in constitutional matters and functions as a court of appeal in the second instance.

Mining conflicts that touch upon Constitutional rights fall in the jurisdiction of the Constitutional Court of South Africa.

A traditional judiciary system is also in place in South Africa, but does not have the jurisdiction over mining licenses and land access issues.

Alternative Dispute Resolution mechanisms are available within the South African justice system, but their use is not obligatory or specifically encouraged for mining license or land access disputes.

On the international level, South Africa has neither signed nor enacted the ICSID convention. In the decade after the Apartheid regime South Africa has negotiated over 40 bilateral investment treaties, 20 of which have entered into force. Despite the fact that South Africa is not an ICSID member state those treaties provide for investor-state arbitration, e.g. before ICSID and under UNCITRAL rules.

A recent review has led to the termination of some of the bilateral investment treaties and the renegotiation of others. This process aims to conclude more equitable bilateral investment treaties as the South African administration feels that the first-generation bilateral investment treaties were concluded in a hurry.

Legal stability contracts or similar offers to maintain the legal framework of the time of the investment are not available to foreign investors.

On the national level, Colombia has not established specialized courts for conflicts regarding mining licenses or land access.

Disputes regarding mining licenses fall under the jurisdiction of the administrative courts, with the Administrative Court as the first instance and the Consejo de Estado [State Council] as appellate body. This includes disputes with Indian/Afro-Colombian mining zone rights holders.

Disputes over land access regarding both Indians/Afro-Colombians and any other land owner fall under the jurisdiction of the civil courts.

The court of first instances is the "*Juece civile del circuito en primera instancia*" [Circuit Court judges in first instance] and the court of appeal is "*La Corte Suprema de Justicia*" [The Supreme Court of Justice].

Regarding land access there is an obligatory administrative review process in place that requires an application to the mayor of the respective mining area before civil court judiciary review can be obtained.

Mining conflicts that touch upon Constitutional rights fall in the jurisdiction of the Constitutional Court of Colombia. There is also a traditional justice system for Indians/Afro-Colombians. This justice system does not apply to mining licenses or land access issues.

Alternative Dispute Resolution mechanisms are available within the Colombian justice system, but their use is not obligatory or specifically encouraged for mining license or land access disputes.

On an international level, Colombia signed and enacted the ICSID convention in 1993. Before the 1990s, foreign investment was not protected to the same extent as today. Colombia has now concluded bilateral investment treaties with several countries. The bilateral investment treaties with the United States and the European Union are still being negotiated. The bilateral investment treaties in place include either an ICSID or an UNICTRAL arbitration clause.

Colombia has established the possibility of concluding legal stability contracts with the aim of promoting new investment and expanding existing investments in the country. It makes frequent use of this opportunity.

Those legal stability contracts, although subject of proceedings before the Constitutional Court of Colombia, were declared constitutional and remain in force.

Foreign investment in mining projects is prone to conflict due to the potential socio-economic and environmental impacts of mining projects. There are two common trends on how the analysed countries address this:

On a national level, some governments have begun to include special provisions regarding mining specific conflict resolution in their mining codes, but disputes are generally still referred to the general national judiciary (South Africa, Colombia). Australia takes a different approach and has established a specific judiciary for conflicts around mining projects in the form of the Land Court. Considering the complexity and specifics of conflicts regarding mining projects, this development is likely to continue.

On an international level, states reconsider/adjust their approach to international arbitration such as ICSID and respective clauses in bilateral investment treaties and investor-state contracts (South Africa) or cease to include arbitration clauses in their bilateral investment treaties and investor-state contracts (Australia). In general it can be said that currently the countries analysed become more hostile towards international arbitration with Colombia being the exception.

On the national levels there is a clear trend from regulating mining related questions of the law from the general public law to specific laws, specifically designed to govern mining projects. The same can be seen in regards to conflicts in the mining sphere. Whilst originally decided by the general judiciary, now specialized mining courts and mining specific procedural codes are becoming more and more common. This has to do with the specific questions mining related conflicts ask to have resolved: numerous stakeholders with different levels of capacity and different cultural backgrounds, the mining specific technical expertise necessary to determine questions regarding licenses e.g. overlapping tenures, liability, sharing of profits, and the interconnection with other uses of the land. The level of such specialization broadly mirrors the history and experience nations have with mining. In Australia, the most developed of the three analyzed countries the substantive law and the conflict resolution has created mining specific frameworks and processes, whilst South Africa and Colombia are still in the process of developing such specific expertise.

On the international level the willingness to accept international jurisdiction such as the ICSID system, appears to directly relate to the perceived benefit or detriments achieved through opting for or against such international arbitration procedures. When countries decide to join ICSID there is a focus on the perceived benefits, such as the additional trust from foreign investors. When they leave ICSID again the focus has often shifted on the importance of national sovereignty.

Australia (re: *Cigarette plain packaging*) and South Africa (re: *Broad-Based Black Economic Empowerment*) did have to painfully notice the pitfalls of succumbing to ICSID and now are trying to find ways to avoid further ICSID clauses (Australia) and/or to renegotiate the contracts (South Africa). It has to be seen whether the investor-friendly pro-international arbitration approach in Colombia will remain when an ICSID case is brought against Colombia under an arbitration clause. The analysis points to the fact that if a government feels that it has the trust of the foreign investor or it can afford to not attract further investment the motivation to succumb to international arbitration such as ICSID is rather limited.

While international arbitration is still the preferred conflict resolution mechanism in mining related conflicts that involve the relationship between the foreign investor and the host government, the specialization and professionalization of the national mining laws and jurisdiction might open new ways for resolving such conflicts. Also, the example of the specialized conflict resolution mechanism in the

Energy Charter that governs foreign investments in the energy sector[2] might be a precedent for a specialized international mining investment conflict resolution mechanism to come in the future.

12.10 Applying for the Social License to Operate by Corporate Social Responsibility Policies and Actions

The development of comprehensive Corporate Social Responsibility policies are an approach practiced in Australia, South Africa and Colombia alike and aim to create certainty in the process of acquiring and maintaining the Social License to Operate.

There is neither national nor state legislation in place that would force mining companies to develop a specific set of CSR policies.

Corporate Social Responsibility in the Australian mining industry does have a long history though and has undergone substantive change. For the example of the employment of local, specifically indigenous personnel, the *Mabo case* and the increasing necessity to negotiate native title agreements brought substantive change to the approach of major mining companies.

The Australian Employment Covenant, an Australian-wide initiative to foster the employment of Indigenous Australians, only started nearly two decades after the *Mabo case*. It did show strong result focusing the attention of mining companies towards employing Indigenous Australians in their mining projects. It can now be considered a good practice for Australian mining companies to address the questions arising in the realm of the Social License to Operate with CSR policies and actions in regards to the employment of local, specifically indigenous personnel and beyond.

Corporate Social Responsibility was not a predominant focus either for mining companies or for the South African government before the end of Apartheid. CSR quickly developed with the arrival of foreign investment and post-Apartheid demands of South African society. Litigation had challenged the notion of CSR on the grounds that a director must only focus on what is best for the company. These legal challenges have now been resolved. The new notion is rather that a director would breach his duties if he does not take into account the socio-economic impact of the company's actions, e.g. by requiring a public or state owned company to establish a social and ethics committee as a part of its governance arrangements. For the example of employment of HDSAs there is now substantive national legislation in place that requires mining companies to address it and other socio-economic factors, e.g. via provisions in the South African Mining Code.

The Mining Charter, once started as a non-enforceable coordinated governmental-industry initiative to address the inequalities derived from the Apartheid regime has now been reformed to be an enforceable legislative measure. It can now be considered a must for foreign investors in South African mining projects to

[2] Energy Charter (2014), *Dispute Resolution*.

address the questions arising in the realm of the Social License to Operate with CSR policies and actions.

In Colombia the notion of Responsabilidad Social Corporativa [Corporate Social Responsibility] has a long history in Colombia. In the last decades, much of the development of CSR policies and initiatives derived from the engagement of foreign investors, especially from Spain. Neither positive nor negative influences of the judiciary on CSR policies of mining companies could be found. In regards to the example of employment of Indian/Afro-Colombian workers there is no national or state legislation in place that requires mining companies to address the in their CSR policies.

It can be considered good practice for foreign investors in Colombian mining projects to address the questions arising in the realm of the social license to operate with CSR policies and actions.

The demand to acquire a Social License to operate to successfully realize an international mining project has led to a proactive approach of mining companies.

Unlike in South Africa, in Australia and Colombia there are no specific laws in place that would force mining to develop substantial CSR policies. In South Africa the Mining Charter developed from a list of suggestions to a list of must-dos in respect to the creation of CSR policies. The mining companies in Australia and Colombia decided to develop substantive CSR policies anyhow.

The legal framework for foreign investments in mining projects so far included aspects of International Business Law, Public International Law and National Mining Laws. It was therefore solely determined by governments, their contractual interrelations and by International Organizations.

The Corporate Social Responsibility policies provide a policy framework determined by the Mining Companies themselves. Such CSR policy frameworks were developed by the mining companies, whether required by law or not.

Global mining companies such as AngloGold Ashanti, Anglo American, BHP and Rio Tinto often operate in remote areas and in developing countries with little capacity to address crucial issues, such as providing employment, etc. The financial power of international mining companies and the impact of mining projects on the job market give CSR policies, e.g. CSR policies regarding employment of certain groups of the population as analyzed supra, a regulatory power that is sometimes even comparable to the regulatory power of the laws of host countries.[3]

[3] While the author considers the term "*Soft Law*" to vague, considering the importance of the Corporate Social responsibility policy answers of the international mining companies to the question of the Social License to Operate some might call CSR policies "*International Mining Investment Soft Law*". Soft Law is usually used to describe non-binding recommendations, resolutions and declarations of bodies, organs and special organizations of the United Nations. The term Soft Law aims to grasp the regulatory power of such recommendations, resolutions and declarations despite their lack of judicial enforceability. In a study called Mining, Environment and Development, published by the United Nations Commission for Trade and Development ("UNCTAD"), the International Soft Law of mining is defined as including demands of international conferences and agreements such as the 1972 Stockholm principles, the United Nations Conference on Environment and Development ("UNCED") Rio declaration and the UNCED

But even in industrialized countries the behavior of mining companies is heavily influenced by its Corporate Social Responsibility policies. Corporate Social Responsibility policies and programs have developed in such way that they are now addressing many of the same issues prevalent in host-states law and governmental policies. Provisions such as the global Community and Environment Management Standards of AngloGold Ashanti encompass many key issues of the legal framework for foreign investments in mining projects, such as Land Access, Local employment and procurement and even dispute resolution mechanisms.[4]

In the context of foreign investments in mining projects the CSR policies of mining companies are at least as important for the actual dealings of a mining company as codes of conducts such as the UN Global Compact. In fact, some mining companies list their CSR policies and their pledge to code of conducts and global indexes rolled into one.[5]

There is also an interrelation of CSR policies with international codes of conduct's in place as can be seen from the cross reference of CSR policies to the International Council on Mining and Metals ("***ICMM***") Position statement on mining: "*Partnerships for Development 2010*".[6]

The special interest of foreign investors to add CSR as a component to the existing legal framework for foreign investments derives from the fact that the CSR framework increases the likelihood to be awarded and to maintain the Social License to Operate—and thereby the chances for an interruption-free realization of a mining project.

Whether CSR policies are established to avoid state control,[7] to avoid conflicts with the local population or derives from a genuine interest to be a good corporate citizen will not be able to be finally determined in this work, but the structured approaches of international mining companies rather suggest a mixture of various motivations.

All of this shows the now accepted realization of the mining companies that the SLO needs to be applied for and maintained to successfully realize a mining project.

While the CSR is mainly targeted at the local stakeholders, the global attention towards the actions of mining firms abroad has further increased the need to develop and implement CSR policies—the SLO is therefore being applied for locally in the host state, but is necessary to acquire and maintain it on a global level.

Agenda 21. In the context of international business law and foreign investments, international codes of conduct are considered to be International Business Soft Law. They might be suggested by international organizations or NGOs, often with participation of the respective industry. Those international codes of conducts include the Berlin Guidelines, the ISO 14000 standards and the UN Global Compact.

[4] AngloGold Ashanti (2013).

[5] AngloGold Ashanti (2014); Rio Tinto (2013).

[6] ICMM (2014).

[7] Pulido and Ramiro (2014), p. 107.

References

AngloGold Ashanti (2013) Community and environment management standards. Available online at: http://www.anglogoldashanti.com/NR/rdonlyres/91825948-F0BF-40CA-AA0E-D43024F2DD26/0/CommunityandEnvironmentManagementStandards.pdf, updated on 9/20/2013, last checked on 15 February 2014

AngloGold Ashanti (2014) United Nations Global Compact. Available online at: http://www.anglogold.com/Sustainability/Global+initiatives/UNGlobalCompact.htm, last checked on 15 February 2014

Bungenberg M, Hobe S (eds) (2015) Permanent sovereignty over natural resources. Springer International Publishing Switzerland, Cham [u.a.]

Energy Charter (2014) Dispute settlement. Available online at: http://www.encharter.org/index.php?id=269, last checked 01.03.2015

ICMM (2014) Mining: partnerships for development position statement. Available online at: http://www.icmm.com/page/17427/mining-partnerships-for-development-position-statement, last checked on 15 February 2014

Pulido A, Ramiro P (2014) La Responsabilidad Social Corporativa de las Multinacionales Españoles en Colombia. Available online at: http://web.usbmed.edu.co/usbmed/elagora/htm/v10nro1/pdf/7.pdf, last checked on 15 February 2014

Rio Tinto (2013) Ethical indexes & awards - sustainable development 2012 - Rio Tinto. Available online at: http://www.riotinto.com/sustainabledevelopment2012/performance/ethical_indexes_awards.html, updated on 3/14/2013, checked on 2/11/2014

Chapter 13
Conclusion: On the Path to an International Mining Investment Law

The hypothesis is (i) that the realization of and the investment in international mining projects creates complex legal challenges, (ii) that these challenges are similar wherever the international mining investments take place; and (iii) that these specific legal challenges cannot sufficiently be analyzed by the legal framework provided for by general foreign investment law.

As exemplarily shown for Australia, South Africa and Colombia it holds true that (i) the realisation of and the investment in international mining projects creates complex legal challenges and (ii) these legal challenges are similar notwithstanding the countries analysed.

In regards to the hypothesis that (iii) these specific legal challenges cannot sufficiently be analysed by the legal framework provided for by general foreign investment law this holds true only for some of the analysed questions, but not for others.

The conclusion will first list questions where the international mining investment specific differences are minor—and the application of general Foreign Investment Law suffices to analyse and answer the legal challenges posed.

The conclusion will then outline the questions where the specific challenges of investments in mining projects have led to legal differences so substantial that questions and legal answers of the analysed countries could not sufficiently be analysed by general Foreign Investment Law.

These differences are so substantial that the author suggests introducing a new sub-category of academic research, "***International Mining Investment Law***" ("***IMIL***").

R.W. Roeder, *Foreign Mining Investment Law*, DOI 10.1007/978-3-319-31217-0_13

13.1 International Mining Investment Specific Differences Minor: General International Investment Law Suffices

It has been shown that the admission of foreign investments in mining projects often undergo more scrutiny and receives more public attention than investments in other industries. This can be explained with the size and the impact of mining projects, especially on the local communities around a mining site. However, the admission of foreign investments in mining projects is not regulated substantially different from the admission of foreign investments in other types of projects and industries. Neither are specific screening processes in place, nor do foreign investors in mining projects have rights and obligations that go beyond other foreign investors.

The same holds true for corporate structure requirements imposed on international mining investments. While some forms of corporate structures, such as farm-in agreements and joint-ventures might be more common for foreign investments in mining projects, such structures may and are being used in other forms of investments as well.

In the case of performance requirements once again the public focus might lay on mining related performance requirements, e.g. B-BBEE employment regulations in South Africa. But this is as of their visibility and importance to the South African economy. Such performance requirements are not handled any different than for other types of industries. In South Africa for example, they are also in place for the South African tourism, forestry, transport, finance and information technology sector and other industries.

Finally, the regulation of repatriation of foreign investments in mining projects is not regulated any differently than the repatriation of other focus of foreign investments.

13.2 International Mining Investment Specific Differences Substantial: International Mining Investment Law Required

The questions where the specific challenges of investments in mining projects have led to legal differences so substantial that questions and legal answers of the analysed countries could not sufficiently be analysed by general foreign investment law are the questions of ownership of minerals and mineral rights, the licensing regime, the land access regime, the distribution of profits, national and international conflict resolution and in the discussion on the Social License to Operate and the CSR policy answers of mining companies.

13.2.1 Mining Investment Specific Ownership Regime

As shown, the intense discussions regarding public versus private ownership of minerals and mineral rights is unique when compared to investments in the services industry or other types of production facility.

First and foremost the intense public discussions arise from the fact that minerals are a depletable resource. Decisions made today will impact irrevocably on future generations to come. The shown mining specific rights, obligations and restrictions imposed upon ownership of minerals are a result of this need for additional control and the freedom to revise decisions made today in future generations.

Mining furthermore is an extremely capital intensive endeavour. The necessity for private and foreign investments to realize the capital intensive mining activities have led to several unique legal solutions, such as the South African custodianship over Natural Resources described supra.

The question of the ownership regime regarding minerals therefore requires specific academic attention.

13.2.2 Mining Investment Specific Licences System

The necessity for a license to conduct certain types of economic activities is common. The shown complexity of the mining license regime of the analysed jurisdictions is unique. The very complex mining laws include mining investment specific rights, obligations and restrictions for foreign investors and thereby influence the current regime for foreign investments. Such differences result, inter alia, from the long-term of the investment, which led to the split between exploration and production licenses discussed supra, as well as the retention license regime, the massive impact on the socio-economic, environmental and cultural setting in the area of the mining site. As shown, resource rich host nations open or restrict access to national mineral wealth not only on the level governed by general International Investment Law and through bilateral investment treaties, but—protected by the Principle of Permanent Sovereignty over their natural resources—also on a national level through national mining laws, inter alia by restricting access to mining licenses and increasing the barriers to land access and associated approvals necessary to realize mining projects.

The general legal framework for foreign investments is therefore by no means sufficient to provide the answers required.

13.2.3 Mining Investment Specific Land Access Regime

The legal challenges posed by mining activities to the land access regimes are unique. First, land access will be required in the form of test drilling and other exploration activities even before the choice is made to actual conduct mining activities. At this point, and often even after that point the land in question will also be used for other activities, such as housing, agriculture activities or have a spiritual, historical or cultural use. The affected parties are also manifold: The actual owner of the land, indigenous tribes and the local governments to just name a few all requests a say in the use of the land. The license provided by the national government might often be a starting point, but by no means is sufficient for mining activities to be conducted without disruption. The analyzed countries have answered the legal questions posed with complex and mining specific land access regimes, that try to balance the various interests of the involved parties.

13.2.4 Mining Investment Specific Distribution of Profits

Nations face specific challenges when taxing foreign mining investments. The tax regime will have to address the discussed *Resource Curse* to avoid a weakening of other industries as of a stronger exchange rate.

Secondly, foreign investors are fully aware that notions of "*Resource Nationalism*" weakened the legal framework provided by general International Investment Law. "*Resource Nationalism*" has been described as "*a government's effort to gain greater benefit from its natural resources — sometimes to the detriment of private companies*".[1] Measures of Resource Nationalism can take the form of nationalization, expropriation of the assets of a single mining project or creeping expropriation such as the increase of taxes and royalties after the foreign investment was made.[2] Considering the long-term nature of mining investments the legal framework for foreign investments for mining investments will have to eminently address the fear of a foreign investor that taxes might be raised in the case of a change of government, while the host state will have to establish a regime that allows it to react flexible in the case of a change of resource prices as of the cyclic nature of the commodity industry.

[1] Morris (2014).

[2] Leon (2009).

13.2.5 *Mining Investment Specific Conflict Resolution Mechanisms*

As shown, the host states have realized that the general public law and the general judiciary was not capable of handling the complex questions and multitude of stakeholder interest created by mining investments. They have reacted on a national level to develop substantive mining codes and a specialized judiciary system that involves elements of Alternative Dispute Resolution Mechanisms, in order to manage the conflicts created by foreign mining investments. At the same time where national capacity in solving mining conflicts is built up, on an international level the analyzed host states, at least in the case of Australia and South Africa, have started to leave or restrict the ICSID system that used to govern conflicts in foreign investments. The example of the specialized conflict resolution mechanism in the Energy Charter that governs foreign investments in the energy sector[3] might be a precedent for a specialized international mining investment conflict resolution mechanism.

13.2.6 *Mining Specific SLO Requirement CSR Policies*

As highlighted several times, mining activities impact on the local community to an extend that very little other industry do. It is therefore not a surprise, that the discussion of the requirement of a Social License to Operate and attempts of the mining companies to provide an answer to this requirement with the establishment of CSR policies is specifically frequent in relation to mining activities. The global reach of mining companies and the discussed quasi-regulatory power of such CSR policies in some areas is not sufficiently addressed by general Foreign Investment Law and requires further attention. That way it could be analyzed what regulatory power such CSR policies have, whether their implementation is an attempt to avoid state control or an outcry pointing to the lack of sufficient regulation of international mining investments.

13.3 Consequences

The questions arises what those international mining investment specific findings mean for the further study of the legal framework for foreign investment in mining projects especially in relation to the legal analysis of foreign investments under general foreign investment law.

[3] Energy Charter (2014).

General Foreign Investment Law has been defined as consisting of: "*(...) layers of general international law, general standards of international economic law and distinct rules peculiar to its domain.*"[4] It also has been noted that the "*(...) interplay between the relevant domestic rules of the host state and applicable rules of international law may become central to the required analysis of a case*"[5] and that "*(...) the line between international law and domestic law becomes blurred*",[6] making the "*(...) classical separation between public and private law*"[7] as different fields of study an insufficient point of focus.[8]

It has been said that "*(...) because of these peculiarities general (...) investment law has acquired distinct characteristics, the understanding of which requires a separate field of study from general international law and general standards of international economic law.*"[9]

The same has become true for the legal framework for foreign investments in mining projects.

As stated infra it has been noted that general International Investment Law, besides being based upon general international law and general standards of international economic law, "*(...) by necessity also incorporate aspects of the laws of the host state.*"[10] and that: "*(...) the interplay between relevant domestic rules of the host state and applicable rules of international law may become central to the required analyses (...);*"[11]

For the legal framework for foreign investments in mining projects "*the interplay between relevant domestic rules of the host state and applicable rules of international law is also central to the required analyses*",[12] but the focus and the point of view is different:

While general International Investment Law has a focus on international law and General Standards of International Economic Law and aims to determine how these influence domestic rules, the legal framework for foreign investments in mining projects has its focus on both international law and general standards of International Economic Law as well as national mining laws (the "*domestic rules*") and aims to determine how the interplay between those various fields of the law creates a distinct legal framework for foreign investments in mining projects.

The existence of and the discussion around the Principle of Permanent Sovereignty over Natural Resources[13]—now rightly so recognized as part of

[4] Dolzer and Schreuer (2008), p. 3.

[5] Dolzer and Schreuer (2008), p. 3.

[6] Dolzer and Schreuer (2008), p. 3.

[7] Dolzer and Schreuer (2008), p. 3.

[8] Dolzer and Schreuer (2008), p. 3.

[9] Dolzer and Schreuer (2008), p. 3.

[10] Dolzer and Schreuer (2008), p. 3.

[11] Dolzer and Schreuer (2008), p. 3.

[12] Dolzer and Schreuer (2008), p. 3.

[13] For a comprehensive discussion see: Hobe and Bungenberg (2015).

customary international law[14]—also demands a different and more focussed academic lens:

In regards to foreign investment law the Principle of Permanent Sovereignty over Natural Resources, states that "*exploration, development and disposition of such resource, as well as the import of the foreign capital required for these purposes, should be in conformity with the rules and conditions which the peoples and nations freely consider to be necessary or desirable with regards to the authorization, restriction or prohibition of such activities*".[15]

This also explains the analysed importance and persistency of national laws in the legal framework for foreign investments in mining projects when comparing to more general frameworks for foreign investments in other sectors. While authors of general International Investment Law increasingly question the notion of an absolute veil of sovereignty of nations, the Sovereignty over Natural Resources is specifically discussed to be "*permanent*".[16]

The focus on the specifics of legal framework for foreign investments in mining projects against its broad analysis under general International Investment Law is therefore an attempt to provide a more focussed view on an area of the law that "*lacks clarity*",[17] by separating a distinct, yet substantial type of foreign investments—foreign investments in the mining sector—for a more profound and concentrated analyses. As stated, the author suggests undertaking such analysis under the term "***International Mining Investment Law***" ("***IMIL***") to adequately address and analyse the specific legal questions raised by foreign investments in mining projects.

The development of such specifics of International Investment Law in the Area of Natural Resources has already been acknowledged.[18]

For International Energy Investment Law—being another distinct category from the more general International Investment Law—the importance to focus the light of academic attention to the specifics of the legal framework for International Energy Investments has been recognized.[19] It has come the time to do so for the specifics of the legal framework for International Mining Investments as well.

The analysed questions of the ownership of minerals and mineral rights, the mining licenses regime, the land access for mining activities, the distribution of profits from mining investments, the resolution of mining investment related conflicts and CSR policies and the requirement of Social License to Operate

---

[14] Hobe and Bungenberg (2015), p. 12.

[15] UNGA Resolution 1803 (XVII) on the Permanent Sovereignty over Natural Resources of 14.12.1962.

[16] Ferreira-Snyman (2007), p. 406; Jackson (2006); for a comprehensive discussion on how "*permanent*" the sovereignty is today: Hobe and Bungenberg (2015).

[17] Sornarajah (2010), p. 33.

[18] Bungenberg in Hobe and Bungenberg (2015), p. 127.

[19] Cameron (2010); Erkan (2011); a Google search of March 1st, 2015 showed numerous results for "International *Energy* Investment Law", but not a single entry for "International *Mining* Investment Law".

could be a basic outline of such International Mining Investment Law and a starting point for further academic discussion.

References

Cameron PD (2010) International energy investment law. The pursuit of stability. Oxford University Press, Oxford

Dolzer R, Schreuer C (2008) Principles of international investment law. Oxford University Press, Oxford

Energy Charter (2014) Dispute settlement. Available online at: http://www.encharter.org/index.php?id=269. Last checked 01.03.2015

Erkan M (2011) International energy investment law. Stability through contractual clauses. Alphen aan den Rijn: Wolters Kluwer (Energy and environmental law & policy series, 15)

Ferreira-Snyman A (2007) Sovereignty and the changing nature of public international law. Towards a world law? Compar Int Law J S Afr 40(3):395–424

Hobe S, Bungenberg M (eds) (2015) Permanent sovereignty over natural resources. Springer International Publishing Switzerland, Cham [u.a.].

Jackson JH (2006) Sovereignty, the WTO and changing fundamentals of international law. 1. publ. Cambridge University Press (Hersch Lauterpacht memorial lectures, [18]), Cambridge

Leon P (2009) Creeping expropriation of mining investments - an African perspective. Int Bar Assoc J Energy Nat Resour Law 27(4):597

Morris J (2014) Why resource nationalism could be increasing. In CNBC. Available online at: http://www.cnbc.com/id/101399000. Last checked on 15 February 2014

Sornarajah M (2010) The international law on foreign investment, 3rd edn. Cambridge University Press, Cambridge

CPSIA information can be obtained
at www.ICGtesting.com
Printed in the USA
LVHW011651041118
595903LV00013B/926/P

9 783319 312163